Additional Praise for *Preaching Must Die!*

"Writing in a vivid style, Jacob D. Myers challenges homiletics to trouble its fealty to both theology and philosophy, so as to assist preaching in dying a certain death. Myers engages the work of Derrida, Irigaray, and other thinkers of deconstruction in order to show how the preacher's use of language, the preacher's self-understanding, and the preacher's relationship to Scripture and to God must be subjected to radical critique, a critique that frees preaching truly to bear witness to and make space for the divine and human other. This book sparkles with wit, and displays Myers's broad reading in theology, philosophy, and homiletics, as well as his facility in making links to popular culture and current events. I highly recommend this book to both scholars and preachers, indeed to any who want to grapple deeply with the paradox of preaching's impossibility and its necessity."
Ruthanna Hooke
Associate Dean of Chapel and the Associate Professor of Homiletics
Virginia Theological Seminary

"*Preaching Must Die!* is a crucial addition to the conversation about postmodernity and preaching. In this well-researched book Myers chronicles the final death throes of preaching at the end of its long captivity to modernity. He deconstructs modern preaching's linguistic, metaphysical, political, and theological assumptions, and observes vital signs of a "bold humility" through which preaching might be resurrected in the pluralistic and postmodern context we have now entered."
John S. McClure
Charles G. Finney Professor of Preaching and Worship
Vanderbilt Divinity School

"Much ink has been spilled in the name of postmodern homiletics. But Jacob D. Myers's book lives into that phrase with new and devastating effect. There is something here to trouble just about everybody. This "stiff drink of homiletical hemlock" is all the more unsettling because it goes down so easily. The writing is lively, clear, and riveting. Preachers and homileticians will be wrestling with this landmark book for years to come."

Ted A. Smith
Associate Professor of Preaching and Ethics
Candler School of Theology

"In *Preaching Must Die!*, readers will find more than deconstruction of pulpit biases associated with language, identity, scripture, and even God, but a guide, built upon engaging a veritable who's who from contemporary homiletics and modern philosophy, for proclamation that gets real. Myers makes an uncompromising, original, and spicy statement about why preaching must meet its maker in order to incarnate the impossible and enunciate humble dreams of welcome for a divine that might arrive at any moment."

Gerald C. Liu
Assistant Professor of Worship and Preaching
Princeton Theological Seminary

Preaching Must Die!

Preaching Must Die!

Troubling Homiletical Theology

Jacob D. Myers

Fortress Press
Minneapolis

PREACHING MUST DIE!

Troubling Homiletical Theology

Cover image: Thinkstock 2017; Vandelism by Valeri_Shanin

Cover design: Alisha Lofgren

Print ISBN: 978-1-5064-1186-6

eBook ISBN: 978-1-5064-1187-3

The paper used in this publication meets the minimum requirements of American National Standard for Information Sciences — Permanence of Paper for Printed Library Materials, ANSI Z329.48-1984.

Manufactured in the U.S.A.

This book was produced using Pressbooks.com, and PDF rendering was done by PrinceXML.

For Tom Long,
with gratitude

To die, to sleep,
To sleep, perchance to Dream; aye, there's the rub,
For in that sleep of death, what dreams may come,
When we have shuffled off this mortal coil,
Must give us pause.

—Shakespeare, *Hamlet*, Act III, Scene I

Contents

Acknowledgments

To begin, I would like to thank the people at Fortress Press for their fine work and commitment to scholarship that serves both the academy and the church. I am especially appreciative to my editor, Michael Gibson, for encouraging this project and for his prompt turnaround with his suggestions for improvement.

I wish to thank my colleague and friend Anna Carter Florence—for her lovingkindness and wonderful insights as she slogged through my earliest attempts at this book. I wish also to thank my friends who provided much feedback on chapters in various states of awfulness and for their encouragement through the editing process. These are Eric Barreto, Brennan Breed, Melissa Browning, Carolyn Helsel, David Lott, Brandon Maxwell, Raj Nadella, Nikki Roberts, and Andrea White. You have taught me so much, and this book is all the better for your insights—even when I failed to heed your counsel.

I could not have written this book without the support of my Columbia Theological Seminary community. In particular, I wish to thank President Leanne Van Dyk and Dean Deborah Flemister Mullen and Dean Christine Roy Yoder for fostering an atmosphere conducive for scholarship. I wish to express much thanks and appreciation for the John Bulow Campbell Library staff led by Dean Kelly Campbell: to Bob Craigmile for keeping me digitally connected to our library databases, even at 4 a.m.; to Wendy Dewberry and Tammy Johnson for acquiring far more philosophy books than any homiletician deserves; to Griselda Lartey for her timeliness in connecting me with books and articles through interlibrary loan; and to Mary Martha Riviere and Erica Durham for their alacrity and hospitality.

Lastly, I want to thank two people who read this book in its entirety prior to submission. Abby Myers, my life partner and editor-in-chief, helped me retain some semblance of intelligibility when my thoughts drifted toward obscurity. Lauren Patrus, one of my star homiletics students, spotted innumerable errors and indexed this book. May God bless you both for your patience!

I wish to dedicate this book to my *Doktorvater*, Tom Long. Tom, you told me once that you sought to teach me the rules of the game so that I could change the game. I hope that this book lives up to that charge and proves worthy of the time and energy you've invested in me over the years. I am thankful for your scholarship, your instruction, your passion, and your kindness.

Introduction: Preaching Must Die!

We will never revive the pulpit with a few fancy pulpit tricks and new preaching styles. We need theological support that goes as deep as the Word itself, because only a theology of the Word that resists idolatry will resist the idolatries of preaching.

—Anna Carter Florence[1]

It is indeed precisely philosophical discourse that we have to challenge, and disrupt, inasmuch as this discourse sets forth the law for all others, inasmuch as it constitutes the discourse on discourse.

—Luce Irigaray[2]

Homiletics exists to free preaching from theology. Homiletics is neither words about God nor God's "Word," if there *is* such a *thing*. Homiletics, like theology, like preaching, can have no life in and of itself. I believe that homiletics' sole purpose is to help preaching die a good death.

Unfortunately, in its quest for academic and ecclesial respectability, homiletics has made a pact with theology: contemporary homiletics presents itself to the world as "theology in the form of sermon preparation."[3] Homiletics has sold its birthright for a bowl of stew. Such is theology's deviousness. Homiletics has failed to notice that theology's duplicitousness stems from its dual allegiance to God and to philosophy. If theology were a Norse god, it could only be Loki.

Theology is always already philosophy. This ought not alarm us. As

1. Anna Carter Florence, *Preaching as Testimony* (Louisville: Westminster John Knox, 2007), 103.
2. Luce Irigaray, "The Power of Discourse," in *This Sex Which is Not One*, trans. Catherine Porter (Ithaca, NY: Cornell University Press, 1985), 74.
3. David Schnasa Jacobsen, "Promise and Cross: Homiletical Theology, the Vocative Word *Extra Nos*, and the Task of a Revisionist Eschatology," in *Homiletical Theology in Action: The Unfinished Theological Task of Preaching*, ed. David Schnasa Jacobsen (Eugene, OR: Cascade Books, 2015), 109.

Herbert McCabe OP puts it, "[The] philosophical task may seem rather distant from doing theology as such, but if faith is 'seeking understanding' it had better not be confused about understanding."[4] Theology, moreover, is not a Christian word, but a loan word from Western philosophy. The word appears nowhere in the Bible, and it is doubtful that Jesus would have employed such a term. Coined by Plato, the term theology was later adopted by Aristotle to differentiate the myths about the gods from philosophy proper.[5] The solution is not, contra Barth, to cleanse or purge theology of philosophy.[6] Rather, we must re-cognize theology—and homiletical theologies most of all—as philosophy. Such is the central preoccupation of this book.   ᵛⁱᵉˢᵗᵉⁱⁿ pʰⁱˡ

As much as some homileticians hate to admit it, the central features of preaching are philosophical before they are baptized as theology. Evangelical homiletics, for instance, operates according to a correspondence theory of truth à la Bertrand Russell and the early Ludwig Wittgenstein. Post-liberal homiletics abides by Wittgenstein's later work, particularly his concept of "language games" (Sprachspiel). Narrative/inductive homiletics rests on a Heideggerian infrastructure. Liberationist homiletics reiterate the suppositions of critical theory. I could go on.

The point here is not to criticize homiletics for its reliance upon philosophical concepts but to suggest that homiletics, like theology, is always and necessarily philosophical. The question we must ask ourselves is what our respective philosophies commit us to homiletically. (I wish I could change my job title to "homilosopher." But, alas.) Are the laws (nomoi) of our homiletical houses (oikoi) just? Does such an eco-

---

4. Herbert McCabe OP, "The Eucharist as Language," Modern Theology 15, no. 2 (April 1999): 133.

5. See Plato, Republic, trans. Paul Shorey (Cambridge, MA: Harvard University Press, 1930), Bk. II, 379 a, p. 182. Plato, speaking to Adeimantus, describes theology as that which arises from the ancient poets about the gods (contra philosophy, which gets at the true essence of things). Few Christian theologians would ascribe to Plato's conclusion: "[god] is the author of only a small part of human affairs . . . the good things we must ascribe to no other than god, while we must seek elsewhere, and not in him [sic], the causes of the harmful things" (379 c). Aristotle, in a derisive tone, challenges the theologoi (whom Hugh Tredennick curiously translates as "cosmologists") vis-à-vis his own philosophical account for metaphysics. See Aristotle, Metaphysics, trans. H. Tredennick (Cambridge, MA: Harvard University Press, 1935), Bk. XII, 1071 b 27, p. 142.

6. "Theology can become noticed by philosophy only after that moment when it no longer seeks to be interesting. Its relation to philosophy can become positive and fruitful only after it resolutely refuses to be itself a philosophy and refuses to demonstrate and base its existence upon a principle with, or alongside of, philosophy." Karl Barth, God in Action: Theological Addresses (Eugene, OR: Wipf & Stock, 2005), 42. Elsewhere Barth declares, "If we open our mouths, we find ourselves in the province of philosophy." Barth, Credo (Eugene, OR: Wipf & Stock, 2005), 183. The tension between these quotations lends support to Kenneth Oakes's argument that "Barth never settles upon one stable or cogent understanding of this topic [the relationship between theology and philosophy], even while he constantly emphasizes theology's independence." Karl Barth on Theology and Philosophy (Oxford: Oxford University Press, 2012), 17.

nomy lead us toward God, or does it inadvertently frustrate the possibility of encountering God in and through preaching?[7]

The Trouble with Preaching

Homiletics troubles preaching, which, in turn, troubles homiletics. Like siblings, homiletics and preaching share a peculiar relationship. They love each other at all times, yet oftentimes they can't stand each other. Homiletics is the younger of the two by (at least) four hundred years[8]; and yet, like Jacob to Esau, Rachel to Leah, or like the Prodigal Son to his brother who remained on the farm, the younger tends to supplant the elder. Either by intent or happenstance, the lure of usurpation is commonplace; the second-born seeks the elder's position and rights as firstborn. Equally precocious and plucky, little brother homiletics likes to tell his big sister preaching how to think (theology) and what to say (rhetoric).[9] Homiletics lurks in preaching's shadow, ever watchful to keep preaching out of trouble. For the most part, preaching has tolerated this with grace and insouciance.

But preaching *is* trouble. At its core. Originarily.[10]

Feminist philosopher Judith Butler opens her classic text *Gender Trouble* with a helpful reflection on the nature of trouble. She urges her readers not to be too quick to cast trouble with a negative valance. Trouble, as such, vacillates between agency and passivity. One can *make*

7. This problem corresponds with the muddled historical and theological division between the private and public spheres and the church's position among them. The household (*oikos*), as Hannah Arendt observes, was restricted to the private sphere in classical societies. The state (*polis*), on the other hand, was conceived as the realm of freedom and public action. *The Human Condition*, 2nd ed. (Chicago: University of Chicago Press, 1998), 28–30. She states that with the rise of society—viz., economic activities beyond the household—any serious division between the social and political realms is impossible: "In the modern world, the two realms indeed constantly flow into each other like waves in the never-resting stream of the life process itself" (33).
8. Many regard St. Augustine's *De Doctrina Christiana*, which was finalized in 426 CE, as the first homiletics text. Much of Book IV of this work draws from classical rhetoric, especially Cicero and Quintilian.
9. This, precisely, is how Sally Brown and Luke Powery orient their readers to the task of preaching: "There are many ways to begin a book about preaching. We chose to begin by reflecting on preaching from both *theological* and *rhetorical* points of view. . . . [In preaching] the human tongue speaks (rhetoric) and the life-giving promise of God sounds (theology)." Sally A. Brown and Luke A. Powery, *Ways of the Word: Learning to Preach for Your Time and Place* (Minneapolis: Fortress Press, 2016), 1, 4. So, too, Frank A. Thomas, *Introduction to the Practice of African American Preaching* (Nashville: Abingdon, 2016), 5, 6, 7, 55.
10. The word *originarily* is a favored term in poststructural philosophies. It is similar though different to the word *originally*. The former resembles the later in regard to that which is temporally prior. Where the terms differ, however, is that the word *original* presumes an origin, a point and place of beginning; the words *original* and its adjectival derivative signify the possibility of isolating and locating an origin. The term *originarily*, by contrast, points to an always already aspect that subverts the possibility of an origin that can ground a concept.

3

trouble, which is a surefire way *to get into trouble*. Butler observes that both rebellion and reprimand are caught up in the same terms, the "subtle ruse of power: the prevailing law threatened one with trouble, even put one in trouble, all to keep one out of trouble." It will remain the task of this book to interrogate the "prevailing laws" of preaching that homiletics establishes and works to enforce, challenging the latter's "ruse of power."[11]

Butler is right. Trouble is inevitable. Preaching is always already in trouble, and I want to make sure it's in trouble for the right reasons. This book presents my efforts to interrogate the constitutive elements of preaching, those aspects of preaching apart from which preaching could not "exist." These are *language, the preacher, scripture,* and *God.* There are other elements we might rightly consider; but, at minimum, and as preaching's conditions of possibility (if preaching is, in fact, *possible*), apart from these four factors preaching could not exist (if preaching does, in fact, *exist*)—see, we've barely begun and already we're causing trouble.

Our task herein is to discern together how best *to make* trouble homiletically and the best ways *to be* in trouble kerygmatically.[12] This book aims to think through the possibility of subverting homiletics *through* preaching. At the same time, this book seeks to displace those naturalized and reified notions of preaching that bolster a certain Western, modernist, theological hegemony: in short, to help homiletics (re)orient itself *as* trouble for preaching. Any strategies that may arise from this investigation do not purport to deliver preaching to some "utopian beyond," as if we could ever arrive at such a place. Rather, it aims to *mobilize, subvert, confuse,* and *proliferate* those constitutive homiletical impulses that aim to keep preaching in check, to keep it out of trouble. Accordingly, this book participates in kerygmatic deconstruction, troubling the "foundational illusions" that bolster contemporary preaching styles.[13]

---

11. Judith Butler, *Gender Trouble: Feminism and the Subversion of Identity*, 2nd ed. (New York: Routledge, 1990), xxix.
12. A brief note on terminology. When employed adjectivally or adverbially, I take "homiletical(ly)" to modify the structures and discourses pertaining to homiletics, which governs the development and delivery of sermons. The modifier "kerygmatic(ally)" relates to preaching in conventional parlance: the *act* of Christian proclamation.
13. This is all drawn from Butler, to whom my debt is great. She writes, "This text continues, then, as an effort to think through the possibility of subverting and displacing those naturalized and reified notions of gender that support masculine hegemony and heterosexist power, to make gender trouble, not through the strategies that figure a utopian beyond, but through the mobilization, subversive confusion, and proliferation of precisely those constitutive categories that seek

4

Biblical Subversions of Homiletics

By way of confession, my understanding of preaching is guided by two biblical scenes—scenes that trouble my understanding of preaching, troubling my understanding of homiletics as a result.

God said to Abraham, "Take your son, your only son Isaac, whom you love, and go to the land of Moriah, and offer him there as a burnt offering on one of the mountains of which I shall tell you" (Gen 22:2). God's calling here is at once monstrous and impossible. It bears witness either to a God who is diabolical or a God who abides by a different rationality than we humans can fathom. All the while, "God keeps silent about [God's] reasons."[14] The calling of God is impossibly absolute and absolutely impossible. The calling of God harbors a secret.

To preach is to heed a summons that defies logic, that defies knowledge. To the degree that preaching "is" anything, it is an attempt to articulate the secret of God, which, as I explain in chapter 4, is another way of saying the "Word" of God. Preaching emerges between the silent and secret call (of God) and our human response, which is neither silent nor secret.

As we witness here in the *Akedah*, the "binding" of Isaac, preaching takes shape as a kind of binding, indeed, a double-bind. In response to God's call (Abraham's theological response), Abraham presents himself. "Here I am," he says. In response to Isaac's call, Abraham presents himself in the same way (his ethical response). Abraham asserts himself in relation to both his theological and his ethical responsibility. Either response fails the test of God's testing (v. 1), because the test was always already rigged. Even in winning he loses. All roads lead to death, barring a miraculous intervention, which must always possibly *not* arrive.

This narrative informs my understanding of preaching as a "leap of faith," to borrow Kierkegaard's famous phrase, which is at the same time a leap of death. Preaching is a summons to die. It is here, at this moment of undecidability, at this moment between a monstrous possibility and a divine impossibility, that preaching exposes itself to *the*

---

to keep gender in its place by posturing as the foundational illusions of identity." *Gender Trouble*, 46.

14. Jacques Derrida, *The Gift of Death and Literature in Secret*, trans. David Willis, 2nd ed. (Chicago: University of Chicago Press, 2008), 59. See also Søren Kierkegaard, *Fear and Trembling*, vol. 6: *Repetition*, Kierkegaard's Writings, trans. Edna H. Hong and Howard V. Hong (Princeton, NJ: Princeton University Press, 1983). It is no wonder that Kierkegaard signs his text under the pseudonym Johannes de Silentio. The "John" who is summoned to speak is summoned out of and into a certain silence.

secret, which is to say, the *Word* of God. It is only into and out of death that the secret *may be* heard. Movement toward death in hope of life inaugurates the possibility of a "new modality of the True," a modality beyond "Truth."[15] In other words, preaching into death provides the ultimate test of our faithfulness, "hoping beyond hope" for God to intervene in a miraculous way.[16]

A second framing text for my understanding of preaching is Mark 9:1–10. Here, Jesus is transfigured in the presence of Peter, James, and John. Within Mark's Gospel, this pericope functions as a kind of hinge. Prior to chapter nine, Jesus's ministry is all about callings and healings and parabolic musings on the kingdom of God. The progression of scenes leads to Jesus's declaration that all who wish to be his followers must deny their selfhood and take up their cross (Mark 8:34). And then Jesus climbs a mountain.

Given the significance of Jesus's transformation and the ghostly apparitions of Moses and Elijah, we, like Peter, might expect some denouement in the Jesus tale that Mark tells. Mark leaves us disappointed. What follows in Mark's narration is very much like that which preceded this mountaintop experience. Jesus continues his ministry of healing and teaching and calling. The rise and fall of his narrative, marked at this pinnacle, this mountaintop, leads us to a state of undecidability. What is the significance of Jesus's transfiguration? What did Jesus discuss with Moses and Elijah? What does this mean for we who have heard Jesus's summons to follow?

Added to this is the voice and presence of God shrouded in a cloud, commanding the disciples to listen to Jesus. They heed this divine admonition and follow Jesus's instructions as they descend from the mountain to tell no one about what they have seen and heard. The summons is to silence; the following is to death. A case could be made that the effect of Jesus's transfiguration—the form of his transfiguration—has less to do with a change in Jesus's essential being than with our perceptions of him. The same could be said about preaching.

---

15. See Emmanuel Levinas, *Proper Names*, trans. Michael B. Smith (Stanford: Stanford University Press, 1996), 77–79.
16. This turn of phrase is Caputo's, following Derrida: "The impossible is not the simple logical contradiction of the possible, but the terminus of a hope beyond hope, of a hope against hope, of a faith in what we cannot imagine or in any way foresee, a *tout autre*, beyond any present horizon of expectation. This is the common coin of deconstruction and mystical prayer, the common aspiration of what I dare call deconstructive prayer and mystical prayer, and the common reason that they drive language to its limits." John D. Caputo, "The Prayers and Tears of Devilish Hermeneutics: Derrida and Meister Eckhart," in *More Radical Hermeneutics: On Not Knowing Who We Are* (Bloomington: Indiana University Press, 2000), 263.

God's transfiguration of Jesus informs my understanding of preaching in that neither leaves a trace—at least not one that lingers. Even as we "speak" with Moses and Elijah in sermon development, our preaching produces no new tabernacles. It is a summons to obey God: to listen and to follow Jesus to a cross, to death. Resurrection may take place, and Mark leaves this possibility open. It's as if he's saying that resurrection is God's business. Ours is death. Preaching that listens to Jesus and follows him down the mountain leads only to death.

So, how might homiletics prepare preaching and preachers to climb these two mountains, these twin peaks that rise to meet death and descend toward death? Homiletics has tended to avoid this question. It wants to ensure a long and healthy life for preaching. It loves preaching too much to watch it die. Homiletics seeks life for preaching, and that, precisely, is its problem.

Homiletics Goes to Hogwarts

Facing preaching's quietus, I feel a bit like Albus Dumbledore when he receives news that his pet phoenix has just died. "At last," Dumbledore says, "He's been looking dreadful for days." Of course, it's natural for a phoenix to burst into flames at the end of its life and arise to new life out of its own ashes. What if preaching is the same way? What if its purpose is to meet its Maker? What if preaching was *born* to die?

Following in Fred Craddock's footsteps, the guild of homiletics has gone to great lengths to keep preaching alive. The situation reminds me of a central plot line from the final two *Harry Potter* books. Lord Voldemort, the darkest of all dark wizards, has discovered a way to live forever. Through his mastery of the dark arts, Voldemort learned how to create horcruxes. A horcrux is an object in which a wizard may conceal a part of his soul; that way, if the wizard is attacked, he will live on despite his bodily demise. A horcrux is a means of avoiding death.

In some respects, homiletics—the academic discipline that bolsters the theoretical, theological, and practical guidelines for the practice of preaching—isn't all that different from Voldemort. Hear me out. While homiletics shares no part in Voldemort's will to power and domination, homiletics has partitioned off its soul (viz., preaching) to ensure its own survival.

One horcrux that homiletics has created to buffer preaching from death is that of dogma. Dogma is a set of propositional claims about God—often held to be incontrovertible. In some church traditions, preaching has become less about embracing an encounter with God through the Spirit and more about pushing dogmatic conformity.[17] This is a classic case of putting the cart before the horse. Karl Barth rightly argues that dogmatics ought to arise out of preaching, not the other way around. Said differently, preaching gives rise to dogma; dogma is not the source content for preaching.[18] Dogma functions as a horcrux for preaching when preachers feel the need to spend their twenty minutes (or forty-five minutes!) defending so-called truths about God against preaching's "cultured despisers," to borrow a phrase from Schleiermacher.

At its core, dogma is a form of argumentation. But, following St. Ambrose, "God has no desire to save His [sic] people through argument. The kingdom of God is found in simple faith and not in verbal disputes."[19] Preaching as dogma commits itself to the gods of logical positivism rather than the God of Abraham, Isaac, and Jacob. Inasmuch as it *is* anything, preaching is a radical, foolish act of faith—and I particularly appreciate Richard Kearney's conception of faith as "knowing you don't know anything absolutely about absolutes."[20] Reasoned argument supplants faith with logic. But faith-ful preaching is tenuous by design. It's like a baby giraffe attempting its first steps . . . on ice . . . in roller skates. No matter how much the preacher seethes about God's "truth," and regardless of the seeming unassailability of the preacher's logic, preaching is always more than dogma or it is nothing at all.[21]

---

17. See Donald English, *An Evangelical Theology of Preaching* (Nashville: Abingdon, 1996), which is less of a theology *of* preaching than an apology for preaching *on* doctrine.
18. Karl Barth, *The Church Dogmatics*, I/1, ed. Geoffrey W. Bromiley and Thomas F. Torrance, trans. Geoffrey W. Bromiley (Edinburgh: T & T Clark, 1975), 47: "Talk about God in the Church seeks to be proclamation to the extent that in the form of preaching and sacrament it is directed to man [sic] with the claim and expectation that in accordance with its commission it has to speak to him the Word of God to be heard in faith. Inasmuch as it is a human word in spite of this claim and expectation, it is the material of dogmatics, i.e., of the investigation of its responsibility as measured by the Word of God which it seeks to proclaim."
19. St. Ambrose, "De Fide Ad Gratianum," in *Nicene and Post-Nicene Fathers*, series 2, ed. Philip Schaff, trans. H. de Romestin, vol. 10, *Ambrose: Selected Works and Letters* (Edinburgh: T & T Clark, 2009), I.5.42, p. 366.
20. Richard Kearney, *Anatheism: Returning to God After God* (New York: Columbia University Press, 2011), 170.
21. Or, as Thomas G. Long so aptly puts it, "The least effective preaching, in my view, occurs when the preacher tries to rise above the grit of everyday existence, attempts to assume the voice of the pop philosopher or the broad culture critic, and pumps out expansive observations about great themes and overarching concepts, whether these be of the evangelical variety ('God's Plan for Salvation') or the more liberal sort ('The Call to Live for Peace and Justice.')." Thomas G. Long, "Can I Get a Witness?" *Vision* 10, no. 1 (Spring 2009): 21–22.
   Dogmatic preaching takes many forms, and David Lose has even found a way to commend dogmatic preaching in a "postmodern" vein. For Lose, doctrine functions like a motion sickness pill, settling the listener's stomach from a kind of postmodern indigestion. He argues that preachers ought to smuggle doctrine into preaching under pretense of attending to the hearer's experience.

A second horcrux that homiletics has created is that of biblical exposition. This betrays an epistemological assumption that collapses the difference between the words of scripture and the "Word" of God, if such a thing *exists*. The Bible bears witness to God's radical holiness. Holy Scripture is only *Holy* to the extent that it exposes us to God's holiness. The Bible's holiness is not innate. Inasmuch as scripture participates in God's radical otherness, it is a miracle.[22]

If our words about God are always already adulterated by a thoroughly human mode of discourse—tenuously held together according to socio-symbolic matrixes we call language (see chapter 1)—how might we understand the Bible to be anything more than attempts at uttering the name "God," but human attempts nonetheless? Before the God who has revealed Godself as worthy of worship and honor, what word-offerings are sufficient to the revealed majesty and holiness of such a God? Does not the deconstruction always already taking place within contemporary modes of thought and discourse make the task of preaching all the more impossible? Would not Wittgenstein's admonition to silence be most apropos for preachers?[23]

David J. Lose, *Preaching at the Crossroads: How the World—and Our Preaching—Is Changing* (Minneapolis: Fortress Press, 2013), 27. In spite of his intentions, which are quite admirable, Lose belies his anti-foundational claims by employing a foundation to undergird his project, a bait-and-switch tactic that radically underestimates the ability of congregants—particularly Millennials—to call bullshit. A "flexible foundation" is still a foundation (see pp. 20–21).

22. As Barth puts it, "[The one] who says 'God,' always says 'miracle'... [For] humanity has no sensible organ wherewith to perceive the miracle. Human experience and human perception end where God begins" Karl Barth, *The Epistle to the Romans*, 6th ed., trans. Edwyn C. Hoskyns (London: Oxford University Press, 1933), 120, (translation modified). Stephen Smith gets it right when he observes that Barth's "Other" is "not, strictly speaking, *anything*: it is only a *way* to speak of *something else*, something that may be quite definite but must remain, for one reason or another, out of direct view." Smith continues, "For Barth the 'something else' is the God revealed in Christ, the Creator incommensurable with the creature, who nevertheless makes himself known to us, in a manner lacking all analogy in our experience." Steven G. Smith, *The Argument to the Other: Reason Beyond Reason in the Thought of Karl Barth and Emmanuel Levinas*, American Academy of Religion Academy Series, no. 42 (Chico, CA: Scholars Press, 1983), 5. See also his latter insight: "Barth's argument is not that God *is* the Wholly Other. Such a statement, like any other direct theological predication, cannot stand before God. Barth's point is that we must speak of God *as* the Wholly Other because of the actual position in which we find ourselves, in the light of revelation" (46).

Or, as Barth puts it elsewhere, "Again it is quite impossible that there should be a direct identity between the human word of Holy Scripture and the Word of God, and therefore between the creaturely reality in itself and as such and the reality of God the Creator. It is impossible that there should have been a transmutation of the one into the other or an admixture of the one with the other. This is not the case even in the person of Christ where the identity between God and man, in all the originality and indissolubility in which it confronts us, is an assumed identity, one specially willed, created and effected by God, and to that extent indirect, i.e., resting neither in the essence of God nor in that of man, but in a decision and act of God to man. When we necessarily allow for inherent differences, it is exactly the same with the unity of the divine and human word in Holy Scripture." Karl Barth, *The Church Dogmatics*, I/2, ed. Geoffrey W. Bromiley and Thomas F. Torrance, trans. George Thomas Thomson and Harold Knight (Edinburgh: T & T Clark, 1956), 499.

23. Ludwig Wittgenstein, *Tractatus Logico-Philosophicus*, trans. B. F. McGuinness and D. F. Pears (Lon-

Biblical exposition is not preaching. It is a substitute for preaching, a homiletical surrogate. Hereby, the preacher is so afraid to trust preaching as proclamation of God's "Word" that he reduces it to mere explanation and application. Preaching and teaching are not the same thing. To be clear, biblical exposition is an important—nay, vital—task of pastoral ministry. But it ought not supplant preaching.[24]

One of the leading homiletical proponents of preaching as teaching is Bryan Chapell. He writes, "In the pulpit, we are expositors, not authors. Sermons explain what the Bible says."[25] But preachers are authors. We write, or at least speak, *beyond* what scripture declares. Furthermore, the impulse to explain what the Bible means robs preaching of its lively, unwieldy, and oftentimes uncanny undecidability. Timothy Keller, a popular expository preacher, argues that exposition "grounds the message in the text so that all the sermon's points are points in the text, and it majors in the text's major ideas."[26] Nope. That's a horcrux. Ideas won't save us. Scripture isn't a foundation upon which we may *ground* anything. The Bible is quicksand.

Anna Carter Florence draws an important distinction along these lines between a *Mary Preacher* and a *Zechariah Preacher*. The former receives God's annunciation with wonder, asking, "How can this *be*?" The latter, by contrast, fights to ground God's in-breaking epistemologically, asking, "How can I *know* this?" Florence warns us of the dangers of forcing scripture to conform to our human metrics and rationalities. She writes, "Zechariah Preachers . . . want certainty, absolutes, answers, explanations; they want proof texts. If they cannot find those

don: Routledge, 1961), 3: "What can be said at all can be said clearly and what we cannot talk about we must pass over in silence."
24. Ebeling draws a helpful distinction here: "[T]he sermon as a sermon is not exposition of the text as past proclamation, but is itself proclamation in the present—and that means, then, that *the sermon is* EXECUTION *of the text.* It carries into execution the aim of the text. It is proclamation of what the text has proclaimed." Gerhard Ebeling, "Word of God and Hermeneutics," in *Word and Faith* (Philadelphia: Fortress Press, 1963), 327. Later, he writes, "*Thus the text by means of the sermon becomes a hermeneutic aid in the understanding of present experience.* Where that happens radically, there true word is uttered, and that in fact means God's Word" (331).
25. Bryan Chapell, *Christ-Centered Preaching: Redeeming the Expository Sermon*, 2nd ed. (Grand Rapids, MI: Baker Academic, 2005), 59. Thomas Long rightly challenges a simple or mechanical logic that would collapse biblical meaning in contemporary exposition. Rather, he urges us to think of preaching as "an imaginative regeneration of a biblical text [that] opens our eyes to the role played by imagination both in the creation and canonization of the text itself and in the minds of those who hear the sermon." Thomas G. Long, "The Use of Scripture in Contemporary Preaching," *Interpretation* 44, no. 4 (October 1990): 348.
26. Timothy Keller, *Preaching: Communicating Faith in an Age of Skepticism* (New York: Viking, 2015), 39. He continues, "It aligns the interpretation of the text with the doctrinal truths of the rest of the Bible (being sensitive to systematic theology). And it always situates the passage within the Bible's narrative, showing how Christ is the final fulfillment of the text's theme (being sensitive to biblical theology)."

10

things, they fear they will not be real preachers—or *good* ones, at any rate. Actually, the truth is that they will not be preachers, period."[27] Scripture may most certainly be a starting point for preaching; but it cannot serve as a prophylactic to guard preaching from extrabiblical infection. Contamination has always already taken hold.[28]

A third horcrux homiletics has fabricated to stave off preaching's demise is practical wisdom. Practical wisdom has a long tradition in the pulpit. For instance, way back in 1928, the famed Baptist preacher Harry Emerson Fosdick published an article poignantly titled, "What's the Matter with Preaching?" Fosdick diagnosed the preaching of his day as being irrelevant insofar as it missed the "true concerns" of congregants and parishioners. He wrote, "Every sermon should have for its main business the solving of some problem . . . and any sermon which thus does tackle a real problem, throw even a little light on it, and help some individuals practically to find their way through it cannot be altogether uninteresting."[29] In essence, the solution Fosdick proffered to solve the problem of preaching was to give the people what they need, or believe they need.[30]

Here's the problem with this horcrux: preaching is not wisdom. At most, it bears witness to a wisdom that troubles all worldly conceptions of wisdom (cf. 1 Cor 2:1-16).[31] Many megachurch pastors have followed in Fosdick's footsteps, succumbing to the lure of what Thomas Long labels the "sage tradition" of preaching. Such preachers merely capitulate to capitalist ideals, neoliberal ideologies, and late-Modern values. By this I mean that they focus on the use-value of the gospel and

---

27. Florence, *Preaching as Testimony*, 116. I find a similar approach in the work of Richard Voelz, who employs the "critical pedagogy" of Henry Giroux as a mode of questioning and challenging discursive/pedagogical possibilities. Richard Voelz, "Reconsidering the Image of Preacher-as-Teacher: Intersections between Henry Giroux's Critical Pedagogy and Homiletics," *Practical Matters Journal* (March 1, 2014), http://wp.me/p6QAmj-a7.

28. On the necessary possibility of contamination, see Jacques Derrida, *Speech and Phenomena: And Other Essays on Husserl's Theory of Signs*, trans. David B. Allison (Evanston, IL: Northwestern University Press, 1973), 17–26.

29. Harry Emerson Fosdick, "What's The Matter With Preaching?" *Harper's* (July 1928): 134.

30. Ibid.: "Any preacher who even with moderate skill is thus helping folk to solve their real problems . . . is doing the one thing that is a preacher's business. He is delivering the goods that the community has a right to expect from the pulpit as much as it has a right to expect shoes from a cobbler. And if any preacher is not doing this, even though he have at his disposal both erudition and oratory, he is not functioning at all."

31. Thomas G. Long, *The Witness of Preaching*, 3rd ed. (Louisville: Westminster John Knox, 2016), 39: "[W]e do not go to the Scripture to gain more information about life as we know it, but rather to have our fundamental understandings of life altered. The task of preaching is not to set out some reality in life and then go to the Bible to find extra wisdom. It is instead to tell the story of the Bible so clearly that it calls into question and ultimately redefines what we think we know of reality and what we call wisdom in the first place. The Bible becomes the key to unlock the true nature of life, not vice versa."

appear more concerned with empire building than in participating in the queendom of God, which transcends particular ecclesial contexts. Offering step-by-step guides for the faithful to shed their "lesser loser life" or to overcome "enemies of the heart" may be great for church small groups or spiritual edification, but they have no business in the pulpit.[32]

Homiletics must abandon its horcruxes. Like Harry Potter in the final book of the series that bears his name, we have to find a way to welcome death. Homiletics must embrace preaching's passing—not just acknowledge it, but embrace it—as preaching's "ownmost possibility."[33] Clinging to Dumbledore's words, "To the well-organized mind, death is but the next great adventure," or—more apropos—to Jesus's words, "Whoever might desire to save his life will lose it; but whoever might lose his life on account of me will save it" (Luke 9:24).

Preaching Meets Its Maker

Humans are obsessed with life. But we will die. All of us. We employ every means at our disposal to stave off the inevitability of our demise.[34] Before our own mortality we are like a cat chasing the beam of a flashlight—gazing, crouching, leaping, seizing. But, like the cat, we never take hold of that which consumes our attention. When we unclench our calico mittens, we find nothing but our own flesh, the sign of our being and doing, the mark of our fragility.

Of course, all this talk of death, dying, and bucket-kicking in homiletics is metaphorical; but the metaphor cashes in on a literal preoccupation: we don't want to die. Ever. But we know that we will die, and this fear animates our desires and consumes our ways of thinking, being, and belonging. This is not the way of Jesus to which homileticians and preachers have been called.

The way of Jesus is the way of bold abnegation; it is an obdurate middle finger to unjust and oppressive social, political, and religious struc-

32. See Steven Furtick, *Greater: Dream Bigger. Start Smaller. Ignite God's Vision for Your Life* (Colorado Springs: Multnomah Books, 2012); Andy Stanley, *Enemies of the Heart: Breaking Free from the Four Emotions That Control You* (Colorado Springs: Multnomah Books, 2011).
33. Cf. Paul Ricoeur, "The Hermeneutical Function of Distanciation," in *Hermeneutics and the Human Sciences: Essays on Language, Action, and Interpretation*, ed. and trans. John B. Thompson (Cambridge: Cambridge University Press, 1981), 142: "the moment of 'understanding' [à la Heidegger, *Being and Time*] corresponds dialectically to being in a situation: it is the projection of our ownmost possibilities at the very heart of a situation in which we find ourselves."
34. "Writing is learning to die. It's learning not to be afraid, in other words to live at the extremity of life, which is what the dead, death, give us." Hélène Cixous, *Three Steps on the Ladder of Writing*, trans. Sarah Cornell and Susan Sellers (New York: Columbia University Press, 1993), 10.

tures; *and* at the same time, it is an opening of the self beyond itself, a rending of oneself that is paradoxical in a very gospelish way: in seeking, we find; in giving, we gain; in losing, we win.[35]

In this book, I invite you to help me roll away the stone of contemporary homiletical theology to enter the cave of deconstruction. Herein, I wish to expose some of the constitutive components of preaching (viz., language, personhood, scripture, and God) to those philosophical elements that homileticians have ignored or rejected outright.[36] Deconstruction, to be clear, is not something I'm going to *do* to preaching. Deconstruction is always already at work *within* preaching.[37] I'm going to show you how and why it matters for homiletical theologies.

Like the ancient Israelites, our (epistemological) liberation from

35. As Karmen MacKendrick writes, "The sacrificial death of God, irredeemable except as self-redeeming (not after or despite, but *in* its mortal violence), opens the space for the movement beyond subjectivity into the opening of the self. The contestation of the subject, the ripping-open of the self, comes out of that subject's own agony of desire. The finitude of the self, the boundaries that make it, open to the infinity of the divine, shattering in flesh and blood the order of the profane—in imitation of the mortal wounds of the bleeding, dying, glorified God. Here the sacred is not 'set apart,' but that which is neither apart nor contained." Karmen MacKendrick, "Sharing God's Wounds: Laceration, Communication, and Stigmata," in *The Obsessions of Georges Bataille: Community and Communication*, ed. Andrew J. Mitchell and Jason Kemp Vinfree (Albany: SUNY Press, 2009), 138.

36. If we had the time and space, we might include other elements: the congregation, sermon delivery, and the world beyond the church in need of God's liberation are some that come to mind. While these and other elements are not treated explicitly, they are implicit: speech necessitates proximity, which implies those gathered to hear a "Word" from the Lord; language, scripture, and theology apart from the world God loves are vapid, if not impossible.

37. ". . . the very condition of a deconstruction may be at work, in the work, *within* the system to be deconstructed; it may *already* be located there, already at work, not at the center but in an eccentric center, in a corner whose eccentricity assures the solid concentration of the system, participating in the construction of what it at the same time threatens to deconstruct. One might then be inclined to reach this conclusion: deconstruction is not an operation that supervenes *afterwards*, from the outside, one fine day; it is always already at work in the work; one must just know how to identify the right or wrong element, the right or wrong stone—the right one, of course, always proves to be, precisely, the wrong one. Since the disruptive force of deconstruction is always already contained within the architecture of the work, all one would finally have to do to be able to deconstruct, given this *always already*, is to do memory work." Jacques Derrida, *Memoires for Paul de Man*, trans. Cecile Lindsay, Jonathan Culler, and Eduardo Cadava (New York: Columbia University Press, 1986), 73. For more clarity on Derrida's use of the term *deconstruction*, see Jacques Derrida, "Letter to a Japanese Friend," in *A Derrida Reader: Between the Blinds*, ed. Peggy Kamuf, trans. David Wood and Andrew Benjamin (New York: Columbia University Press, 1991), 269–76; John D. Caputo, *Deconstruction in a Nutshell: A Conversation with Jacques Derrida* (New York: Fordham University Press, 1997); and Geoffrey Bennington, "'Jacques Derrida,'" in *Interrupting Derrida* (London: Routledge, 2000), 7–17.
    This is where, despite his important advances, Phil Snider's work is off. He writes, "Deconstruction was not sent into the world in order to confirm and ordain the present powers that be, but rather to open them up, to provoke them, to disturb them, which is not entirely unlike what Jesus did when he was said to be going about his father's business." *Preaching After God: Derrida, Caputo and the Language of Postmodern Homiletics* (Eugene, OR: Cascade Books, 2012), 117. Within a Derridian *frame*—if we may speak of a frame, or speak beyond a frame, or a Derridian *anything*, Derrida might counter—it is incorrect to think of deconstruction as that which was "sent into the world." Deconstruction does not arrive on the scene from some outside one fine day, but is always already present on the inside—indeed, in the very separation of an outside from an inside.

(metaphysical) bondage necessitates a certain desert wandering. But very much *unlike* the Israelites, our search can in no way deliver us to a (homiletical) promised land. Deconstruction cannot even lead us to a new starting point for Christian proclamation—except as a way of tripping up every strategy for starting. Deconstruction invites us to the threshold of our theological liberation, our liberation from theo-logy as such, to imagine a new mode of homiletical being in the world. It makes no promises. Deconstruction cannot become the *Sache* (theme or subject) of Christian proclamation, nor can it offer a viable *method* for sermon development and delivery. Rather, in keeping with the words of Walter Lowe, deconstruction helps theology to "clean house," to help theology "identify and expel from its vocabulary that entire lexicon of terms which serve the metaphysics of presence."[38] Lowe offers a glimpse of a theology keen to the philosophical commitments that work against the values it proclaims most resolutely. Deconstruction can thus be understood as a tool for such liberative work.[39] Accordingly, deconstruction unwittingly serves homiletics by pointing to the cracks and fissures plastered over by centuries of philosophical spackle and layers of theological wallpaper. There are a few points that I wish to clarify before we begin.

First, deconstruction troubles thought and discourse from within. When we open our eyes to the deconstruction taking place on the *inside* of preaching, we witness a certain troubling always already at work within Western thought—and homiletics in the wake of postmodernity. As the eminent philosopher Jacques Derrida writes, "The movements of deconstruction do not destroy structures from the outside. They are not possible and effective, nor can they take accurate aim, except by inhabiting those structures. Inhabiting them *in a certain way,* because one always inhabits, and all the more when one does not suspect it."[40] Herein, we shall follow Derrida's admonition and thereby

38. Walter Lowe, *Theology and Difference: The Wound of Reason* (Bloomington: Indiana University Press, 1993), 17.
39. Anna Carter Florence has also recognized that deconstruction can be used to liberate the "enslaved logic" at work in our preaching. She writes, "ready or not, like it or not, when we deconstruct a thing, we *will* see ourselves more clearly. Deconstruction, like therapy, permits us to uncover the masked priorities and power dynamics of a text that may warp its authority structures, and so create ingrown systems that lead to oppression and suffering. Or, to put it another way, when we deconstruct something, such as preaching, we allow it to *show itself more clearly* so that we can see the things that make it what it is." *Preaching as Testimony*, xv. See also Ronald J. Allen, *Preaching and the Other: Studies of Postmodern Insights* (St. Louis: Chalice, 2009), 46–74.
40. Jacques Derrida, *Of Grammatology*, trans. Gayatri Chakravorty Spivak, corr. ed. (Baltimore: Johns Hopkins University Press, 1997), 24. This is not a "radical rupture and discontinuity" that some criticize. See Andreas Huyssen, *After the Great Divide: Modernism, Mass Culture, Postmodernism* (Bloomington: Indiana University Press, 1986), 207. In his essay, "The Ends of Man," in *Margins*

"inhabit" the foundational elements of preaching in order to trouble homiletical theologies.

Second, deconstruction helps us attend to a necessary otherness or alterity that has been segregated and silenced by Western thought. Deconstruction helps us lean more robustly into the Great Commandment. Deconstruction helps us chip away at the structural elements that thwart love of neighbor. In our time of rabid xenophobia on both sides of the Atlantic, preachers need help to invent language that can empower us to receive the other as neighbor, rather than foreigner. However, as novelist and philosopher Hélène Cixous reminds us, "there is no *invention* possible, whether it be philosophical or poetic, without the presence in the inventing subject of an abundance of the other, of the diverse."[41] Deconstruction opens us to such diversity, helping us to embrace ways of speaking and writing that open up rather than shut down alterity.

Third, deconstruction is not to be mistaken for destruction; rather, it exposes us to an alternative way of being in the world. Jesus liked to call this mode of being the kingdom of God. Operative within every construction is the necessary possibility of deconstruction. All homiletical theologies arise out of a desire for God's will to be done on earth as it is in heaven—or at least I'm giving them the benefit of the doubt. And thus the words of philosopher John Caputo are apropos: "The good news deconstruction bears to the church is to provide the hermeneutics of the kingdom of God." He continues,

> The deconstruction of Christianity is not an attack on the church but a critique of the idols to which it is vulnerable—the literalism and authoritarianism, the sexism and racism, the militarism and imperialism, and the love of unrestrained capitalism with which the church in its various forms has today and for too long been entangled, any one of which is toxic to the kingdom of God.[42]

In a similar way, the deconstruction of homiletics, wherein homiletics is at once subject and object, works to smash our theological and philosophical idols in hope of a preaching to come.

This book forwards a homiletical theology of trouble that both trou-

of Philosophy, trans. Alan Bass (Chicago: University of Chicago Press, 1982), 134–35, Derrida differentiates between a *trembling* and a *radical trembling*: "A radical trembling can only come from the *outside*. Therefore, the trembling of which I speak derives no more than any other from some spontaneous decision or philosophical thought after some internal maturation of its history."
41. Hélène Cixous, "Sorties," in *New French Feminisms: An Anthology*, ed. Elaine Marks and Isabelle de Courtivron, trans. Ann Liddle (New York: Schocken Books, 1981), 97.
42. John D. Caputo, *What Would Jesus Deconstruct? The Good News of Postmodernism for the Church* (Grand Rapids, MI: Baker Academic, 2007), 137.

bles homiletics and gets it into trouble in the hope that preaching will meet its Maker.[43] This homiletical trouble/ing is necessary because homiletics is not preaching's maker. And it is precisely in the service of preaching that homiletics must help preaching to die. My aim is to submit homiletical theologies to the deconstruction at work within them. When homiletical theologies—every homiletics as theo-*logy*, with their respective philosophical-metaphysical commitments harbored in a *logos* that always already structures the reception of *theos*—shifts from striving to keep preaching alive to helping preaching die a good death, we liberate preaching to what dreams may come.

---

43. Caputo writes, "My own idea . . . is to stick with the hermeneutics of trouble, to proceed on the assumption that we get the best results by staying on the trail of trouble, by facing up to the difficulty of life, by swallowing the pills of a ruthless problematizing, however bitter, even if this 'perhaps' seems like poison." John D. Caputo, *The Insistence of God: A Theology of Perhaps* (Bloomington: Indiana University Press, 2013), 189.

1

———

Before One's Time: Troubling Language

The house of language has become a kind of tomb . . . The closure of the logos of the world, calls for contraries, oppositions, conflicts.(Y)

—Luce Irigaray[1]

The 2016 film *Arrival* shows how language structures our relationships with others—and what is preaching if not a particular use of language to relate with others around the Absolute Other, God? The film features Dr. Louise Banks, a linguist recruited by the military to attempt to communicate with one of twelve alien spaceships that have recently arrived on earth.

In their first encounter, the humans and aliens attempt to communicate orally/aurally. Dr. Banks quickly determines, however, that the aliens are conveying too much information at once for the human ear to decipher. This is a limit of spoken discourse: sounds don't like to hang around. What is more, if too many sounds are working to transfer information at once, we lose the capacity for understanding; words melt into a flood of sound devoid of meaning.

Dr. Banks attempts inscribed discourse next. This giving and receiving of *written* signs proves far more effective because writing endures through time. The aliens respond to her discursive efforts by drawing a symbol, a logogram, which is not phonetic but ideographic. Dr. Banks

1. Luce Irigaray, *In the Beginning She Was* (London: Bloomsbury Academic, 2013), 5.

explains to her team that by employing logograms the aliens are displaying a very different understanding of time because logograms represent concepts rather than sounds.

As Dr. Banks works to decipher what the aliens are striving to communicate, she learns that the aliens' language allows its user to experience all of time synchronically rather than diachronically. They explain to her that they are here to give this new language to humans, because in three thousand years the aliens will need humanity's aid. But without the linguistic means to communicate beyond the dualities of time, humanity won't be around to help.

As the narrative unfolds, we learn that what language delimits—and what the aliens are here to give us—is the possibility of language as a *non zero-sum game*. The spatiotemporal finitude of discourse forces our words to silence those of others. Not only this: language wires our minds in particular ways. Holding the reins of language allows me to bend meaning to my will. What *Arrival* surfaces is that language itself forces me to turn the other into an alien, an enemy. Communication is only necessary on account of otherness. If you and I shared a mind, there would be no reason to work to understand each other—or for me to write this book.

But there's a problem. In desiring to communicate, I tend to force what the other is trying to say into *my* language, *my* ways of thinking. But the other wants to maintain her *transcendence*, her *otherness*. The eminent psychoanalytic philosopher Luce Irigaray helps us here. She writes, "Desire that wants only the same cannot escape conflict in order to appropriate the other's transcendence."[2] So, ironically, the very means we employ to bridge the gap between disparate minds (language) ends up widening that gap because what we receive is not the other's transcendence but an abrogation of the other's otherness via appropriation.

What Dr. Banks intuits, and what contemporary homileticians and preachers must learn, is that languages are not mere add-ons to thought. Language shapes thought as such.[3] So, to really understand

---

2. Luce Irigaray, *To Be Two*, trans. Monique M. Rhodes (New York: Routledge, 2001), 18.

3. "In itself, thought is like a swirling cloud, where no shape is intrinsically determinate. No ideas are established in advance, and nothing is distinct, before the introduction of linguistic structure." Ferdinand de Saussure, *Course in General Linguistics,* ed. Charles Bally, Albert Sechehaye, and Albert Riedlinger, trans. Roy Harris (Chicago: Open Court, 1983), 110.

At the opening of his influential text *The Homiletical Plot: The Sermon as Narrated Art Form*, exp. ed. (Louisville: Westminster John Knox, 2001), Eugene Lowry writes, "[W]e take our language for granted. We do not stop to consider the fact that our language has individual letters that are collected into words, and words into phrases and phrases into sentences, etc. We just do it that

another, we must submit our ways of thinking to those of the other. How we embark upon this task is what this chapter is all about.

Section One: Language *in* Trouble

If anyone can understand how a word can be, not only before it is spoken aloud but even before the image of its sounds are turned over in thought—this is the word that belongs to no language.

— St. Augustine[4]

Paul Scott Wilson argues that "preachers who are unaware how language works can fall into traps of their own making."[5] This statement is true, but not quite in the way Wilson suggests. Here he gives far too much credit to preachers and far too little credit to language. He would have us hold language on a leash, unaware that on the other end rests a dragon. The words of the literary critic and writer Jean Paulhan are closer to the truth: *"Run away from language and it will come after you. Go after language and it will run away from you."*[6] For Paulhan and others, lan-

way—and presume everyone else does too. But everyone doesn't! (For example, many languages such as Chinese use pictures or ideograms instead of letters.) And those who do it differently, think differently" (4). So, if different languages mean differently, is it appropriate for theological and homiletical notions developed within one language system to be normative within different language systems?

4. St. Augustine, *On the Trinity*, trans. Stephen McKenna (Washington, DC: Catholic University of America Press, 1963), XV.19, p. 523.

5. Paul Scott Wilson, *Preaching as Poetry: Goodness, Beauty, and Truth in Every Sermon* (Nashville: Abingdon, 2014), 57. Here, Wilson falls squarely under Irigaray's indictment: "Man has become estranged from his to be and thinks in an improper fashion. He considers himself to be the master of the very thing which dominates him." Irigaray, *To Be Two*, 70.

James F. Kay, *Preaching and Theology* (St. Louis: Chalice, 2007), says much the same thing as Wilson. Kay opens his text thusly: "'You poor preachers. You only have words!' This reproach rings truer of the Christian pulpit than a certain defensiveness might otherwise allow. Yes, we preachers work largely with words. And words are problematic. Sometimes they seem scarcely up to the job. Sometimes they wander and hide from their subject matter—or get lost. Through repeated use and overuse their meanings cease to challenge us to further reflection or needed action. . . . No less than ourselves, words are fallen into the grips of a power, traditionally termed sin, that corrupts and kills them even while enticing them into its service and frequently in the name of religion or God. For this reason, thinking critically and theologically is necessary for preaching to proceed with honesty, integrity, and faithfulness to the Christian message" (vii).

The significance of Kay's prefatory remarks is profound: 1) We are limited by the linguistic constraints in which we find ourselves; 2) Our words, in spite of our best attempts, never quite do the job of communicating because they are somehow "fallen"; and 3) If we will but employ critical, theological thinking we will be able to overcome the "grips of power" that "corrupts and kills" our words about God. With these opening remarks, Kay seems to be seeking a secret passage into a linguistic Eden. The only problem with this is that Kay has forgotten about the cherubim and flaming sword flashing back and forth to guard the way (Gen 3:24).

While I immensely appreciate Kay's insights at the intersection of preaching and theology, this initial gesture belies the difficulty—nay, impossibility—of such a task. What troubles me about Kay's text is that his attempt to return to the prelapsarian state of language by way of theology (as opposed to poetics or rhetoric) ignores the philosophical difficulties that haunt his journey at every step.

guage possesses an innate strength that surpasses the capacities of its user to fully master. This is true even for the preacher—maybe especially for the preacher.

For the past fifty or so years, mainline homiletics has stressed the *eventfulness* of kerygmatic discourse. How and to what degree preaching is an "event"—or even an "Event"—is up for debate. In general, when homiletical theologians talk about "the event of preaching" they are talking about one of two things: 1) the Event of God's self-revelation in/as Jesus Christ to which preaching *bears witness*; or, 2) preaching as an *event in language* that takes shape in the context of Christian worship. Both of these theological arguments are grounded in philosophy.[7]

---

6. Jean Paulhan, *The Flowers of Tarbes*, trans. Michael Syrotinski (Urbana: University of Illinois Press, 2006), 82.

7. That is when we are being clear about our understanding of said "event." Many homileticians talk about "the preaching event" with little or no comment about what they mean by this. This has a long history in homiletics. See William L. Malcolmson, *The Preaching Event* (Philadelphia: Westminster, 1968), who argues for preaching as a "communicative event" contra discourse concerning events; John R. Claypool, *The Preaching Event* (Waco, TX: Word Books, 1980), where "the preaching event" is conceived as confessionalism, that is, a "grappling with our own woundedness"; and Henry H. Mitchell, *Black Preaching: The Recovery of a Powerful Art* (Nashville: Abingdon, 1990), 100. Amid this vagueness we can appreciate Wilson's precision: "The Christ event occurred at a particular time and place in history, and the same event, centered on the cross and resurrection, can encounter us in and through preaching now." Paul Scott Wilson, "Preaching as God's Event," *Vision* 10, no. 1 (Spring 2009): 13.

Dialectical theology finds its philosophical grounding in Kant's method of interrogating judgments, which resemble truth but are in fact illusory. In this usage, adopted by Barth and his fellow "dialectical theologians," the goal is not to arrive at a "synthesis" (an *Aufhebung* à la Hegel); rather, it is to expose false epistemologies. In Kant's words: "Since [transcendental logic] should properly be only a canon for the assessment of empirical use, it is misused if one lets it count as the organon of a general and unrestricted use, and dares to synthetically judge, assert, and decide about objects in general with the pure understanding alone. The use of the pure understanding would in this case therefore be dialectical. The second part of the transcendental logic must therefore be a critique of this dialectical illusion, and is called transcendental dialectic, not as an art of dogmatically arousing such illusion (an unfortunately highly prevalent art among the manifold works of metaphysical jugglery), but rather as a critique of the understanding and reason in regard to their hyperphysical use, in order to uncover the false illusion of their groundless pretentions and to reduce their claims to invention and amplification, putatively to be attained through transcendental principles, to the mere assessment and evaluation of the pure understanding, guarding it against sophistical tricks." Immanuel Kant, *Critique of Pure Reason*, ed. and trans. Paul Guyer and Allen W. Wood (Cambridge: Cambridge University Press, 1998), A64, p. 200.

The notion that language is inherently event-ful, as espoused by proponents of the New Homiletic, arises out of Heidegger's philosophy. Language is understood here as the privileged mode of announcing Being as "Event" or "Appropriation" (*Ereignis*). Heidegger explains, "Appropriation, in beholding human nature, makes mortals appropriate for that which avows itself from everywhere to man in Saying, which points toward the concealed. . . . It is: the sounding of the word. The encountering saying of mortals is answering. Every spoken word is already an answer: counter-saying, coming to the encounter, listening Saying. When mortals are made appropriate for Saying, human nature is released into that needfulness out of which man is used for bringing soundless Saying to the sound of language. Appropriation, needing and using man's appropriations, allows Saying to reach speech. The way to language belongs to Saying determined by Appropriation. Within this way, which belongs to the reality of language, the peculiar property of language is concealed. The way is appropriating." Martin Heidegger, *On the Way to Language*, trans. Peter D. Hertz (New York: Harper & Row, 1982), 129.

For "dialectical" theologians like Karl Barth and Emil Brunner, the "event/Event" signifies God's action of self-disclosure, apart from which we would not know God.[8] Brunner contends that "Jesus Christ is the revelation; He is the Love of God in Person. . . . The perception of this love is bound up with the event of revelation, or, as we have already said, this love does not define itself in intellectual terms, but in an Event."[9] Barth argues that while all knowledge of God is at once within historical time, such can only ever be known as an Event beyond history; the Event of revelation occurs beyond time when God both presents Godself to be known by humanity *and* validates this knowledge as such.[10] For Barth, preaching is not quite an *Event* in this special sense. Preaching arises out of and in response to the Event of God's self-revelation. It "can only be a human repetition referring us to the event of the preceding revelation," which Barth labels preaching's "unconditional whence."[11]

For those like Fred Craddock, who constitute the New Homiletic, language itself is eventful: a Word-event. Craddock asserts that language is "not only the supreme event of human existence, but the very being of humanity is founded in language."[12] Similarly, David James Randolph argues that to understand preaching in its "uniqueness"—in contradistinction to other modes of discourse—is to understand it as an *event*: "a

---

8. Of course, this gets a bit slippery in the famous debate between Barth and Brunner in 1934 concerning the *analogia entis*, or "analogy of being," by which we humans might have the "capacity" to obtain knowledge of God apart from divine revelation. See Karl Barth, "No! Answer to Emil Brunner," in *Karl Barth: Theologian of Freedom*, ed. Clifford Green (Minneapolis: Fortress Press, 1991), 151–67.

9. Emil Brunner, *The Christian Doctrine of God*, vol. 1, *Dogmatics*, trans. Olive Wyon (Eugene, OR: Wipf & Stock, 2014), 187–88. He continues, "The God of revelation, that is, the God whose Nature it is to impart Himself [sic], can only be known in this event of self-revelation; a God who cannot be known *thus*, is *eo ipso* not this God" (188).

10. See Barth, *CD* I/1, 42, 143, 165 and Barth, *CD* II/1, 181. It is on account of God's desire to be known that the church "should testify to this event and its content (Jesus Christ) and speak to itself and to all the world about it. For in virtue of what takes place and what is contained, this event and content constitute a gospel which wills to go forth, and which cannot be and cannot be understood except as a gospel that goes forth" (*CD* I/2, 848).

11. Karl Barth, *Homiletics*, trans. Geoffrey W. Bromiley and Donald E. Daniels (Louisville: Westminster John Knox, 1991), 61, 51. See also Karl Barth, *The Epistle to the Romans*, 6th ed., trans. Edwyn C. Hoskyns (London: Oxford University Press, 1933), 28: "The Gospel is not one thing in the midst of other things, to be directly apprehended and comprehended. The Gospel is the Word of the Primal Origin of all things, the Word which, since it is ever new, must ever be received with renewed fear and trembling. The Gospel is therefore not an event, nor an experience, nor an emotion—however delicate! Rather, it is the clear and objective perception of what eye hath not seen nor ear heard."

12. Fred B. Craddock, *As One Without Authority*, rev. ed. (St. Louis: Chalice, 2001), 31. Also, "Let those who oppose the preaching ministry with phrases such as 'the acts of God' and 'salvation events' recall the role of spoken words within those events that gave them their character and the role of spoken words in sharing the benefits of those events. There is in our experience no event so profound as speaking one with another" (36).

form of discourse designed to bring the word of God to expression in the concrete situation of the hearers."[13]

Irigaray notes, however, that much of what passes as "discourse" in the West never really takes place as such. Because discourse "closes upon itself through strategies of conflicting oppositions," it causes language to "take place between oneself and oneself, within or between the same one(s), and truth and language begin to speak from themselves, on themselves, without any source in an other or return to an other." The Western linguistic tradition cuts off man—and Irigaray means *man*—from the real and from the other as real: "A tautology of words, of truth locks the speaking subjects—master and disciple—in a shelter, a universe, a logic which is intended to duplicate what belongs to their birth, their growth, their natural reality."[14]

So, here's my claim: *Before God may speak, language has already spoken; God's "Word" is already and always human words.* In this section, I wish to trouble popular homiletical notions of language in general—or, better, I seek to show how language itself is always already undergoing its own trouble. I don't believe we must choose between theological orthodoxy and cultural relevance, and I believe that the path toward such a third way begins with language.

How Language Works: Linguistics 101

So, how *does* language work? Well, that depends on whom you ask. Wishing neither to overcomplicate nor oversimplify matters, we would do well to think of language as "working" in one of three ways. The first perspective on linguistic meaning is called *representationalism*. This one has been around for centuries. It posits that expressions (oral, written, gestural, etc.) are meaningful in virtue of representing worldly objects or states of affairs. The key here is *representation*. So, in the early work of the famed Austrian philosopher Ludwig Wittgenstein we read, "A name means an object. The object is its meaning. . . . In a proposition a name is the representative of an object."[15] Words mean because they *represent* a reality that preexists them.

This view of language has a rich theological history. In his *Confessions*, for instance, Augustine describes how he came to understand

13. David James Randolph, *The Renewal of Preaching in the Twenty-First Century*, 2nd ed., with commentary by Robert Stephen Reid (Eugene, OR: Wipf & Stock, 2008), 15.
14. Irigaray, *In the Beginning*, 3–4.
15. Ludwig Wittgenstein, *Tractatus Logico-Philosophicus*, trans. D. F. Pears and B. F. McGuiness (New York: Routledge Classics, 2001), §§3.203; 3.22, p. 15.

the inner workings of language by observing children. From watching them he perceived that gestural signs resemble internal desires. Children cry, however, because between their internal desires and external sounds there is "no real resemblance."[16] In other words, one of our most primal experiences in this world is of epistemological alienation; others lack access to our hearts and minds. That is why we speak.

A second take on how language functions is called *linguistic pragmatism*. Folks in this camp are less concerned with representation than they are with *language use*, that is, how particular linguistic expressions correspond with the sociolinguistic milieu in which it is being used. Meaning, by this account, is not conceptually autonomous but grounded within "certain fields of experience" that manifest themselves between a word and its meaning.[17] It is here that Wittgenstein would abandon his earlier (representationalist) view of language for this pragmatic understanding. He argues that "the general concept of the meaning of a word surrounds the working of language with such a haze which makes clear vision impossible." Pragmatisim clears up this confusion: "It disperses the fog if we study the phenomena of language in primitive kinds of *use* in which one can clearly survey the purpose and functioning of the words."[18]

We find this linguistic pragmatism put to great use by one of the progenitors of postliberal theology, George Lindbeck. He explains, "The function of church doctrines that becomes most prominent . . . is their *use*, not as expressive symbols or as truth claims, but as communally authoritative rules of discourse, attitude, and action."[19] Lindbeck's "cultural-linguistic" mode of theology, along with its pragmatist linguistic assumptions, would go on to shape the thinking of many prominent voices in homiletics that constitute the postliberal "school" of homiletics.

A third effort to articulate how language works is called *structuralism*. I find this theory most illuminating because it helps us to ask more fundamental questions about language and knowledge than either representationalism or pragmatism. Moreover, it corresponds most closely to the way that many Westerners learn language—even if the

---

16. St. Augustine, *Confessions*, trans. Henry Chadwick (Oxford: Oxford University Press, 2009), I.8, p. 7.
17. G.H. Mead, *G.H. Mead: A Reader*, ed. Filipe Carreira da Silva (London: Routledge, 2012), 9.
18. Ludwig Wittgenstein, *Philosophical Investigations*, trans. G. E. M. Anscombe, P. M. S. Hacker, and Joachim Schulte, 4th ed. (Malden, MA: Wiley-Blackwell, 2009), ¶7, p. 5. Emphasis added.
19. George A. Lindbeck, *The Nature of Doctrine: Religion and Theology in a Postliberal Age* (Louisville: Westminster John Knox, 1984), 18. Emphasis added.

representationalist and pragmatist views are probably the most widely assumed.

In the West, we learn language by mastering rules that tether particular sound patterns to particular letters and letter combinations. Linguists label this *phonology*, the systematic organization of sounds in languages. As language users, we learn to work with language before we understand how it works. Think back to first grade, when your teacher wrote the letter *D* on the board. Together you worked on the [D] sound. You learned to differentiate this sound from other sounds we use in English. *[D] is for dog. Log? No, not [L]; [D]. Door. Day. Desk.*

Through phonology, linguists attend to the adhesive power of a language system between the realm of *thought* and the realm of *sound*, the content of which is *structural* rather than *concrete*. In other words, we learn a language by mastering the formal (aka structural) relations of linguistic signs (e.g., letters, words), which are *internal* to the language system. Mastering these relations is equivalent to "cracking the code" that makes a language meaningful. As philosophical theologian Herbert McCabe OP puts it, "A meaning is always the role or function of some part in an *organized structure*—as, for instance, the meaning of a word is *the part it plays* in the language. . . . For the meanings of words are their *roles* not within the structure of any individual body but within the *structure of language*, which is in principle (in order to be language at all) shared by all."[20] The structure of languages determines meaning as such.

The thing we might not recognize while we are learning a language is that our language system is inherently arbitrary.[21] In other words, there is no *necessary* and *absolute* reason why any particular sound or inscription should conjoin with any particular thought. It is not the *givenness* of a particular sound or inscription per se that gives it meaning; rather, meaning is structured by the *differences* between sounds and inscriptions. In other words, "Languages differ by differentiating differently."[22]

20. Herbert McCabe OP, "The Logic of Mysticism," in *God Still Matters* (London: Continuum, 2005), 25. Emphasis added.
21. NB. This is not original to Saussure. See Aristotle, *On Interpretation*, in *Categories. On Interpretation. Prior Analytics*, Loeb Classical Library, vol. 325, trans. H. P. Cooke and H. Tredennick (Cambridge, MA: Harvard University Press, 1938), 117: "A noun is a sound having meaning established by convention alone but no reference whatever to time, while no part of it has any meaning, considered apart from the whole." See also John Locke, *An Essay Concerning Human Understanding*, ed. Peter Nidditch (Oxford: Oxford University Press, 1979), III/§8, p. 408: "Words by long and familiar use, as has been said, come to excite in Men certain Ideas, so constantly and readily, that they are apt to suppose a natural connexion [*sic*] between them. But that they signify only Men's peculiar Ideas, and that by a perfectly arbitrary Imposition, is evident . . ."

Let's start where our first grade teacher started: with letters. Each of the twenty-six letters that make up the English alphabet is tethered to a sound pattern, or phoneme. Take, for instance, the sound patterns we represent as [d] and as [ð]. The sound [d] occurs at the beginning of the word *den*, while the sound [ð] occurs at the beginning of the word *then*. Because these two sounds may be differentiated from one another, we can say that they possess different *values*; in other words, they "count" as different in English. If they didn't, we wouldn't be able to tell them apart. The sounds [d] and [ð] belong, in English, to two different structural units, which we in turn represent grammatically as /d/ and /th/, so that *den* and *then* are represented phonemically as /den/ and /ðen/.

By contrast, the sounds [d] and [ð] do not "count" the same in Spanish, even though both sounds exist in Spanish. The sounds behave differently between Spanish and English on account of their different structural relations *within* their respective language systems. It is these systems that ascribe them their value. So, for instance, in Spanish, [ð] can occur only in certain positions, notably between vowels, as in *deðo*, "finger," while [d] can never occur in these positions. Thus, the word *dama*, "lady," starts with a [d], but because Spanish requires a [ð] rather than a [d] between vowels, when used with its definite article *dama* becomes *la ðama*. In English and Spanish the phoneme [ð] exists, but it "counts" differently in English because the structural relationship is different in the two language systems.

All this is to say that languages operate according to structural relations. There are no *objective* or *absolute* phonetic truths. There is no *necessary* reason why the phoneme [ð] ought to sound as it does in English. To say otherwise, by rational deduction, is to say that Spanish pronounces this sound incorrectly. Of course, such an assertion would be ludicrous—*both* pronunciations are correct relative to their respective system of structural relations. This same structural principle of difference and arbitrariness applies to words as well.

Words aren't real. You can't find them roaming the wilds of New Zealand or floating with prehistoric jellyfish in the ocean's depths. *Words are abstractions from reality.*[23] Words don't *stand for* things in the world, either. Those things we see in the world do not exist,

---

22. John Passmore, *Recent Philosophers* (London: Duckworth, 1985), 24.
23. Maurice Blanchot, "Mystery in Literature," in *The Work of Fire*, trans. Charlotte Mandell (Stanford: Stanford University Press, 1995), 49: "words vanish from the scene to make the thing enter, but since this thing is itself no more than an absence, . . . it is an absence of words and an absence of thing, a simultaneous emptiness, nothing supported by nothing."

linguistically speaking, prior to being labeled with words.[24] A simple correspondence between word and referent is a fantasy that we must dispel.

For starters, the communicative function of a language system requires the scope of reference to be much greater than the particularity of its individual instance. We employ concepts like *leaves* and *smiles* to stand in for all kinds of leaves and facial expressions that share certain characteristics. (If we had to come up with a new word for every *single* leaf and every *particular* smile, we'd never get this language thing off the ground.) Thus, reference is always to *classes* of things and *concepts* rather than *particular* objects we encounter in the world.

Language, at base, defines the linkage between signifiers (e.g., written words, gestures, sounds) and mental concepts. So, when I mount the pulpit and declare with John the Baptist that "the axe is already laid at the roots of the tree" (Luke 3:9), an *actual* tree does not miraculously appear before us (nor an *actual* axe). Language doesn't get us from the word *tree* to an actual substance found in nature that's covered in bark and sprouts limbs and leaves. Language only governs the *connection* between the inscription /tree/ or sound pattern [trē] and the idea of a tree. Accordingly, /God/ ≠ God.

Said differently, *all of language is structured by signification: signs pointing to other signs.* At no point on the inside of language (as if we could somehow get outside of language) does the play of signification rest. If we are to interrogate preaching's relationship to language, we must understand that language is at root *sign* language—that is, an arbitrary and differential structure of significations.[25]

Sign Language

In English, the sound [dôg] conjures in your mind an animal that barks

---

24. This is not to say that things don't exist. What I'm trying to say is that ontology and semiology ought not be confused. Again, McCabe helps us here: "It is not simply in our capacity to use signs, our ability, for example, to understand words, but in our actual use of them to say what is the case that we have need of and lay hold on the *esse* [being] of things. It is only by analogy that we can speak of the 'concept' of *esse*, we do not have a concept of existence as we have a concept of greenness or prevarication or polar bears." McCabe, "The Logic of Mysticism," 13–14.

25. An interesting point to note in passing is that American Sign Language (ASL), which is its own complete and complex language system, is less arbitrary, though just as differential, as the English language from which it was developed. The iterability of each *sign* requires sufficient differentiation from all of the other signs that make up ASL; however, many signs employed in ASL *do* bear a resemblance to objects in the world. For example, the sign for *tree* looks like a tree waving above the ground. To make the *tree* sign, one extends her weak hand flat across her body to make the ground. Then she stands her strong hand up at a right angle with her fingers extended and shaking them back and forth—like branches swaying in the wind.

and wags its tail when it's happy because a certain sonic materiality syncs with an image of this lovable creature. The sound pattern [dôg] doesn't *have* to signify as it does. The relationship is *arbitrary*. In German, the sign [*Hund*] works just as well; in Spanish, the sign [*perro*] does the job. However, within the English language system we've decided—by convention—that a particular sound will signify the idea of a particular creature.[26] Moreover, the linkage works because the sound [dôg] is sufficiently *different* from all other sounds that constitute English as such. Signification only ever works as a result of its structural difference from all other sounds within a respective system.[27]

Language shapes, and even determines, thought. The eminent Swiss linguist Ferdinand de Saussure puts it this way: "In itself, thought is like a swirling cloud, where no shape is intrinsically determinate. No ideas are established in advance, and nothing is distinct, before the introduction of linguistic structure."[28] This was a revolutionary claim one hundred years ago, and its impact is still felt in contemporary contexts where notions of meaning and truth are maintained as somehow preexisting human thought.

As an example, consider the vitriol and consternation arising from folks who insist that only the masculine pronoun be used in reference

26. Jonathan D. Culler, *Ferdinand De Saussure*, rev. ed. (Ithaca, NY: Cornell University Press, 1986), 29. Culler writes, "Since I speak English I may use the signifier represented by *dog* to talk about an animal of a particular species, but this sequence of sounds is no better suited to this purpose than another sequence. *Lod, tet,* or *bloop* would serve equally well if it were accepted by members of my speech community. There is no intrinsic reason why one of these signifiers rather than the other should be linked with the concept of 'dog.'" *Chien* also signifies a furry animal that barks and wags its tail when it's excited. The sounds are different, but that is irrelevant; what matters is the *connection* between the sound and the mental image it renders within its system of signification.
27. Saussure writes, "The content of a word is determined in the final analysis not by what it contains but by what exists outside it. As an element in a system, the word has not only a meaning but also—above all—a value. And that is something quite different." *Course in General Linguistics*, 114. Or, as Luce Irigaray will put it many years after Saussure, "As set, the phoneme is defined by a network of relations with respect to a set or to a field of differential traits, just as it circumscribes, in a play of relations to other phonemes, other sub-sets of pertinent traits or empty sub-sets. Bundle of differences, the phenomena is itself the knot in a network of differences that articulate it, as a site of references, into the set of distinctive traits, and with the other phonemes. Not one, the phoneme is also not unique. Or at least its singularity is criss-crossed with relations of identity and non-identity to other phonemes, with inclusion or exclusion of differences, with their neutralization." "The Rape of the Letter," in *To Speak is Never Neutral*, trans. Gail Schwab (New York: Routledge, 2002), 126.
28. Saussure, *Course in General Linguistic*, 66. I employ ascriptions such as "Saussure writes" for ease of communication. The text of his *Course* was published posthumously by several of Saussure's students from lecture notes. There is, thus, a problem with identifying Saussure with the *Course* uncritically. Nevertheless, it is not Saussure's reconstructive work through comparative linguistics that gained him the attention of scores of commentators, but the ideas in his *Course*. Thus, following the scholarly convention, I identify Saussure with the ideas expressed through the *Course*. See Jacques Derrida, *Of Grammatology*, trans. Gayatri Chakravorty Spivak, corrected ed. (Baltimore: Johns Hopkins University Press, 1997), 329n38.

to God. Is God a *He/Him*? Really? Might this traditional designation arise out of a language system where no divine pronoun exists? Our choices (in English) are masculine, feminine, or neuter. Surely God is not an *It*. But why not *She/Her*? Why not the non-binary gender designation, *Their*? More perniciously, might this phenomenon mask political commitments that value the masculine over the feminine (and exclude anything that fails to conform to this binary)? This is what philosophers of language teach us: *language does not merely represent pre-existing thought; it shapes thought from the beginning.*

More recently, linguists and philosophers of language have verified through empirical research the truthfulness of Saussure's assertion about language shaping thought. Cognitive research studies prove that language not only gives expression to thought, it also plays a *causal role in shaping cognition.* Russian, for example, makes an extra distinction between light and dark blue; thus, Russian speakers are better able to visually discriminate between shades of blue. Similarly, the Piraha, a tribe in Brazil, whose language only has terms like *few* and *many* instead of numerals, are not able to keep track of exact quantities.[29]

Cognitive psychologists Lera Boroditsky of Stanford University and Alice Gaby of the University of California, Berkeley, recently conducted an experiment with speakers of English, Hebrew, and Kuuk Thaayorre (the language spoken in Pormpuraaw, a small Aboriginal community on the western edge of Cape York in northern Australia), showing how the languages we speak affect our perceptions of the world.[30] In the experiment, they gave speakers sets of pictures that showed temporal progressions—a man aging, a crocodile growing, a banana being eaten, and so on. They then asked the participants to arrange the shuffled photographs on the ground to indicate the correct temporal order.

Boroditsky and Gaby tested each person several times, each time facing in a different cardinal direction. They found that the English speakers given this task would arrange the cards so that the temporal sequencing depicted in the images proceeded from left to right. Conversely, Hebrew speakers tended to lay out the cards from right to left, showing that writing direction in a language influences how we organize time (Hebrew is written from right to left). The Kuuk Thaayorre, however, did not routinely arrange the cards from left to right or

---

29. Lera Boroditsky, "Lost in Translation" *The Wall Street Journal*, July 23, 2010, https://tinyurl.com/lvgb6ec.
30. Lera Boroditsky and Alice Gaby, "Remembrances of Times East: Absolute Spatial Representations of Time in an Australian Aboriginal Community," *Psychological Science* 21, no. 11 (November 2010): 1635–39.

right to left. They arranged them from east to west. That is, when they were seated facing south, the cards went left to right. When they faced north, the cards went from right to left. When they faced east, the cards were directed toward the body, and so on. The researchers never told any of the participants which direction they were facing—the Kuuk Thaayorre intuited their cardinal position and spontaneously used this spatial orientation to construct their representations of time.[31]

At this point, you may be asking yourself what this has to do with homiletical theologies. Well, consider this: if language is *arbitrary*, then its structural relations cannot be "right," "objective," or "true." Language is not a *neutral* mechanism for communicating our thoughts about God but actually *shapes* those thoughts; therefore, any serious consideration of God-talk—theo-logy—necessitates a critical examination of the languages we employ to speak (about) God. Language itself *produces* meanings; it does not represent pre-packaged thought.[32]

Homiletics has picked up some bad habits from Western ways of thinking.[33] For millennia, Western thinkers have operated under the assumption that through the careful reconstruction of ancient languages (especially Indo-European, the parent language of Greek and Latin), one could gain access to the *purity* of language, could get at *primal signification*. This view of language is known as the *atomistic* approach to language structure, that is, one that perceives language as primarily a collection of objects (e.g., sounds, words, grammatical endings) rather than a socio-symbolic structure of relations. If you've been to, or are currently attending, seminary or Bible college, I won't need to convince you that this view of language is still very much in oper-

---

31. In subsequent studies, Boroditsky and her team have shown that language affects eyewitness memory and conceptions of time. See Caitlin M. Fausey and Lera Boroditsky, "Who Dunnit? Cross-Linguistic Differences in Eye-Witness Memory," *Psychon Bull Rev* 18 (2011): 150–57 and Lera Boroditsky, Orly Fuhrman, and Kelly McCormick, "Do English and Mandarin Speakers Think About Time Differently?" *Cognition* 118 (2011): 123–29.

32. Thus, it is not the case that "[o]rdinary, simple words have been kidnapped and their meanings pressed into service by powers foreign to their original intention." Richard Lischer, *A Theology of Preaching: The Dynamics of the Gospel* (Nashville: Abingdon, 1981), 88. No words are *ordinary* or *simple*; nor do words possess *innate* meanings apart from their use *in language*. We have no access to an "original intention" hidden behind words. McCabe is closer to the truth when he writes that "human language itself, whether of flags or of words, is a kind of mystery, something that in a way transcends our understanding even while being the means of our understanding." Herbert McCabe OP, "The Eucharist as Language," *Modern Theology* 15, no. 2 (April 1999): 132.

33. See, for example, William H. Willimon, *Peculiar Speech: Preaching to the Baptized* (Grand Rapids, MI: Eerdmans, 1992), 23: "Too much of our theology and preaching has acted as if we need new language in order to maintain our old, conventional means of human gatherings. Biblical language has shown, time and again, that it has power, like the sacrament of baptism itself, to evoke that of which it speaks."

ation. We study ancient Hebrew and Koine Greek to gain access to the ways of thinking and being of biblical characters and authors. I'm not challenging this practice. I do, however, wish to challenge the linguistic assumptions such models reinforce.

Language and translation skills grant us access to other thought-worlds; but at no point is the veil of meaning ever lifted. The Martiniqan philosopher and revolutionary Frantz Fanon once observed that when we possess a language, we gain access to the world expressed and implied by this language.[34] This is true, but it misses what Fanon understood better than most: language also possesses us. We see but through a glass darkly—no matter the strength of our grammatical ninjitsu. If we want to speak (about) God, we need to hone a particular way with words by which we may interrogate language itself. Homileticians assert that God speaks to us through preaching; but rarely do we take the time to consider how language commits us to certain ways of thinking and what such epistemologies commit us to theologically.

The Sexualization of Discourse

Difference without positive terms means that nothing of language is given in advance. And yet, paradoxically, language is precisely that which gives itself in advance of discourse. To ascertain what is going on *in* language we must work to uncover the dynamics *of* language that bolster individual utterances. Such work is not simple. How do you interrogate the foundations of language when you require language to do the work of interrogation? It's like trying to bite your own neck.

This is where Luce Irigaray's work is so important. As a trained psychoanalyst, she approaches language differently than the theologian or homiletician. We learn much by attending to how she troubles her discipline's use of language. Psychoanalysis, as a science, is governed by *scientific* rhetorical conventions. Irigaray identifies these rules as "unavowed" techniques that cannot distinguish themselves from "so-called truth."[35] By this she means that science privileges *neutral, objective* language. Through its efforts toward neutrality and objectivity, it refuses "the imperialism of the 'I' that is the paradigm of all speaking subjects."[36]

34. Frantz Fanon, *Black Skin, White Masks*, trans. Richard Philcox (New York: Grove, 2008), 2.
35. Irigaray, *To Speak is Never Neutral*, 3.
36. Ibid. Elsewhere, she puts it this way: "If I begin to question discourse—beginning with the language that I speak and that has made me a subject—I shall observe that the neuter is apparently a

But here's the rub: it is science that proves that sexuality is determined by biology—the cerebral cortex, to be specific. How, then, can science insist that its discourse ought to be neuter? Irigaray writes, "We learn that the left and right sides of the brain are not the same in men as in women, but that, nevertheless, the two sexes speak the same language, and that no other language could possibly exist." She then asks, "By what grace, or what necessity, is it possible to speak the same language without having the same brain?"[37] Accordingly, Irigaray's writings question the language of science and its supposed neutrality, arguing that the sexualization of language undermines any pretense of neutrality.

Irigaray contends that the sexualization of discourse is "not a matter of a few words here and there, even though the fact that certain words do not exist in the *lexicon* can be structurally significant." Gender difference encoded in language enforces the submission of one sex to the other.[38] Man—and she means *man*—seeks to mimic nature, to exert a certain power that is universal and radically beyond human control. Irigaray shows how this is hardwired into our language by evoking the neuter gender (e.g., "*one* reasons that . . ." or "*it* is necessary to . . .").

Gender is less conspicuous in English than it is in French because English neither mandates the presence of an article (*the, a*) to accompany a noun, nor does English gender its adjectives in accordance with the nouns they modify.[39] We move seamlessly through language from abstract, impersonal forces of nature (e.g., "it is snowing," "it is windy," "it is thundering") to non-gendered assertions that present themselves grammatically as powers unto themselves (e.g., "it is nec-

matter of *nature* in the first instance." Luce Irigaray, "The Three Genders," in *Sexes and Genealogies*, trans. Gillian C. Gill (New York: Columbia University Press, 1993), 170.

37. Irigaray, *To Speak is Never Neutral*, 3. Note that this is not just a problem of speech as such. See Irigaray's illuminating essay, "The Rape of the Letter," 121–37. Herein she writes, "Without doubt, the letter informs whomever gives it form; it is formed by that upon which it confers form" (123); "Thus deprived of all signifying aim, of all intent to convey a meaningful message, the scribe notes after the fact the effect of sense and non-sense of the inscription, or rather the effect that precedes that dichotomy. It is constituted as form, as matrix, where meaning can inscribe itself or be inscribed. . . . the letter outlines the writer as an arbitrary, distinct, discontinuous form, the space of suspension, space deferring time, the becoming of time" (125).

38. Irigaray, "The Three Genders," 173.

39. In French, the definite articles (*le, la*) and indefinite articles (*un, une*) must precede every noun unless some other modifier is employed (e.g., *des*/some, *plusieur*/several). Adjectives must agree with the nouns they modify in gender and number, which can result in minor or significant changes in the adjective. For instance, the adjective "fat" in its masculine form is *gros* and *grosse* in its feminine form; the adjective "soft" shifts between *doux* (m) and *douce* (f). When it comes to pronouns, English is more explicit than French. In English, we employ "he" or "she" in reference to masculine or feminine *subjects* and "it" in place of non-gendered *objects*. In French, the words "*elle*" or "*la*" are used in place of feminine nouns, but the words "*il*" or "*le*" are used to substitute for both masculine and neuter nouns.

31

essary," "it is true," "it is false"). To this linguistic phenomenon Irigaray writes, "This order of laws is intended to be neuter but carries the brand of the man who produced it. . . . Things of our era command a language that sometimes overwhelms us, annihilates us, and whose noise can be heard loud and clear of the sound of the silence of the natural order."[40] This, precisely, is what homiletics has refused to hear: its own silence. Homiletics is so focused on teaching preaching how to *communicate* that it misses the communion with the other that it purports to enact.[41]

So, if the first problem of (Western) language is its drive toward a universal neutrality that would be equally meaningful and accessible to *all* people, regardless of sex, the second is the truth this primary drive masks: language is always already *masculine language*. Irigaray avers,

> Man gives his own gender to the universe as he intends to give his name to his children and his possessions. Everything man considers of value has to be of his gender. The feminine is a merger of secondariness, of subordination to the principle gender. The *neuter* is reserved for specific and variable areas in different languages. . . . The *it is necessary* refers to a duty or an order that has been laid down by one sex only, one gender only. It has only the appearance of being neuter or neutral, and in French at any rate it has the same form as the masculine.[42]

This is not a matter of concern for women alone. Men—and non-binary identifying persons—are just as enslaved to "masculine" ways of thinking that are hardwired to our language. Men, too, are "dragged down, or swallowed up, by repetitions and formulas, by graphisms" in which we do not recognize ourselves, but which control us, nevertheless.[43] There is an irony here: the very thing preachers most need in order to

40. Irigaray, "The Three Genders," 170–71.
41. This is a problem in some of Paul Scott Wilson's work. He maintains that the *summum bonum* of preaching is that listeners can understand a sermon's meaning. He assumes that "meaningful communication" arises when "sentences link to sentences, paragraphs link to paragraphs, and sections link to sections until a whole is produced in which the parts and whole contribute to each other." Wilson, *Preaching and Homiletical Theory*, 21. Sometimes the most meaningful forms of communication transcend communication and belie meaning. Again, McCabe guides us: "Although we do not understand what [our assertions] refer to in God, they are our way of asserting that the riches of religious imagery are more than the art-form of a particular culture (though, of course, they are that) but are part of our access to a mystery beyond our understanding which we do not create, but which rather creates us and our understanding and our whole world." McCabe, *God Still Matters*, 28.
42. Irigaray, "The Three Genders," 173. Elsewhere she writes, "Of course, we must first remember that language is not neutral and that its rules weigh heavily on the constitution of a female identity and on women's relationships with one another." Luce Irigaray, *Thinking the Difference: For a Peaceful Revolution*, trans. Karin Montin (New York: Routledge, 1994), 27.
43. Irigaray, *To Speak is Never Neutral*, 6.

preach is the thing over which we have the least control. "Masculine" biases within language trouble preaching before we even get started.

The "Event" of Preaching

There is no such thing as a preaching *event*. Whatever we can say (through language) is impossible to say in such a way that would set it apart from discourse in general.[44] Homileticians evoke this event-language to privilege preaching as *holy* discourse. However, as discourse, all preaching words must pre-exist their kerygmatic appropriation. On a linguistic level, sermonic words and word-forms (rhetoric) are no more holy or event-ful than any other words that rely upon that which must be able to be repeated. If anything we might say in a sermon could be repeated, there can be no way of elevating sermonic speech as an *event* in any special sense.

Perhaps preaching is an event on a theological level; but then we must articulate how to differentiate theological language from language in general. We must provide a sufficient defense for how theological language is anything other, or more, than a rhetorical style. Just to be clear: I believe that God's incarnation in the person of Jesus Christ through the Spirit's power at work within Mary qualifies as an *event*. The problem is that we have no access to this event—not even through scripture. Scripture tosses us back into the sea of language—to signification, tropes, and iterability. It is semantically vacuous to declare, as does Haddon Robinson, that "[i]n spite of the 'bad-mouthing' of preaching and preachers, no one who takes the Bible seriously should count preaching out. To the New Testament writers, preaching stood as the event through which God works."[45] I have no doubt that the biblical writers believed this, but this belief alone is insufficient for overcoming linguistic iterability, which precludes any *event* of language.

I can already hear a rebuttal building in your chest: *But if preaching is the work of the Holy Spirit, then it is more event-ful than language as such.* Indeed. The problem for homiletical theologies, and where homileticians often overstep our bounds, is that we have no noumenal barom-

44. This is as true for preaching as it is for psychoanalysis: "Impossible *to say* it now, because the permission to speak, the incitement to speak, and the perspective of speaking and saying everything . . . without interdiction, paradoxically ends up in *nothing to say*. . . . Impossible to say it *now*, because the inter-diction cannot be presented, expressed as present, or as presence, cannot be uttered in any remark proffered as present." Luce Irigaray, "Sex as Sign," in *To Speak is Never Neutral*, 137.

45. Haddon W. Robinson, *Biblical Preaching: The Development and Delivery of Expository Messages*, 3rd ed. (Grand Rapids, MI: Baker Academic, 2014), 2.

eter, no *geistlich* Geiger counter.[46] Fred Craddock reminds us that "it is too much to guarantee the Spirit's presence [in preaching], as though we had an effective technology in matters of the Spirit, creating the conditions that assure the Spirit's arrival among us. . . . The Spirit is *of God* and not contingent upon our willing or doing." He goes on to observe that *after* the fact we may sometimes assert, "Yes. The Spirit of God was here. Just now." This acknowledgement of uncertainty corresponds in no way with a lack of faith, Craddock argues; rather, it is "a hesitation to walk too far on a path where certainty shades into blasphemy."[47] So, in a very real sense, the *event* of preaching never takes place; it never happens except in a happening that is never fully accessible *in the present*, as an *event*. To assert *ex nihilo* that there is an event of preaching is either to say too much or to say nothing.[48]

Meaning-making only ever takes place *within* a given system of signification, which means that no event is possible in any special or privileged sense. There is no linguistic outside to preaching. Even other means of human communication that we preachers employ (e.g., gesture, facial expression, eye contact, vocal intonation) still participate in the same kind of arbitrary and differential structures that govern language in general. Homileticians must do something with the fact that, within language, signs point to other signs; signifiers signal other signifiers.[49] We don't ever escape the play of signification; we never get

46. On the significance of *geistlich*, which is quite relevant here, see Karl Barth, *The Church Dogmatics: Lecture Fragments*, IV/4, trans. Geoffrey W. Bromiley (Grand Rapids, MI: Eerdmans, 1981), 92: "In modern usage the term 'spiritual' has wrongly been put in embarrassing proximity to the word 'religious.' It should be related to this word only indirectly and not very firmly. What has been forgotten is that, among Christians at least, the word 'spiritual' can denote only a new definition of the human spirit, of the whole of this spirit, by the Holy Spirit, so that it cannot refer to a variation or modification of human spiritual activity as such. *Geistlich* and *geistig*, which, unfortunately, like *Geschichte* and *Historie*, can be distinguished linguistically only in German, denote two different things. *Geistig* denotes the capacity for orientation to something transcendent, and it thus implies a religious life in some sense and to some degree. But in the use of this capacity, what is *geistig* is not necessarily *geistlich*. The *geistlich* has contacts with it. It operates in its sphere. It uses its possibilities. It determines, controls, and penetrates it. Yet it has and retains its own individuality, distinctiveness, and movement in relation to the religious life as well as the scientific, moral, political, and aesthetic life. It has no special affinity to the religious life."
47. Fred Craddock, *Preaching*, 25th ann. ed. (Nashville: Abingdon, 2010), 29. This observation notwithstanding, Craddock views preaching as an "acoustical event." He writes, "The actual preaching of a sermon is a non-repeatable, non-portable event" (31–32). But, by this measure, *every* utterance would qualify as an *event*.
48. An exception to this would be certain kinds of Pentecostal preaching that refuse to conform to preestablished rhetorical and linguistic paradigms. See Ashon Crawley, "Breathing Flesh and the Sound of Black Pentecostalism," *Theology and Sexuality* 19, no. 1 (2013): 49-60. See also Luce Irigaray, "The Way of Breath," in *Between East and West: From Singularity to Community*, trans. Stephen Pluháek (New York: Columbia University Press, 2002), 73–93.
49. ". . . the signified always already functions as a signifier. The secondary that it seemed possible to ascribe to writing alone affects all the signifieds in general, affects them always already, the moment they *enter the game*. There is not a single signified that escapes, even if recaptured, the

from the sound [trē] to an *actual* tree. This is the basic movement of language *at its origin*, and because homiletics has largely forgotten or erased its own constituting origin *in* language, it is content to evoke the *event* of preaching as a kind of hocus pocus that's supposed to settle the matter before we have time to consider it.[50]

The words we employ to speak about God must be *iterable*. What this means is that for any sound pattern, written inscription, or gesture—any sign—to *make* meaning it must be both *repeatable* and *distinguishable*. If a word is only ever used once, what function would it serve within a language system? Moreover, since we've already discussed that for any sign to signify it needs to be *different* from the other signs that make up the system of signification, those differences must be discernible.[51] Thus, a general a-temporality necessarily and structurally troubles preaching as an event of particular speech-acts in time.

In their recent introductory homiletics text *Ways of the Word: Learning to Preach for Your Time and Place*, Sally Brown and Luke Powery offer much in the service of preaching. I particularly appreciate their attention to the myriad ways that sexual and racial difference shapes preaching. Along the way, however, they argue in defense of preaching as an event.

To begin, Brown and Powery define preaching as an "event of spoken communication" that is split between theological (i.e., God-controlled) and rhetorical (i.e., human-controlled) elements.[52] They seek to affirm the "core rhetoric" of Christian preaching as 1) Declaring God's promises; 2) Renaming and re-narrating the world through cross and resurrection; and 3) Imaginative rehearsal for action in the world.

play of signifying references that constitute language. The advent of writing is the advent of this play; today such a play is coming into its own, effacing the limit starting from which one had thought to regulate the circulation of signs, drawing along with it all the reassuring signifieds, reducing all the strongholds, all the out-of-bounds shelters that watched over the field of language. This strictly speaking, amounts to destroying the concept of 'sign' and its entire logic." Derrida, *Of Grammatology*, 7.
50. This is not the case for all homileticians. David Buttrick asks, "Why is preaching a 'Word of God?'" To this he answers, "Preaching is a word of God *only* if it serves God's redemptive purposes." *A Captive Voice: The Liberation of Preaching* (Louisville: Westminster John Knox, 1994), 30. Consider also the indictment of Wilson: "Current textbooks in preaching pay almost no attention to how students are to preach the gospel. Preach-the-text operates uncritically on the assumption that text yields the Word of God and that this Word is the gospel." Paul Scott Wilson, *The Practice of Preaching*, 2nd ed. (Nashville: Abingdon, 2007), 157.
51. "A phoneme or grapheme is necessarily always to some extent different each time that it is presented in an operation or a perception. But, it can function as a sign, and in general as language, only if a formal identity enables it to be issued again and to be recognized." Derrida, *Speech and Phenomena*, 50.
52. Sally A. Brown and Luke A. Powery, *Ways of the Word: Learning to Preach for Your Time and Place* (Minneapolis: Fortress Press, 2016), 13.

Though this book is helpful in many ways, the division Brown and Powery create between theology and rhetoric is not one of them. Theology is already rhetoric, and herein lies the tension they produce in their discussion of preaching as an event: if preaching is an event *theologically*, it must be utterly novel and unexpected, unknown in advance; but preaching cannot be an event *rhetorically* because rhetoric is already committed to conventionality, to patterns and forms of "proper" speech, to that which has already been experienced.[53] To be clear, I have no problem with teaching rhetoric in homiletics classrooms. I do not believe, however, that it can be so cleanly separated from theology or that preaching coincides with any *event* worthy of the name, at least not one that homiletics can anticipate.

Many homiletics texts advancing an African-American mode of preaching exhibit a similar tension. In his informative book, *Introduction to the Practice of African American Preaching*, Frank Thomas differentiates between rhetorical patterns employed in predominantly Euro-American contexts (so-called "standard" English) and a "second language" shared among African Americans. This latter style is called *signifying*, a term he borrows from Henry Louis Gates. I do not wish to challenge the presence of both rhetorical styles and their use in preaching; rather, I want to point out that even as signifying is privileged in African-American preaching it has no privileged access to anything beyond language.

Signifying is no more an event than any other form of rhetoric. As a "rhetorical practice," signifying's emphasis on improvisation, verbal dexterity, and creative expression tethers it to an identifiable form of language that may be intuited, taught, and learned.[54] It is right and crucial for African-American preaching to lift up signifying as "a rhetorical strategy whose purpose is to empower cultural definition by claiming space for black presence." Moreover, Thomas is correct to assert

53. Brown and Powery, *Ways of the Word*, 10: "Your *experience* of preaching as a rhetorical event shapes the images you have of preachers and your *expectations* of the effects of preaching has, or should have, on listeners." Emphasis added. Here we can see that the former supervenes upon the latter, disqualifying preaching as an event. For Derrida, the *event*, if there is such a thing, arises in "(sur)passing the aporia" of conditions and conventionality. Jacques Derrida, "*Sauf le nom (Post-Scriptum)*," in *On the Name*, ed. Thomas Dutoit, trans. David Wood, John P. Leavey Jr., and Ian McLeod (Stanford: Stanford University Press, 1995), 54.
54. Thomas writes, "Signifying can only be defined through possibilities of indirection and innuendo because signifying, at its heart, *is* indirection and innuendo. In other words, one has to signify to define signifying." Frank A. Thomas, *Introduction to the Practice of African American Preaching* (Nashville: Abingdon, 2016), 75. Thomas is only able to lift up signifying as an "indirect communicative art" by assuming that so-called "standard" English is somehow more direct or straightforward.

that "rhetoric is not an appendage after the preacher has decided the rational content of what to say: signifying and the like are verbal jabs and rhetorical feints to validate personhood, identity and a sense of being in a world that, in whatever form, seeks to deny fundamental aspects of being human."[55] However, using Thomas's own words, if signifying is evoked as a "strategy" with a particular "purpose" aiming at a certain "presence," it begs the question how far from Euro-American (i.e., Western) thought signifying ventures. Strategies, teleologies, and a metaphysics of presence are features of Western thought par excellence.[56] Signifying is just as axiomatic and taxonomic as so-called "standard" rhetorical paradigms; it too bears a discernible and iterable relation to intra-linguistic modes of signification with concomitant sociocultural conventions. Signifying remains within the powers of language that troubles an *event* as such.[57]

My intention is not to denigrate the fine work of these scholars. I merely wish to argue that homiletics must keep ever in mind that the game of language is rigged. We know better than to bet big in Vegas because we know that the odds of winning are always already skewed in the casino's favor. The same holds true for preaching that hopes to participate in the superabundant logic of Jesus and the prophets. The words we might employ and the rules of language we must use to make meaning possible are *already* in play. By necessity. Moreover, the assumptions that underlie language are *already* committed to certain ways of being that may share little with a Jesus-way of speaking, thinking, and being.

Language is power, and it favors the powerful.[58] Language serves the powers and principalities of this age. You probably haven't even noticed that throughout this chapter I've employed terms like *mastery,*

55. Ibid., 76.
56. See Derrida, "*Ousia* and *Grammē*: A Note on a Note from *Being and Time*," in *Margins of Philosophy,* particularly the section entitled, "The Closure of the Gramme and the Trace of Difference," 63–67.
57. Irigaray's reflections on the linguistic "structure" of schizophrenic discourse are illuminating here. She concludes, "A schizophrenic would then be someone who could not, or who would not, play the game, who recalls what lies underneath, the reverse side, the prerequisites, or the balance, lack of recognition and the price to be paid for it. The schizophrenic would signal (the way toward) the above or the beyond of signs." "Schizophrenics, or the Refusal of Schiz," in *To Speak is Never Neutral,* 191.
58. This is why it is imperative that preachers learn to resist the temptation to view language as utilitarian and instead learn to interrogate language in and beyond "discursive practices" and "enunciative fields" like Michel Foucault taught us. See Foucault, *The Archeology of Knowledge and the Discourse on Language,* trans. Rupert Sawyer (New York: Vintage, 1982). See also Irigaray: Western man "believes himself to be the creator of language, of poetry, of reason, but, in fact, he has only imitated the strength of the universe which surrounds him. He is nothing but an effect of the violence which results from his conquest." *To Be Two,* 71.

order, and *rules* to talk of language *acquisition* and words like *internal*, *necessary*, and *repeatable* to talk about meaning-making. These are Western values. They are hardwired into our language. Masters are valued over slaves; rules and order trump transgression and chaos. That which is internal, necessary, and the same takes precedence over that which is external, ancillary, and different. See? Hierarchy abides. Even as I work to explain language, I am forced to submit to certain ideals and commitments that constitute language itself. This is also the case when we employ language to talk about God.

Words Fall Apart

Language is always *in* trouble. The trembling of language's foundations that preaching has experienced over that past sixty years has merely helped to expose the primary idolatry of homiletics. We have constructed our understanding of God and God's speaking on a system that is always already committed to other gods. I would go so far as to argue that preaching that does not interrogate the philosophical assumptions at work on the inside of its language is guilty of bending the knee to Nebuchadnezzar's gold statue (Daniel 3).

How may we escape from that which binds us? Furthermore, by what means might we venture an escape when the very tools we would employ are already committed to our enslavement? Here's where Irigaray helps us again. She writes, "What is elementary or simple intervenes only as fiction that will have to be unmasked over and over again, deconstructed. . . . If one risks it."[59] And make no mistake: this is risky business. Nevertheless, we must nurture a way with language that demystifies language and does not seek to rule over others through discursive imperialisms. Homiletically, this means that the only way to begin to preach is not to begin.[60]

But here's the thing: now that we know about the un-holy alliance shared between preaching and language, we are in a position to do something about it. The solution is neither to acquiesce to the vernacular nor retreat to the perceived safety of biblical language. *The solution is to embrace preaching's death in and through language.* We ought not

---

59. Irigaray, "The Rape of the Letter," 134. In a later text, Irigaray puts it this way: "In order to get close to the sex dimension of discourse, it is not enough to shift its rules and change its propositions about content, especially historical content. We need to analyze very rigorously the forms that authorize that content." Irigaray, "The Three Genders," 172.

60. Irigaray, *To Be Two*, 19: "Rather than grasping you—with my hand, with my gaze, with my intellect—I must stop before the inappropriable, leaving the transcendence between us to be."

run from such death. We must embrace it. We must orient ourselves to death to rescue preaching from zombiehood.

Preaching must meet its Maker in and through language. This requires us to risk our theologies, our ideologies, and our very selves in the *work* of preaching, a work that is impossible, un-eventful, unwork-able (*désœuvrement*). We would do well to heed the wisdom of Rebecca Chopp. She writes, "If Protestant theology has any identity to find or, more to my interests, anything to contribute to Christian theology and Christianity in general, such a contribution requires a reconsideration of proclamation and the Word."[61] Such a reconsideration leads her to conclude that any theology of proclamation that takes "the Word" seri-ously must result in an understanding of such as a "perfectly open sign," one that is radically open to new significations leading to trans-formation and freedom. To that task we now turn.

Section Two: Language *as* Trouble

You just don't go and do anything with language; it preexists us and it survives us. When you introduce something into language, you have to do it in a refined manner, by respecting through disrespect its secret law. That's what might be called unfaithful fidelity.

— Jacques Derrida[62]

Language may be the "house of [homiletical] being," but it is not our home.[63] In language, preachers are under house arrest. If language pre-exists us—if it has already set the rules of the game that we must fol-low—how are we to employ language in Christian preaching that is not always already subservient to said language?[64] We can't escape lan-guage, and there is nowhere that we might preserve or protect ser-monic language from the vicissitudes and injustices at work within

61. Rebecca S. Chopp, *The Power to Speak: Feminism, Language, God* (New York: Crossroad, 1989), 5.
62. Jacques Derrida and Jean Birnbaum, *Learning to Live Finally: The Last Interview*, trans. Pascale-Anne Brault and Michael Naas (Brooklyn: Melville House, 2007), 36.
63. "Contemporary leaders seem to be trapped in the language and culture they have produced as if caught in a net or sinking in quicksand. They are prisoners of their own civilization." Irigaray, *Thinking the Difference*, 29.
64. Language is "purely immanent," writes the influential Soviet/Russian linguist Valentin Nikolae-vich Voloshinov. In his book *Marxism and the Philosophy of Language*, trans. Ladislav Matejka and I. R. Titanic (Cambridge, MA: Harvard University Press, 1986), he concludes, "The individual must accept and assimilate this system [of language] entirely as it is; there is no place in it for evalua-tive, ideological discriminations—such as whether something is better, worse, beautiful, ugly, or the like. In fact, there is only one linguistic criterion: correct versus incorrect, wherein *linguisti-cally correct* is understood to mean only the *correspondence of a given form to the normative system of language*" (54).

language. We can't just hightail it to the sanctity of biblical or ecclesial language. These, too, are always already committed to socio-symbolic networks that are not politically neutral.

Mary Lin Hudson gets it right when she declares that "words fashion worlds of reality, they selectively shut out competing claims, relegating them to the realm of silence."[65] So, how might we work within language in the hope that our preaching will fashion worlds of reality that reflect the kin(g)dom of God attested by Jesus? Or, to borrow Derrida's words quoted above, how might we practice an "unfaithful fidelity" to language in and through our preaching?

Preaching must learn to embrace the messiness of language.[66] Such is the task of homiletical theologies. Language is always already *in* trouble and so we must employ language *as* trouble in our preaching. We do this by working in and through language with an eye to those hidden commitments and political allegiances that lurk below the surface of our languages, with an ear to those murmurs that disrupt through their excess that which would silence otherness.[67] If language is essentially a code, then we must preach in such a way that we crack the code in service of the gospel.

Thankfully, there is a kind of approach that can facilitate such work. This method—which is not really a method—is called *deconstruction*. Irigaray maps such a non-programmable program with poetic vivacity:

> Turn everything upside down, inside out, back to front. *Rack it with radical convulsions*, carry back, reimport, those cries that her "body" suffers in her impotence to say what disturbs her. Insist also and deliberately upon those *blanks* in discourse which recall the places of her exclusion and which, by their *silent plasticity*, ensure the cohesion, the articulation, the coherent expansion of established forms. Reinscribe them hither and thither *as divergencies*, otherwise and elsewhere than they are expected, in *ellipses* and *eclipses* that deconstruct the logical grid of reader-writer, drive him out of his mind, trouble his vision to the point of incurable diplopia at least.[68]

---

65. Mary Lin Hudson, "To Die and Rise Again: Preaching the Gospel for Liberation," in *Preaching as a Theological Task: World, Gospel, Scripture: In Honor of David Buttrick*, ed. Thomas G. Long and Edward Farley (Louisville: Westminster John Knox, 1996), 113.
66. See Jacob D. Myers, *Making Love with Scripture: Why The Bible Doesn't Mean How You Think It Means* (Minneapolis: Fortress Press, 2015), chapters 9 and 10.
67. Irigaray speaks of such an approach in terms of "jamming the theoretical machinery," by attending to a "disruptive excess" that phallogocentrism has suppressed. Irigaray, "The Power of Discourse," 78.
68. Luce Irigaray, *Speculum of the Other Woman*, trans. Gillian C. Gill (Ithaca, NY: Cornell University Press, 1985), 142.

Such an approach, in other words, disturbs thought from within by allowing that which has been occluded and silenced by language to be seen and heard.

Deconstruction "is" (and I use scare quotes here to destabilize from the get-go that deconstruction may be reduced to a thing, being, or ontology) a way of seeing and hearing that gets at what I believe Jesus is talking about when he blesses those with eyes to see and those with ears to hear (Mark 8:18; Matt 13:16). Deconstruction is a way of seeing in, through, and beyond mundane vision. We might go so far as to say that deconstruction is synonymous with faith, albeit a faith understood as a "passion for the impossible," to borrow John Caputo's phrase.[69] Deconstruction is a way of enacting an unfaithful fidelity to language in preaching.

Now You See Me

Deconstruction is not any *thing*. Deconstruction happens. It's an *event* (if there "is" such a thing). It arises unexpectedly, beyond even the horizon of expectation. Deconstruction arises within, behind, and around the boundaries—the interpretive horizon—of language. It makes itself visible and audible at those moments of rupture, where language throws itself into doubt. As Derrida puts it, "Deconstruction takes place, it is an event that does not await the deliberation, consciousness, or organization of a subject, or even of modernity. It deconstructs itself."[70] This last sentence is key.

To say that deconstruction deconstructs *itself* is to say that we have no control over it. Deconstruction is not quite a *method* or *theory*, which gives us the sense that we can wield it and employ it for our predetermined ends.[71] It's better to understand deconstruction as an *attitude*, a *sensibility*, or a *way of seeing and hearing* that is wide-awake to the constructed nature of *all* languages—even biblical language. What

69. "The passion for the impossible is the passion of faith. Not only does deconstruction reinscribe the determinable faiths within undecidability, which is a very salutary reminder, but deconstruction's undecidability goes hand in hand with a certain faith, *sans savoir, sans avoir, sans voir* and a certain passion of non-knowing." John D. Caputo, *The Prayers and Tears of Jacques Derrida: Religion without Religion* (Bloomington: Indiana University Press, 1997), 63–64.
70. Derrida, "Letter to a Japanese Friend," 274. See also Derrida, *Memoires for Paul de Man*, 73: "The disruptive force of deconstruction is always already contained within the architecture of the work."
71. Irigaray asks, "How to reveal what can be revealed only outside this autological circle? What cannot even come to be until after escaping from these times of logic? . . . What method will allow this question even to be heard?" She answers, "I will here indicate, modestly, certain applications and implications of the—male—sexualization of discourse, and *employ in part its own methods in order to expose its always occulted presuppositions*." "The Language of Man," in *To Speak is Never Neutral*, 228. Emphasis added.

this means for us is that we need to help preachers understand *how* the architectonics of language are always already coming undone by the very measures established to build them up. In the pages that follow, I want to carry forward a kind of homiletical deconstruction according to certain ways of seeing. In the following section I shall offer the same in relation to hearing, which has been subordinated to seeing in Western practice even as, ironically, speech has been privileged over writing. To the degree that deconstruction *is* anything, it's a way of seeing *and* hearing.

Nearsighted Deconstruction: There's No Outside Text

Folks who are nearsighted possess very good vision at close range, whereas objects that are far away appear blurry unless corrected by glasses or contact lenses. What I am labeling *nearsighted deconstruction* is a way of seeing that attends very closely to *language use itself*. It allows us to see the governing logics of language in spite of their invisibility, which are often also invisible to their author.[72] By attending to a certain troubling of language, nearsighted deconstruction may open up our facility with language in and through Christian preaching.

Nearsighted deconstruction arises out of a *transgression* of language; that is, a use of language that infringes upon linguistic codes. Preachers who adopt this way of seeing will begin to detect philosophical and theological commitments underwriting certain patterns of dis-course and they will seek to insert themselves upon those codes in fidelity to the gospel of liberation. This is why so many so-called "postmodern" theologians and philosophers employ hyphens, parentheses, and slashes in their writing. Such thinkers are simultaneously employing language and transgressing upon language itself. They do this by recognizing what is going on in language in spite of what they might wish to say. For example, the word *discourse* signifies spoken or written communication; but by adding a hyphen, the writer is able to *also* signify that what we understand as discourse is also *dis-course* by drawing attention to the negative or negating quality of discourse (*dis*) that also shapes the route or trajectory (*course*) of thought.

In order to transgress boundaries and borders, the preacher must go

---

72. See Derrida, *Of Grammatology*, 158: "[T]he writer writes *in* a language and *in* a logic whose proper system, laws, and life his discourse by definition cannot dominate absolutely. He uses them only by letting himself . . . be governed by the system. And the reading [aka deconstruction] must always aim at a certain relationship, unperceived by the writer, between what he commands and what he does not command of the patterns of the language that he uses."

rogue, or even become a kind of rogue for the sake of the gospel.[73] The roguish preacher who leans into a certain transgression of language will recognize that the dividing lines or borders at work within signi-fication are *active:* they have *agency.* The boundary line itself *makes* the distinction we have been taught to discern between text and context, fiction and reality.[74] By transgressing the boundaries, the preacher is able to enter this *other* world of language in *a certain way.* This attitude or approach of exploration, of wanting to discern what is hidden, what is present in its absence, what is necessarily excluded, what is *other* in the world of language features centrally in nearsighted deconstruction. This may seem impossible for homiletical theologies; but I contend that its very im-possibility is what drives homiletical deconstruction (mad). Is not preaching both impossible and that which transgresses (upon) the impossible?[75]

To illustrate, consider the vitriol these days animating the political dis-course between Republicans and Democrats, between conserva-tives and liberals. Mark C. Taylor describes the "oppositional logic" of contemporary political discourse, which attempts to secure a discur-sive position by negating the other. What neither side understands, Taylor argues, is that such struggles are always self-defeating: "to negate the other without whom one cannot be what one is, is to negate the self."[76] We must teach preachers to transgress the philosophical structures underwriting homiletics in order to help them catch sight of something in and beyond language.

Nearsighted deconstruction is also hyper-vigilant to how language structures reality. This drives to the heart of deconstruction's provoca-tive, and often misunderstood, tagline: "there is no outside-text."[77] This doesn't mean that there is no such thing as reality, or that all is

---

73. See Jacques Derrida, "The Rogue That I Am," in *Rogues: Two Essays on Reason*, trans. Pascale-Anne Brault and Michael Naas (Stanford: Stanford University Press, 2005), 63–70.
74. "If we are to approach a text, it must have an edge. . . . [But] a 'text'. . . is henceforth no longer a finished corpus of writing, some content enclosed in a book or its margins, but a differential network, a fabric of traces referring endlessly to something other than itself, to other differential traces. Thus the text overruns all the limits assigned to it . . ." Derrida, "Living On: Border Lines," in *Between the Blinds*, 256–57.
75. See Jacques Derrida, "Psyche: Inventions of the Other," in *Psyche: Inventions of the Other*, vol. 1, ed. Peggy Kamuf and Elizabeth Rottenberg, trans. Catherine Porter (Stanford: Stanford Univer-sity Press, 2007), 15: "And I would say that deconstruction loses nothing from admitting that it is impossible. . . . For a deconstructive operation *possibility* would rather be the danger, the danger of becoming an available set of rule-governed procedures, methods, accessible approaches. The interest of deconstruction, of such force and desire as it may have, is a certain experience of the impossible: that is . . . the experience of the other as the invention of the impossible."
76. Mark C. Taylor, *After God* (Chicago: University of Chicago Press, 2007), 349.
77. Derrida, *Of Grammatology*, 158. The French phrase is *il n'y a pas de hors-texte.*

language. Rather, it means that language, as a constant movement of differences in which we find no stable resting point, makes it impossible to appeal to reality as a refuge *independent* of language. Everything acquires the instability and ambiguity that is inherent in language.

Nearsighted deconstruction works to unveil the constructed reality of the fictional, dreamlike world established by language. That which we label *reality* relies upon the very linguistic possibilities by which we label anything. Nearsighted deconstruction blurs the lines between language and reality and between text and context. After all, "every text is a text on a text under a text, without any established hierarchy."[78] Nearsighted deconstruction under-stands that there is no way *outside* of the linguistic world, that the so-called "real" world can in no way supervene upon the "other" world fabricated in and through language. The real world has always already escaped and is beyond our reach amidst the endless play of differences necessary to simulate sameness.

One example of this in popular discourse is found in the heated discussions concerning gender-neutral bathrooms in North Carolina. What some conservative lawmakers fail to see is that the words *man* and *woman* do not point to a simple and stable reality that exists outside of language. Identity markers such as gender and sex are not neutral; they participate in numerous philosophical and sociopolitical alliances. Nearsighted deconstruction discerns the ways in which the inside and outside of language interpenetrate and constitute one another.

Lastly, through a certain way of seeing, through "inhabiting" the logics that underwrite linguistic codes, nearsighted deconstruction attends to the ways that a discourse's animating energy is simultaneously the source of its own deconstruction. "The movements of deconstruction do not destroy structures from the outside. They are not possible and effective, nor can they take accurate aim, except by inhabiting those structures. Inhabiting them *in a certain way*, because one always inhabits, and all the more when one does not suspect it."[79] What

---

78. Geoffrey Bennington and Jacques Derrida, *Jacques Derrida*, trans. Geoffrey Bennington (Chicago and London: The University of Chicago Press, 1993), 92. Bennington continues, "But if we thus place in doubt the distinctions between text and context on the one hand, object-language and metalanguage on the other, we are not flattening everything into a single homogeneous text: on the contrary, we are multiplying differences within the text, whose unity and closure were given only by the context supposed to surround it. . . . the context is already remarked in the text, the object-language already infiltrated with metalanguage: to this extent we ought to be able, up to a point, to find resources for reading 'in' the text being read" (93).

79. Derrida, *Of Grammatology*, 24.

this means is that the thing the writer or speaker seeks to conceal through language—even unconsciously—is the very thing that *cannot* be concealed. The machinations of the author or speaker work against him—not by any act of the reader or hearer, nor by anything *external* to the world of discourse. The world of language harbors the seeds of its *own* deconstruction.

Nearsighted deconstruction attends carefully to the *internal* logic of texts, uncovering their animating principles and underlying foundations. As we will soon see (in chapter 3), this way of seeing opens up biblical texts to trouble their own peculiar logics, their particular economies. Hereby, homiletical theologies may precipitate a kind of kerygmatic vision that may also illuminate contemporary faith and praxis.

Farsighted Deconstruction: The Invisibility of the Too Visible

Homiletical theologies may also learn to nurture a second mode of sight in service of a preaching to come. Hereby, we are invited to see with a certain *farsightedness*. Farsighted people can see distant objects quite well, but have difficulty focusing on objects that are close up. This vision problem occurs when light rays entering the eye focus *behind* the retina, rather than directly upon it.

Here's the insight that farsighted deconstruction contributes to homiletical theologies: we are so immersed in our discursive regimes—our ways of adjudicating what counts as knowledge, rationality, and truth—that we can fail to discern the power dynamics at play *behind* such ways of knowing. Knowledge doesn't emerge spontaneously. It has a history. It evolves. The only way to *really* see the forms of knowledge right in front of our faces—and even then only partially and obliquely—is to look behind what lies before us, to gaze at the architectonics that constitute knowledge as such, the genealogies that made such ways of thinking and speaking possible.[80]

One way to do this is to attend to the underlying "play of forces" that makes all discursive acts (texts, speeches, sermons, etc.) possible. This way of seeing is guided by a certain "care" and is sustained by a certain "curiosity." Such is a readiness to behold that which surrounds us as "strange and odd. . . . to throw off familiar ways of thought and to look

---

80. See Michel Foucault, "The Subject and Power," in *Power: Essential Works of Foucault*, ed. James Faubion, trans. Robert Hurley (New York: New Press, 2000), 326–48.

at the same things in a different way."[81] Here is where scholarly methods serve the preacher.

Here's how farsighted deconstruction takes shape. First off, it's not the same thing as historical study, because the latter is already animated by certain philosophical ideals (e.g., history as descent or emergence; history as a progressive record of causes and effects). Farsighted deconstruction is *meta-historical*, that is, it transcends the "technologies" that produce history and determine it as such.[82] Farsighted deconstruction goes elbows-deep into history's orifices to uncover what lies at the heart of the beast, what drives it and shapes its destiny. It is not history, because it attends less to history's *flow* than to its *ruptures*, the snags in its fabric.

The "stuff" of farsighted deconstruction, if there *is* such a thing, is not found in history books. It is found in "unapproved" locales: archives, cave paintings, rally signs, social media posts—and only then by attending carefully to the "muted voice" and "half silence" of those marginalized by regimes of power.[83] By looking *beyond* history, philosophy, science, and theology one can begin to understand the "play of forces" at work *behind* language that constitute discourse itself.

When we scrutinize the developments *behind* our various modes of communicating, by adopting a certain farsightedness, we are able to discern the "intrinsic intelligibility," the "internal regimes of power" that structure language as knowledge.[84] Such a mode of seeing is oriented by the conviction that what is visible in the present is *too visible.* In other words, it is so utterly and completely obvious that we cannot actually see it for what it is: *an exercise of power.*

Truth is already power.

Nobody *has* power. Power is taken even as it takes hold of us; power

---

81. Michel Foucault, "The Masked Philosopher," in *Ethics, Subjectivity and Truth*, ed. Paul Rabinow, trans. Alan Sheridan (New York: New Press, 1997), 325. In other works, Foucault attends more pointedly to what he labels the "play of forces," that is, those cultural and political commitments that determine what counts as knowledge. See, for example, Michel Foucault, "We Other Victorians," in *The History of Sexuality*, vol. 1, trans. Robert Hurley (New York: Vintage Books, 1990), 12, and Foucault, *Discipline & Punish: The Birth of the Prison*, 2nd ed., trans. Alan Sheridan (New York: Vintage Books, 1995), 27: "power produces knowledge . . . power and knowledge directly imply one another."

82. "Technologies" here does not signify machines or gadgets that make our lives easier. For Foucault, they signify intrinsic, legitimizing energies that bind power, knowledge, and discourse. Technologies (of sexuality, of the self, of the body, etc.) are the operational necessities, tactics, and effects that make certain ways of knowing and speaking/writing possible within a given epoch.

83. Michel Foucault, *History of Madness*, ed. Jean Khalfa, trans. Jonahan Murphy and Jean Khalfa (London: Routledge, 2006), 396.

84. See Michel Foucault, "Truth and Power," in *Power/Knowledge: Selected Interviews and Other Writings, 1972-1977*, ed. Colin Gordon, trans. Alessandro Fontana and Pasquale Pasquino (New York: Pantheon Books, 1980), 112–14.

is snatched out of and snatches us out of the crucible of conflict. The story of humanity "proceeds from domination to domination" and history is written by those who have seized the rules.[85] This means that all forms of knowledge did not appear out of the sky one fine day for no apparent reason. Rather, regimes of knowledge are the *artifacts* of struggles and conflicts waged long ago.

As an example, consider the deconstructive theological treatments of race in the writings of Willie James Jennings and J. Kameron Carter.[86] Each in his own way, the former historically and the latter ideologically, present race as a theological construct and a theological problem. Neither scholar engages *race as such*, that is, on its own terms, as a given that maps cleanly onto skin pigmentation. Rather, they attend to the voices on the margins of history, to those silences, sighs, and ellipses that are not-quite-present and not-quite-absent from the theological, philosophical, and political architectonics that make it even possible for us to talk about a "post-racial America," as incredulous as that sounds. Accordingly, this mode of deconstruction that sees with a certain farsightedness does not seek to emancipate language from particular systems of power (e.g., rationality, human sexuality, God), but of *detaching* the power of truth from the forms of hegemony (e.g. psychology, sociology, theology) within which it operates in the present.

We must exercise extreme caution in attempting to uncover the historical impact on power/knowledge at work in and through language. The ground is tenuous. Seeking to discern power/knowledge relations and their linguistic effects does not mean that we are seeking a new foundation or origin, beyond the present. We are not seeking to structure a *better* system (however *better* may be defined, which is itself power laden). An obvious danger of such an approach is to totalize current effects of power in language according to mythological assessments—the "glory days" of yore or "the troubles" of today so that we may "make America great again." Farsighted deconstruction is more primal than this. It offers us a way of perceiving the present by attending to historical forces ignored or suppressed by history as such.[87]

Arising out of the writings of Michel Foucault, farsighted decon-

---

85. Michel Foucault, "Nietzsche, Genealogy, History," in *Language, Counter-Memory, Practice: Selected Essays and Interviews*, ed. Donald F. Bouchard (Ithaca, NY: Cornell University Press, 1980), 151.
86. Willie James Jennings, *The Christian Imagination: Theology and the Origins of Race* (New Haven, CT: Yale University Press, 2011) and J. Kameron Carter, *Race: A Theological Account* (Oxford: Oxford University Press, 2008).
87. Michel Foucault, "Space, Knowledge, and Power," in *The Foucault Reader*, ed. Paul Rabinow, trans. Christian Hubert (New York: Pantheon Books, 1984), 250.

struction has done much to uncover ways that seemingly unquestionable modern concepts and institutions (e.g., madness, homosexuality, the penal system) are constructs with their own constructed histories. They didn't just drop out of the sky; they were forged by those with the power to adjudicate knowledge and truth at particular points in history. Homiletics may learn greatly from such a way of seeing.

Astigmatic Deconstruction: Splitting Space

As with nearsighted and farsighted vision, a certain way of seeing is manifested in a third deconstructive approach that we can liken to astigmatism. Astigmatism is a condition in which light fails to come to a single point of focus on the retina to produce "clear vision." Instead, *multiple* focus points occur: either in front of the retina, on its periphery, behind it, or on all three at once. Astigmatic deconstruction is a mode of seeing multifarious focal points *simultaneously*. Astigmatic preachers don't just read texts. Such readers have been so shaped by their experiences that their vision *can't not* see texts according to such illumination.

In particular, astigmatic deconstruction entails a set of interpretative optics that arise out of colonial/imperial rule. These are the human consequences of controlling a country and establishing settlers for the economic exploitation of native people and their resources. Such a way of seeing attends to social, economic, cultural, political, and intellectual factors *all at once* because such vision incarnates the interconnections between them. Unfortunately, many who are granted such vision receive this "gift" by growing up under imperial rule or by being forced from their homeland in response to life's vicissitudes—poor educational opportunities, famine, or war. Like Heimdall, the Asgardian protector in the Marvel Comics, folks with the capacity for astigmatic deconstruction possess the ability to see across time and space—in a sense.

For those of you who have not been baptized in comic ink, let me unpack this comparison. Heimdall is able to sense the life essences of the gods throughout the Nine Worlds of Asgard, and has the ability to focus on certain sensory data or block them out of his consciousness at will. There is no origin story for Heimdall in the comics. In the Norse myths we get a bit more. In the poem *Heimdalargaldr*, we read that Heimdall is the son of nine sisters. In another Old Icelandic text, *Skáld-skaparmál*, we learn that Heimdall is the grandson of Aegir and Rán, who bore nine daughters whose names are associated with the waves of the sea. Thus, many Norse scholars believe that Heimdall was somehow born out of the waves of the sea.

As we mash-up these ancient stories about Heimdall, we learn two things. First, we discern an innate plurality, a multiform identity, in Heimdall's person. If we can wrap our minds around how Heimdall's birth could have been divided nine ways (and nine is the number of perfection in ancient Norse culture), at minimum we can see that he is the sum of multiple parts—much like those reared under colonial power or in diasporic communities (cf. the Apostle Paul).[88]

Second, we know from the myths that Aegir is the mighty sea Jötun (aka frost giant). The frost giants are the sworn enemies of the Aesir (the Norse gods who dwell in Asgard). Rán is the goddess of the sea. I highlight Heimdall's lineage because it showcases further his split identity: in his blood flows the histories of both the frost giants *and* the Aesir, the colonized *and* the colonizers, the subjugated *and* the subjugators.

Heimdall is a helpful analogue to those who embody astigmatic deconstruction because he, too, shares a particular way of seeing the world at work in and through language. Like him, such persons are subjects situated *within* particular ways of knowing and being in the world. As one such astigmatic thinker puts it, such folks abide in a "Third Space," an "*inbetween* space." This situatedness makes it possible for them to see *beyond*, *around*, and *through* cultural difference, to "elude the politics of polarity and emerge as the others of our selves."[89]

Astigmatic deconstruction is made possible because such people have split identities. They have been made *objects* of oppression and marginalization by colonial and imperial domination. At the same time, they remain *subjects* who see, know, and speak in a way that is conditioned by their subjugation and totalization. As Fanon, a thinker borne out of such a culture of *hybridity*, puts it: "I came into this world anxious to uncover the meaning of things, my soul desirous to be at the origin of the world, and here I am an object among other objects."[90]

Homiletical theologies can learn much from the words and witness of those reared under colonial and/or imperialistic regimes. Furthermore, homileticians and preachers alike may learn to nurture such a

88. For more on Paul's postcolonial identity, see the illuminating work of Eric D. Barreto, "Negotiating Difference: Theology and Ethnicity in the Acts of the Apostles," *Word and World* 31, no. 2 (Spring 2011): 129–37.
89. Homi K. Bhabha, *The Location of Culture* (London: Routledge, 1994), 53, 56.
90. Fanon, *Black Skins, White Masks*, 98.

way of seeing when we attend to the ways our minds have been colonized by neoliberal ideologies, white supremacy, and heterosexism. This work is ongoing. It is troubling even as it troubles the imagined stability of the preacher's personhood (see chapter 2).

Can You Hear Me Now?

"Opening our eyes," writes Irigaray, ". . . shakes the very foundations of what is given as universal, as beyond the reach of empirical imperatives, or of subjective or historical particularities."[91] And yet, even as deconstruction in and through language shares a relation to sight for Irigaray, a certain kind of listening offers even more.

For starters, hearing and listening are not the same thing, just as seeing is not quite perceiving. Listening, for Irigaray, "does not amount to grasping something in order to integrate and order it into our own world." Such violence silences otherness, and *otherness* cannot speak when *sameness* won't stop prattling. Listening is "opening one's own world to something or someone external and strange to it." Every listening worthy of the name is a "listening-to," meaning, "a way of opening ourselves to the other and of welcoming this other, its truth and its world as different."[92] Embracing language *as* trouble calls preachers to a certain listening.

Homiletics scholars have written much on the importance of listening—both to what the Bible "wants to say" and to what the congregation "wants to hear."[93] As helpful as these texts are, they tend to operate within an occidental frame that reduces otherness to sameness and alterity to appropriation. This is why homileticians need to start reading Irigaray. She teaches us to listen "in silence to a saying different from ours and which questions us about what we think we are or know." Such she describes as a "meeting beyond all mastery of the other and speech, because speech also arises in the exchange with the other. An already existing, already coded tool cannot regulate listening to one another nor the appropriateness of speech that will be addressed to the one or to the other after such listening." Because of our narrow understanding of language, Irigaray presses us to a mode

91. Irigaray, "The Language of Man," 225.
92. Luce Irigaray, "Listening, Thinking, Teaching," in *Luce Irigaray: Teaching*, ed. Luce Irigaray with Mary Green (London: Continuum, 2008), 232.
93. See the essays in *Listening to the Word: Homiletical Case Studies*, ed. John S. McClure (St. Louis: Chalice Press, 2004). See also Lenora Tubbs Tisdale, *Preaching as Local Theology and Folk Art* (Minneapolis: Fortress Press, 1997).

of engagement with human and non-human others (e.g., the environment) that resists the tendency to totalize the other. Instead, she helps
us listen for the "singularity" of the other that is only ever discernable
when we grant to the other a "decisive place of human becoming."[94]
Such would offer a kind of mystical path for homiletical theologies,
teaching preachers to listen beyond assumptions about meaning-making in language that are deaf to difference.

Two final comments about this kind of listening. First, deconstructive listening attends to sex-ual difference in a way that is structurally
impossible for traditional Western epistemologies, governed as they
are between hierarchical binaries (man/woman, straight/gay, etc.). Irigaray writes that men and women have different subjective configurations and ways of speaking. These, she argues, "cannot be attributed
solely to socio-historical determinations, or to an alienation of the feminine which is to be overcome by making it equal to the masculine."
What Irigaray labels "women's language" arises beyond the linguis-
tic-epistemic provenance of man according to a certain "alienation
and inertia, but it also demonstrates a richness of its own which has
nothing to envy in men's language; and, particularly a taste for intersubjectivity which is definitely not to be abandoned in favor of the sub-
ject-object relation dear to men."[95] Hereby, Irigaray is offering a mode
of communication that resists the zero-sum game that governs Western, male-dominated discourse.

Second, deconstructive listening à la Irigaray can lead us further
than Irigaray herself to listen beyond racial and ethnic binaries. Irigaray herself has been heavily criticized, and rightly so, for ignoring
class differences and the intersectionality of race that troubles the sexual difference she inscribes ontologically.[96] In elevating sexual difference as difference par excellence, Irigaray marginalizes, and effectively
silences, racial and ethnic difference. Thus, it is imperative, as a kind of
listening activity in and through language, that we learn from Irigaray

94. Irigaray, *In the Beginning*, 59–60. Or consider the words of Maurice Blanchot: "Speech is not sufficient for the truth it contains. Take the trouble to listen to a single word: in that word, nothing-
ness is struggling and toiling away, it digs tirelessly, doing its utmost to find a way out, nullifying
what encloses it—it is infinite disquiet, formless and nameless vigilance." *The Work of Fire*, 326.
95. Luce Irigaray, "The Question of the Other," in *Democracy Begins Between Two*, trans. Kirsteen Anderson (New York: Routledge, 2001), 137.
96. For helpful overviews of these critiques, see the essays by Naomi Schor, "Previous Engagements:
The Receptions of Irigaray" and "This Essentialism Which Is Not One: Coming to Grips with
Irigaray," in *Engaging with Irigaray: Feminist Philosophy and Modern European Thought*, ed. Carolyn
Burke, Naomi Schor, and Margaret Whitford (New York: Columbia University Press, 1994), 3–15,
57–78.

to embrace the trouble of language in a radical way, which will trouble even the language of those troubling language.

Conclusion

A/way with Words

If we keep on speaking the same language together, we're going to reproduce the same history. Begin the same old stories all over again.
—Luce Irigaray[97]

Language necessitates the death of preaching as hope for preaching. This is neither for pragmatic nor pedagogical reasons. As a discipline oriented to the im-possibility of speaking of God, homiletical theologies must help preaching die for *theological reasons*—albeit beyond every *logos*. If preaching is a *foolish* task, as Charles Campbell and Johan Cilliers contend, then homiletics ought to drop all pretenses about its own respectability.[98] But genuine foolishness ought to be neither a cultural-linguistic ruse, feigning foolishness while obviating folly, nor a rhetorical strategy. You can't teach foolishness because the bona fide *fool* is unteachable.

In order to lead preaching toward a good death, homiletical theologies, too, must die. Each must sacrifice itself upon the altar of linguistic deconstruction. The language that is necessary for us to work together, beyond the zero-sum logic of our world's dominant epistemologies, requires us to open ourselves to the other—and radically so. This is why the film *Arrival* was so helpful in orienting our discussion in this chapter. As Dr. Banks works to accommodate her ways of thinking to the aliens' language—the other par excellence, we might say—she exposes herself to both beauty and pain. She peers into her future and learns that her unborn daughter will die; she learns that her future husband will one day leave her. And yet, she chooses to expose herself to death and loss. This is the ultimate test: can you lay down your life so that others may live?

Contemporary homileticians and preachers must work to trouble the conventional theological and rhetorical standards that adjudicate kerygmatic possibilities. Having now abided for some time in the trou-

---

97. Irigaray, "When Our Lips Speak Together," 205.
98. See Charles L. Campbell and Johan H. Cilliers, *Preaching Fools: The Gospel as a Rhetoric of Folly* (Waco, TX: Baylor University Press, 2012).

ble at work within language, and having leaned into a way of preaching that embraces the death-dealing elements of language, we are now in a position to see that any homiletical attempt to get around language is impossible. I contend that it is more faithful (to God), and to any possible hearing therefrom, that we work with the cracks always already at work in language to facilitate preaching's encounter with its Maker. In teaching preachers to embrace the troubling of language, we remove the scaffolding of Western thought that bolsters contemporary preaching styles. We force them to consider, to borrow Hamlet's line, *what dreams may come*. We ought not, nor can we, answer this question for them.

Homiletics teaches a certain facility with language, *a way* with words. It might seem preposterous for a homiletician such as myself to suggest that preachers embrace the death of language in and for our preaching—that we do *away* with words. But, as Irigaray explains, "We are moulded by language: it is not only a question of understanding each word. . . . Thus the question is not only one of listening to words, but also to the linguistic and cultural context in which they take place, to the world that they compose and construct."[99] Such a listening exposes us to a certain deconstruction always already at work within language. We've got to think more about the spacing, absence, and even death, at work *on the inside* of language. This is what I mean when I insist that preachers must find *a way with words* that does *away with words.*

99. Irigaray, "Listening, Thinking, Teaching," 232.

2

Crossing Over to the Other Side: Troubling the Preacher

Pronouncing one's specificity is not enough if one is to escape the lethal, indistinct confusion of assimilations; this specificity still has to be put into action before consenting to it any outcome.

—Édouard Glissant[1]

Few shows engage the intersecting domains of identity and selfhood as poignantly—or as violently—as HBO's *Game of Thrones*. Nowhere is this confluence seen more clearly than in Arya Stark, who just so happens to be my favorite character in the series. For the uninitiated, Arya is the youngest daughter of Eddard Stark, the Lord of Winterfell.

When we first meet Arya, she is doing everything in her power to denounce her social status and expectations of her gender. Arya doesn't want to be a Lady, which she makes no attempt to conceal through her half-hearted attempts at needlepoint and vaunting exhibitions of her facility with bow and arrow. In subsequent episodes, we observe Arya leaning into various identities (squire, acolyte, beggar,

---

1. Édouard Glissant, *Poetics of Relation,* trans. Betsy Wing (Ann Arbor: University of Michigan Press, 1997), 147.

assassin) and subverting others (Lady, girl, boy—and even personhood altogether) in the *performance* of her identity.[2]

A significant example of such performance occurs when Arya's half-brother John gives her a sword as a parting gift. After handing her the weapon, John informs her that all the best swords have names. To this Arya replies, "Sansa can keep her sewing needles, I've got a Needle of my own." Here we witness a key aspect of selfhood: it arises out of a dialectic of sameness and otherness. She names her sword *Needle*, not only because it is small and fitting for her nine-year-old frame, but also in relation to her sister, Sansa. Arya's sword becomes a mark of her class and gender enculturation, *and* her transgression of such identity markers.

A second aspect of Arya's identity development takes shape as Arya submits herself to the tutelage of a certain Jaqen H'ghar. Jaqen is a member of the Faceless Men, a coterie of religious assassins who serve the Many-Faced God. One of the key aspects of this sect is that they aspire to the total renunciation of selfhood. He teaches Arya that selfhood is antithetical to their sect, and thus he works to purge Arya's identity, forcing her to undergo a kind of death.

"A girl has no name" becomes Arya's mantra. Even as Arya strives to become no one, her thirst to avenge those who've wronged her proves stronger than her desire to abdicate her selfhood. In their final encounter, Jaqen says, "Finally a girl is no one." Arya replies, "A girl is Arya Stark of Winterfell." Her individuality wins out over her quest to expunge her identity. Even as she learns from otherness, she embraces her name and place in the world: sameness.

In following Arya's journey, we witness something homiletics has treated insufficiently. Identity-formation, the very possibility of selfhood, is not simple but is a confluence of passivity and agency. Sometimes we are given identities, other times we pursue them. But more often than not, our subjecthood emerges out of a dialectical tension that is agonistic as well as generative. As Arya learns, circumscribing this process brings dire consequences. It is only according to a certain death, a certain *crossing over to the other side* of identity, that selfhood may emerge.

Attenuated understandings of selfhood and identity foster homilet-

---

2. On the *performance* of identity, see Judith Butler, *Bodies That Matter: On the Discursive Limits of "Sex"* (New York: Routledge, 2011), xvi-ii: "To claim that the subject is itself produced in and as a gendered matrix of relations is not to do away with the subject, but only to ask after the conditions of its emergence and operation."

ical theologies that minimize the sociopolitical significance of the preacher, or worse, erase the preacher altogether.[3] Despite all that they contribute to preaching and the church, most homiletical theologies presume that the preacher is a stable entity, a kind of tabula rasa onto which homiletical strategies may be written. This is wrong. In this chapter, I shall trouble the propensity to take the preacher for granted by exposing preaching to an otherness suppressed by contemporary homiletical theologies. This is not to "solve" the problem of the preacher nor is it to divest the preacher of their [sic] identity; rather, this work responds to a (divine) call to be(for)e the other.[4]

Section One: The Preacher *in* Trouble

We are unable to inscribe or write [because] we don't know who we are, something we never consider since we always take ourselves for ourselves; and from this point on we no longer know anything.
— Hélène Cixous[5]

3. Luke A. Powery, in his chapter entitled, "A Spirit-Driven Theology of Preaching," lifts up the importance of the preacher's identity for sermon development and delivery. He writes, "The gospel truth is connected to particular contextual experiences. As a preacher within a particular cultural context, I realize that I not only come from within particular faith communities but also from within specific cultural communities, not from outside of them. Preachers are located somewhere in time and space from the beginning. Preachers should begin right where they are as homiletical, enfleshed temples of the Spirit, experiencing the world and God" (28). I completely agree. The problem I have with he and Sally A. Brown's introductory preaching text, *Ways of the Word: Learning to Preach for Your Time and Place* (Minneapolis: Fortress Press, 2016), is that the preacher's identity is completely ignored in their chapters on biblical interpretation and sermon design (chs. 5–7). The preacher does resurface in Powery's chapter on "Embodying the Sermon," but this begs the question of how the preacher is supposed to em-body a sermon when the text-to-sermon process has left his/her/their body out of the discussion.
4. In this chapter, and throughout the rest of the book, I will occasionally include the non-binary gender pronouns *they/their* in addition to traditional masculine (he/his/him) and feminine (she/hers/her) pronouns. This is an effort to model a troubling of identity that I have found in no homiletics texts to date.
    The last part of this sentence about responding to a (divine) call to be(for)e the other aims to trouble several matters at once: a simple assimilation of the call to God; the Levinasian recognition of the call of the other as more originary than Being; and the acknowledgement that the site of one's being arises out of encounters with otherness. Each of these matters will become clearer as we proceed. The word *divine* is in parenthesis to mark a kind of dative, indirect relationship between the human subject of discourse who encounters God, perhaps. See Emmanuel Levinas, *Otherwise Than Being: Or, Beyond Essence*, trans. Alphonso Lingis (Pittsburgh: Duquesne University Press, 1998), 144–45: "Substituting itself for the other, a responsibility ordered to the first one on the scene, a responsibility for the neighbor, inspired by the other, I, the same, am torn up from my beginning in myself, my equality with myself. The glory of the Infinite is glorified in this responsibility. It leaves to the subject no refuge in its secrecy that would protect it against being obsessed by the other, and cover over its evasion. . . . The glory of the Infinite is the anarchic identity of the subject flushed out without being able to slip away. It is the ego led to sincerity, making signs to the other, for whom and before whom I am responsible, of this very giving of signs, that is, of this responsibility: 'here I am.'"
5. Hélène Cixous, *Three Steps on the Ladder of Writing*, trans. Sarah Cornell and Susan Sellers (New York: Columbia University Press, 1993), 51.

Preachers are in trouble. In many ways, this goes with the job description—*other duties as assigned*. But the kind of trouble I want to focus on in this chapter has nothing to do with what happened at the last business or session meeting. It's not about whom the preacher forgot to visit at the hospital or how many receipts have yet to make it to the office manager. The kind of trouble preachers are in is a trouble endemic to homiletics itself: the trouble of identity.[6]

But first an important distinction: the difference between selfhood and identity is slight but significant. Selfhood, philosophically or psychologically speaking, is a state of having a *particular* identity, being a *subject* distinct from others: in short, individuality.[7] Identity expresses our similarity or affinity to an ideal; it is the *sameness* we share in relation to perceived norms. Selfhood is more than identity, and, paradoxically, this *more* is also *less*. Always already at work on the inside of selfhood—an inside ineluctably exposed to an outside—is a certain absence, a negation, an alterity that is not otherwise than selfhood but is nevertheless *structurally necessary*. Selfhood is constructed out of identity *and* difference, sameness *and* otherness.[8]

Homiletical theologies tend to bifurcate along the fault line of the preacher. Either the preacher is supposed to radically absent herself from the preaching event (as Barth and Bonhoeffer argue)[9], or the preacher is to exert herself as a crucial element in preaching.[10] What is more, the most influential voices in homiletics rest much of their

---

6. The issue of identity under consideration in this chapter differs markedly from that which Robert Stephen Reid presumes in his edited volume, *Slow of Speech and Unclean Lips: Contemporary Images of Preaching Identity* (Eugene, OR: Cascade Books, 2010). For Reid, in this volume at least, identity is conceived tropologically and agentially. The focus here is upon a preacher's understanding of his/her/their theological function *as* preacher.

7. Another word that captures this concept philosophically is *ipseity*. See the discussion below of Paul Ricoeur's *Oneself as Another*, trans. Kathleen Blamey (Chicago: University of Chicago Press, 1992).

8. For one of the most comprehensive treatments of the relationship between selfhood and identity, which spans three millennia, see Charles Taylor, *Sources of the Self: The Making of Modern Identity* (Cambridge: Cambridge University Press, 1989).

9. Bonhoeffer writes that the "self-movement of the word to the congregation should not be hindered by the preacher but rather should be acknowledged. The preacher should not allow his or her own efforts to get in the way." Dietrich Bonhoeffer, *Worldly Preaching: Lectures on Homiletics*, ed. and trans. Clyde E. Fant (New York: Crossroad, 1991), 102.

10. Too often the preacher's identity is rendered in foundational terms. See Thomas H. Troeger and Leonora Tubbs Tisdale, *A Sermon Workbook: Exercises in the Art and Craft of Preaching* (Nashville: Abingdon, 2013), which states in the first paragraph that the purpose of the workbook is "to help you think like a preacher, write like a preacher, and proclaim the good news with imagination, theological integrity, deepened biblical insight, and heartfelt passion" (1). Nowhere do the authors consider the ways in which the preacher's thinking, writing, proclaiming, and imagining are already structured by their personhood. In a similar way, in her introduction to *Black United Methodists Preach!* (Nashville: Abingdon, 2012), Gennifer Benjamin Brooks flattens race, gender, and class into a monolithic signification: preacher.

CROSSING OVER TO THE OTHER SIDE

homiletical infrastructure on the preacher themself. For instance, in his widely used and extremely helpful introductory preaching text-book, Fred Craddock writes, "All preaching is to some extent self-disclosure by the *preacher* . . . a revelation of *self*."[11] And he is not alone. William Willimon situates the very "nature" of preaching in the embodiment, performance, and incarnation of the preacher. And Frank Thomas advocates "taking the 'I' position in preaching."[12] The preacher, these thinkers seem to imply, emerges onto the homiletical stage fully formed.[13]

Thankfully, this trend is shifting somewhat. In recent years, scholars who are not part of the majority culture have worked to bring the preacher's identity to the fore. Claudio Carvalhaes, for instance, urges us to "be watchful that minority identities are not swallowed up by the identity of more powerful ones."[14] Homileticians and preachers who have endured a certain marginalization of their homiletical subject-hood on account of racial, gendered, and/or sexual difference teach us that these experiences of marginalization are not peripheral matters; they are matters of utmost theological concern for preaching. As Ruthanna Hooke puts it, "God chooses most to be revealed in preaching not when the preacher strives to become invisible, a hollow tube though which the Word comes, but when she is most present in her particular, embodied humanity, meeting the text and God in the

---

11. Fred B. Craddock, *Preaching*, 25th ann. ed. (Nashville: Abingdon, 2010), 23. Emphasis added.
12. William H. Willimon, *Pastor: The Theology and Practice of Ordained Ministry* (Nashville: Abingdon, 2002), 158. Frank A. Thomas, *They Like to Never Quit Praisin' God*, rev. and exp. ed. (Cleveland: Pilgrim, 2013), 80–82.
13. Along with those of the entire congregation, so it would seem: "It is not the preacher who goes to the Scripture; it is the church that goes to the Scripture by means of the preacher. The preacher is a member of the community, set apart by them and sent to the Scripture to search, to study, and to listen obediently on their behalf." Thomas G. Long, *The Witness of Preaching*, 3rd ed. (Louisville: Westminster John Knox, 2016), 54. Henry H. Mitchell, in his book, *Black Preaching: The Recovery of a Powerful Art* (Nashville: Abingdon, 1990), says much the same thing about the importance of culture on preaching, arguing that Black preachers must conform their speech to the "Black English" patois. He writes, "Only a healthy Black identity, born of acute exposure to the Black experience and complete Black self-acceptance, can complete the process of lingual identification and implant Black language naturally on one's tongue" (84). But what is a "healthy Black identity"? Mitchell fails to say.
14. Claudio Carvalhaes, "*Communitas*: Liturgy and Identity," *International Review of Mission* 100, no. 392 (April 2011): 43. See also the work of Jennifer Copeland: "It is incumbent upon a feminist homiletic, therefore, not simply to make sense from a feminist perspective, but to provide an alternative understanding of the homiletical enterprise. . . . The voices of women, therefore, are not added to the homiletical soup in order to balance the flavors by equalizing the hierarchies. The voice of women creates a new soup by transforming the ordered hierarchy of language into a multiplicity of connected differences. . . . Diagnosing the distinctiveness of women's voices and exploring the richness they convey about the presence of God requires taking a detailed look at the meaning-making strategies used by those who preach and those who listen. It requires understanding the register of a sermon." Jennifer E. Copeland, *Feminine Registers: The Importance of Women's Voices for Christian Preaching* (Eugene, OR: Cascade Books, 2014), 46–47.

text."[15] The task remains for us to consider *how* the preacher's "embodied humanity" (aka, identity) is to be made "most present" in her preaching.

There is no "I" in preacher; but that is precisely what mainstream (i.e., mostly white, mostly male, mostly straight) homileticians expect of preachers. Too often, preachers internalize this expectation from their preaching professors, struggling to present themselves as whole, unified, at one with their "self." And so, preachers leave seminary and week after week, they rise from their pew. They make the long, lonely walk from their seat among the congregation, crossing the chancellery abyss, where they take their place behind the pulpit. They stand apart, exposed, and charged with offering *the* "Word" of God for the people of God.[16] They adjust their sermon manuscript or notes, clear their throats. And then . . . they pretend.

Let me pause here to speak directly to members of the majority, who, like myself, are mostly white, mostly straight, mostly male, mostly affluent, and mostly educated. Our status on the side of power and privilege in the present is not ancillary to the so-called authority we wield behind the pulpit. The truth, if we are brave enough to admit it, is that we *also* are strangers to ourselves. But we have become so proficient at ignoring our ruptured sense of selfhood that we are scared to even mention it.[17] We secure ourselves in our dominant position and ignore other elements of our sense of identity.[18] The white, male, heterosexual preacher may also be divorced, or obese, or a Republican, or vegan.

15. Ruthanna B. Hooke, "The Personal and Its Others in the Performance of Preaching," in *Preaching and the Personal*, ed. J. Dwayne Howell (Eugene, OR: Pickwick, 2013), 24. See also Hooke, *Transforming Preaching* (New York: Church, 2010); Teresa Fry Brown, *Weary Throats and New Songs* (Nashville: Abingdon, 2003); Anna Carter Florence, *Preaching as Testimony* (Louisville: Westminster John Knox, 2007); and Angela Yarber, *The Gendered Pulpit: Sex, Body, and Desire in Preaching and Worship* (Cleveland, TN: Parson's Porch Books, 2013).
16. Long, *The Witness of Preaching*, 55: "The witness is also not a neutral observer in the sense that where one stands influences what one sees. The location of the witness, in other words, is critical, and the preacher as witness is one who stands in and with a particular community of faith, deeply involved in the concrete struggles of that community to find meaning, to seek justice, and to be faithful to the gospel. Whether the community of faith to which the witness belongs and from which the witness comes is urban *or* rural, black *or* Asian, rich *or* poor, powerless *or* powerful, these circumstances firmly shape the character of the preacher." Emphasis added. Where I would challenge Long is at the intersection of identity and testimony. If the location of the witness is indeed "critical," then can we really speak of the preacher's identity in such binary and reductionist terms? Moreover, ought not the homiletician urge the preacher to consider constantly his/her/their identity along the path from text to sermon?
17. "Can we be ourselves in the pulpit? Absolutely. In fact, you should be yourself." Ronald J. Allen, *Interpreting the Gospel: An Introduction to Preaching* (St. Louis: Chalice, 1998), 5.
18. James H. Cone, "Theology's Great Sin: Silence in the Face of White Supremacy," *Union Seminary Quarterly Review* 55 (2001): 11, observes, "Although white Christians and other religious communities acknowledge their sinful condition and that their inordinate power as a group makes them more prone toward injustice in relation to other minority groups, they find it nearly impossible

These ways of relating to ourselves and the world around us—though less so than race, gender, and sex/uality—shape approaches to sermon development and delivery. It's time that homiletical theology exposed preaching to the trouble of selfhood.

Selfhood is necessary for preaching—or so we've been led to believe. In truth, the Subject, the "I" in the strong sense established by Descartes and bolstered by Kant, is coming unraveled.[19] This unraveling of selfhood takes many forms, appearing as a mere snag or loose thread to some and a heap of frayed wool to others. It is precisely this unraveling that I'd like us to explore together.

Drowning in the Homiletical Swimming Pool

Contemporary preachers are drowning. In our "sink or swim" society, buttressed as it is by the twin pillars of globalization and neoliberalism, preachers today are ill-equipped to stay afloat on the turbid waters of fear, anxiety, and uncertainty that saturate the present age. In a world where liberty is reduced to individual choice, preachers are just as responsible as the rest of society for putting their lives on display for public consumption. Preachers are performers, and doubly so: they perform their identities in and against their intersecting cultures and perform as preachers vis-à-vis ecclesial cultures.[20] Preaching is performance squared.

The Polish-born sociologist Zygmunt Bauman has articulated these contemporary challenges of identity performance through a metaphor of liquidity.[21] Here Bauman points to the societal drive to continually

to do anything to relinquish their advantage. Individuals are often self-critical, but groups are inevitably selfish and proud."

I am especially thankful for the work of Carolyn Browning Helsel here. See her essay "A Word to the 'Whites': Whites Preaching about Racism in White Congregations," *Word and World* 31, no. 2 (Spring 2011): 196–203. Drawing upon the work of Janet Helms and Beverly Daniel Tatum on racial identity development, Helsel leads white preachers through Helms's six stages of racial understanding toward, in Martin Luther King Jr.'s words, a "humble acknowledgement of guilt and an honest knowledge of self." In Helsel's words, "Preaching with an awareness of racial identity development theory can *expose* the continued problem of racism in predominantly white congregations and *envision* a new reality by helping individuals work towards an antiracist white racial identity, no longer denying the reality of racism and instead feeling empowered to fight it" (203).

19. To this Ricoeur names a "crisis of the cogito," which, in Descartes "is contemporaneous with the positing of the cogito." *Oneself as Another*, 5.

20. Judith Butler teaches us that the appearance of a stable identity is, in fact, a performative project. See her *Gender Trouble* (London: Routledge, 1990), 192: Gender is "a stylized repetition of acts . . . which are internally discontinuous . . . [so that] the appearance of substance is precisely that, a constructed identity, a performative accomplishment which the mundane social audience, including the actors themselves, come to believe and to perform in the mode of belief." To say that gender is performative is to argue that gender is "real only to the extent that it is performed."

21. See Zygmunt Bauman, *Liquid Love: On the Frailty of Human Bonds* (Cambridge: Polity, 2003) and

reinvent ourselves and to constantly redefine ourselves to ourselves and to the world around us. The core of this idea is that a life lived in "liquid modernity" changes too fast for habits and routines to have any chance to solidify. This is the essence of "liquid life," which grants us not freedom but insecurity. The irony, Bauman contends, is that the process of identity construction is sold to us as something that is pleasurable: the apogee of the Enlightenment pursuit of individual liberty. It has become a normal part of life to spend a considerable amount of time, effort, and money constructing, maintaining, and continually transforming one's self. Thanks, Weight Watchers!

Bauman reminds us, however, that although we may think we are free, we are actually obliged to engage in this process of constant reinvention because our social lives are continually in flux. We are slaves to these "liquid times," where our personhoods never have time to solidify.[22] Identities are no longer rooted in the local, the social, or the political. They are *floating* and *transient*, based on fashion, music, and hobbies. Amid this cultural backdrop, preachers fall prey to the "consumerist syndrome" that "judges and evaluates its members mostly by their consumption-related capacities and conduct."[23] You *are* what you *consume*.

Our contemporary cultural realities place enormous pressure on "individuals" to assert their individuality through consumption. It is not, for instance, a matter of processor speed or software interface that leads one to purchase a Mac or a PC. Not really. The question becomes, "Are you a Mac or a Microsoft *person*?" The decision to purchase a Prius or an F-350 King Ranch pickup truck identifies its driver as a *certain kind*

Bauman, *Liquid Modernity* (Cambridge: Polity, 2000). See also Taylor, *Sources of the Self*, where he attempts to counter the instability particular to the modern self by summoning a neo-Lucretian spirit that is able to "remove the burden of impossible aspirations . . . within which something can flower" (346).

22. Zygmunt Bauman, *Liquid Times: Living in an Age of Uncertainty* (Cambridge: Polity, 2006). See also the work of sociologist Erving Goffman, who first proposed the idea of "the presentation of the self in everyday life," noting how we follow dramatic scripts or even scenes in our interactions with others, particularly in social hierarchies or institutional settings. *The Presentation of the Self in Everyday Life* (Garden City, NY: Doubleday, 1959).

23. Bauman, *Liquid Life*, 82. Here Bauman offers insights that may help us understand the rise of celebrity preachers. He reflects upon how the diminution of concerns for eternity and long-term planning has produced a dearth of heroes from the liquid modern consumer societies of the affluent West. He notes how it is now celebrities who provide the focal point for generating communities of collective meaning. Unlike the martyrs and heroes of "solid modernity," celebrities are worthy emblems of "liquid modern" culture as their oscillating notoriety perfectly encapsulates the episodic nature of "liquid life" (39–51). Kenyatta R. Gilbert, *The Journey and Promise of African American Preaching* (Minneapolis: Fortress Press, 2011), 59–60 provides a helpful critique along these lines of churches that have uncritically conformed to what he labels a "business model ideology."

of person—this is often underscored by a "Coexist" or "Yeti" bumper sticker. Make no mistake: selfhood isn't cheap, and it certainly isn't free.

One of the most alarming features of identity consumption is its insatiability. Because there is always something else to buy, some new social media platform to exploit, and some new political slogan to regurgitate, we remain empty even as we gorge ourselves on cultural commodities. The great inversion of our time is that in consuming *we become* commodities.

We are drowning in the pool of identity commodification, and the more fervently we fight against it the quicker we are sucked beneath its surface. This is most noticeable when we attempt to rebel against the system. In his incisive collection of essays entitled *Commodify Your Dissent*, Thomas Frank argues convincingly that the economics of identity swallows us up even when we rebel against it. He writes, "But for us rebellion has come disconnected from the tangible change it once promised. Now it appears publicly as an existential thing, a sort of limp craving for self-expression so closely associated with consumer products and brand loyalty that we are virtually incapable of imagining it without a corporate sponsor of some kind."[24] This is a most pernicious and insidious feature of late capitalism: inverting sociopolitical rebellion into cultural acquiescence. Fredric Jameson concurs, writing that those cultural phenomena that parade themselves under the banner of a "postmodern revolt" are no longer scandalous but are received with "the greatest complacency" and "have themselves become institutionalized and are at one with the official or public culture of Western society."[25] Rebellion, too, has been commodified.

This assimilative posture finds expression in the work of Michel Foucault, who argues that *the individual*, the subject with their identity and characteristics, is the product of relations of power exercised over bodies. And power is central to Foucault's understanding of selfhood:

> The individual is not to be conceived as a sort of elementary nucleus, a primitive atom, a multiple and inert material on which power comes to fasten or against which it happens to strike, and in so doing subdues or crushes individuals. In fact, it is already one of the prime effects of power that certain bodies, certain gestures, certain discourses, certain desires,

---

24. Thomas Frank, "Closing Salvo: Dark Age," in *Commodify Your Dissent: Salvos From the Baffler*, ed. Thomas Frank and Matt Weiland (New York: Norton, 1997), 264–65.
25. Fredric Jameson, *Postmodernism, or, The Cultural Logic of Late Capitalism* (Durham, NC: Duke University Press, 1991), 4.

come to be identified and constituted as individuals. The individual, that is, is not the *vis-à-vis* of power; it is, I believe, one of its prime effects. The individual is an effect of power, and at the same time, or precisely to the extent to which it is that effect, it is the element of its articulation. The individual which power has constituted is at the same time its vehicle.[26]

Neither the MDiv degree nor ordination can insulate the capital-P Preacher from the movement of power exerted on their body, and, accordingly, selfhood. Who we "are" is a function of the power dynamics always already inhabiting our ethnic identities, our gender identities, and our sexual identities. As a mostly white, mostly straight male, for example, the power I wield behind the pulpit is already a function of the power at work within my *whiteness*, my *straightness*, my *maleness*—all of which are mere cultural constructs reinscribed to ensure that those with power retain power. The power my body exerts has huge effects on how my preaching will be received.

Exercises of power on identity can attach to the most seemingly innocuous of personal features. Kenyatta Gilbert, for instance, names with homiletical poignancy the challenges African-American women face in performing their identities as preachers in relation to hair-grooming rituals. Gilbert writes, "Beyond hair hygiene, for many women in the African American village, hair carries a sacred significance deeply connected to a woman's self-esteem and sense of being in a society where the Eurocentric standards of beauty are the most high-ranking." This aspect of performance transcends sociocultural power dynamics and becomes theological behind the pulpit. Gilbert continues, "How does a Black Christian woman reconcile her own belief in the concept of *imago Dei*—'image of God'— if she has become overly concerned or obsessed with self-beautification? Where does one draw the line? The line between care of self and love of self and self-hate is a thin one."[27]

Such insights are all too often missed by mainstream homileticians. Consider one of the most influential definitions of preaching in the modern era: *truth through personality*. In the opening chapter of his *Lectures on Preaching* (1877), the famed Episcopalian preacher Phillips

---

26. Michel Foucault, "Questions on Geography," in *Power/Knowledge: Selected Interviews & Other Writings, 1972-1977*, ed. Colin Gordon (New York: Pantheon Books, 1980), 74, and Foucault, "Two Lectures," in *Power/Knowledge*, 98.

27. Gilbert, *Journey and Promise*, 82–83. See also Amy P. McCullough, "Her Preaching Body: A Qualitative Study of Agency, Meaning and Proclamation in Contemporary Female Preachers (PhD diss., Vanderbilt University, 2012), who investigates matters such as cosmetics, fashion, and jewelry upon the personhood of women preachers.

Brooks offers these words: "Preaching is the communication of truth by man to men. It has in it two essential elements, truth and personality. Neither of these can it spare and still be preaching."[28] It should be stressed that Brooks is not advocating a facile *Just as I am* approach to preaching; rather, personality for Brooks arises out of a certain "kneading and tempering" of the preacher's selfhood "till it becomes of such a consistency and quality as to be capable of transmission."[29] Nevertheless, in grounding preaching in the identity of the preacher, Brooks is heir to a post-Enlightenment foundationalism that I hold partly responsible for the rise of pastoral attrition. Let's trouble this foundationalism philosophically and linguistically.

Notions of selfhood and identity are philosophically fraught. This is particularly troubling when we consider that it was philosophy, beginning with Descartes, that endeavored to establish the subject, the "I," as the *foundation* for knowledge.[30] Foucault situates this complexity for contemporary persons in the inversion of the hierarchy of the two principles of antiquity: "Take care of yourself" and "Know yourself." In Greco-Roman culture, he explains, knowledge of oneself manifested as the consequence of the care of the self. In the modern world, knowledge of oneself constitutes the fundamental principle.[31] The idea of the *person, identity, self*—whatever you wish to call it—is not an absolute concept. The notion of the subject has always been in a state of flux. Selfhood emerges out of discursive practices that are in place *prior* to philosophical considerations of the self. By analogy, it's like trying to understand the physics of jet propulsion while you are already hurtling through space.

Such concerns extend even beyond the self's fragmented construction. In the previous chapter, I identified a certain troubling of language that troubles preaching. We need to reopen that discussion now because selfhood is inextricable from language inasmuch as language

28. Phillips Brooks, *Lectures on Preaching Delivered Before the Divinity School of Yale College in January and February 1877* (New York: E.P. Dutton, 1894), 5.
29. Ibid., 9. I am indebted to my friend and colleague, Ben Anthony, for directing me to consider Brooks in his own words, beyond the homiletical caricature of him. See Benjamin Jay Anthony, "Christ in Boston: The Death and Afterlife of Phillips Brooks" (PhD diss., Vanderbilt University, 2015).
30. See Ricoeur, *Oneself as Another*, 5: "If this ambition of establishing an ultimate foundation has seen itself radicalized from Descartes to Kant, then from Kant to Fichte, and finally to the Husserl of the *Cartesian Meditations*, it nevertheless seems to me that it is enough to focus on its birthplace, in Descartes himself, whose philosophy confirms that the *crisis* of the cogito is contemporary with the *positing* of the cogito."
31. Michel Foucault, "Technologies of the Self," in *Ethics, Subjectivity and Truth: Essential Works of Foucault, 1954–1984*, ed. Paul Rabinow (New York: New Press, 1997), 228.

constitutes thought as such. The French linguist Émile Benveniste helps us here, as he sought to establish the linguistic grounds for subjectivity.

Benveniste argues that subjectivity is a function of language. In other words, the "I" is the one who *says* "I."[32] For Benveniste, subjectivity is not an extra-linguistic category that is manifested *by* language; rather, it is a function *of* language. Thus, he avers that language "is possible only because each speaker sets himself up as a *subject* by referring to himself as *I* in his discourse. Because of this, *I* posits another person, the one who, being, as he is, completely exterior to 'me,' becomes my echo to whom I say *you* and who says *you* to me. This polarity of persons is the fundamental condition in language, of which the process of communication, in which we share, is only a mere pragmatic consequence."[33] Another way of articulating this paradox is that otherness constitutes a sameness that sets itself against otherness; or, I need a "you" to fulfill the discursive needs of the "I" that I "am." Like an echo, there's no *their* there.

When a preacher speaks, she cannot position herself as a speaking subject without conceptualizing herself (linguistically as well as psychologically) in opposition to another who is exterior to her.[34] That is why the capital-P Preacher, as an individual/subject/self *ought* to drown. Through a kind of death, when the preacher's subjecthood decreases so that their modes of identity might increase, we expose our "selves" to a possibility beyond preaching: the possibility of becoming.

Identity Matters for Preaching

Out of the generative work of liberation theologians in the latter half of the twentieth century, ministers and theologians have learned that

---

32. Émile Benveniste, "Subjectivity in Language," in *Problems in General Linguistics*, trans. Mary Elizabeth Meek (Coral Gables, FL: University of Miami Press, 1971), 224. "Language is accordingly the possibility of subjectivity because it always contains the linguistic forms appropriate to the expression of subjectivity, and discourse provokes the emergence of subjectivity because it consists of *discrete* instances. In some way language puts forth 'empty' forms which each speaker, in the exercise of discourse, appropriates to himself and which he relates to his 'person,' at the same time defining himself as *I* and a partner as *you*." (227, emphasis added). It is questionable how "empty" the forms of discourse are. Not all *I*'s maintain the same ability to "fill" the first-person pronoun. For instance, when *I*, as an ordained minister, declare, "I now pronounce you husband and wife" to conclude a wedding ceremony, the words *do* different things than if a truck driver or a plumber says the same words.
33. Ibid., 225.
34. This transcends facile notions of "social location." As Mayra Rivera observes, we are not merely *located* in society, we are *constituted* in relation to the world. *Poetics of the Flesh* (Durham, NC: Duke University Press, 2015), 10.

identity matters for gospel proclamation; indeed, it *matters* for preaching the way that oxygen matters for breathing. The gospel is not a one-size-fits-all garment that can be used to cloak individual differences. On the contrary, the gospel is oriented toward *incarnation*, which is another word for *particularity*. Flesh, if it is anything at all, is situated in and by culture.[35] So-called Christian identity that fails to attend to matters of racial, sexual, gender, socioeconomic, and ethnic particularity fails to incarnate the gospel.

Matters of class are particularly significant, both because they are the means to education and because they can attenuate—though never abrogate—other demographic features such as race, ethnicity, and sex/uality. Liberation theologies expose "the infinite absorptive capacity of capitalism," which dissolves God's unconditional concern for the poor into neoliberal economic ideologies that sustain the myth of a level playing field.[36] One's economic identity is paramount for preaching because it situates the preacher along a spectrum between "wanton misery on one side and scandalous wealth on the other," to borrow Leonardo Boff's terminology.[37] In other words, class determines my level of responsibility to be-for(e) those with fewer economic advantages: to fight on behalf of the economic other before whom I may not turn away in apathy.

Matters of identity trouble homiletical theologies because they force us to factor in those elements that both constitute *and* trouble a preacher's identity. The Christian preacher is not a disembodied mind that can float through time and space unaffected by matters of identity and difference. Before we speak, preachers are breathing air that gives life to sameness *and* otherness. The preacher's race, sexual orientation, and gender identity shape how she will proclaim the good news of God's liberating work in the world in and through Jesus Christ. Such matters will shape how people who are themselves situated by time and space will hear her. The preaching *event*, if there is such a thing, is a potentially powerful encounter of complex identities. Unfortunately, we have not learned to see preaching in this way because we have failed to understand identity itself.

35. Here the work of feminist philosopher Susan Bordo is instructive. See, in particular, *Unbearable Weight: Feminism, Western Culture and the Body* (Berkeley: University of California Press, 1993) and *The Male Body: A New Look at Men in Public and in Private* (New York: Farrar, Straus & Giroux, 1999).
36. Frederick Herzog, *Liberation Theology* (New York: Seabury, 1972), 10.
37. Leonardo Boff, *Church, Charism, and Power: Liberation Theology and the Institutional Church*, trans. John W. Diercksmeier (Eugene, OR: Wipf & Stock, 2012), 20. Accordingly, he presses for a "process of liberation by which the poor regain their dignity and help give birth to a society that is . . . more just and fraternal."

Identity is multifaceted. It is heterogeneous (difference within similarity) and unstable (i.e., not fixed). Identification with a particular group is always relative. Moreover, the different aspects of identity are not developed discretely. The cultural processes that shape our sense of our own gender, sexuality, race, class, ability, and ethnicity are interwoven in such a way that their separation (even if only analytic or strategic) is distorting and politically dangerous, for it occludes relations of interdependence and blocks paths for resistance and subversion.

Along these lines, we must avoid uncritically aligning locatedness and language with identity; we are far more complex than any single strand of identity.[38] Poet and essayist Édouard Glissant helps us here. He presses against a kind of static polarity between sameness and otherness toward non-foundational networks of multiple and varied relations with others. Such is a *questioning* identity, which is in relation with otherness but in an open-ended way that does not totalize identity in sameness.[39]

Glissant draws an important distinction between "root-identity" and "relation-identity."[40] The former is ideological and historical; the latter is experiential and errant (in the sense of journeying, exploring). Root-identity is grounded in the distant past, either historically or mythologically—which are not so easily disentangled. Root-identity is totalizing and delimiting, leading, in extreme cases, to genocide.[41] Root-identity is fixed and inflexible, and it underwrites the essentialist at work within colonialism and identity politics. For instance, the root-identity of America is grounded in myths about religious and economic freedom that mask the sordid history of class and racial bias that simultaneously bolsters the freedom of the few (mostly white, mostly affluent) and frustrates the freedom of the many (mostly brown, mostly poor).[42]

By contrast, relation-identity is not linked to any historical/mythological determinism but to the pliant and contradictory experience of contacts among cultures. It gestures toward a swirling network of

---

38. See also Gayatri Spivak, *The Post-colonial Critic* (New York: Routledge, 1990), 38: "One needs to be vigilant against simple notions of identity which overlap neatly with language or location." Accordingly, we must resist the temptation toward identity politics, whereby we overlook or even suppress otherness in the quest for political capital.

39. Édouard Glissant, *Caribbean Discourse: Selected Essays*, trans. J. Michael Dash (Charlottesville: University of Virginia Press, 1999), 169.

40. See Glissant's distinction between root-identity and relation-identity in *Poetics of Relation*, 143–44.

41. See Édouard Glissant, *Introduction à une poétique du divers* (Paris: Gallimard, 1996), 96, where he holds root-identity responsible for the Rwandan and Bosnian genocides.

42. See Nancy Isenberg, *White Trash: The 400-Year Untold History of Class in America* (New York: Viking, 2016).

connections that does not attempt to ground identity, much less self-hood, in this or that *mark* of difference (e.g., skin color, genitalia, customs). Rather, relation-identity avoids and resists the "always comfortable trap of generalization."[43] Relation attends to the spacing between sameness and otherness, between identities and differences as a "terra incognita," an "inexhaustible sphere of variations" pregnant with possibilities.[44] In other words, a person's identity is not a one-size-fits-all phenomenon. Preaching identities are constantly in flux, moving and bending in response to the cultural forces that mark identities with a coefficient of uncertainty. Homiletical theologies may learn much by considering identity matters from different perspectives. Of course, such analytics cannot lead us to any definitive conclusion; but they can help us move toward a more robust appreciation for intersectionality.

LGBTQ-identifying persons have long described their sense of self-hood as *fractured* and *fraught*. For instance, in his important book *Insult and the Making of the Gay Self*, the French intellectual Didier Eribon describes gay selfhood in terms of "dissociation" and "rupture," noting the dissonance gay-identifying men experience between cultural stigma and cultural appropriation: gay men are at once reviled by segments of society and envied by others, particularly following the emergence of "metrosexual" commodity fetishism.[45] The "gay self" is stuck between abhorrence and adoration—both externally and internally.

In a completely different and yet similar way, many Latinx persons living in America experience their selfhood as a kind of "battleground" or "borderland," where ethnicity, skin pigment, religion, and language structure their identity out of an internal dissonance, a certain disquietude. Such identities are formed "at the margins of an in between others' identities." Such a place of self-understanding, argues biblical scholar Jacqueline Hidalgo, is also a kind of "no place."[46] That is why Chicana scholar and poet Gloria Anzaldúa, argues for a "new consciousness," one that occupies a space "on both shores at once and, at once,

43. Glissant, *Poetics of Relation*, 156.
44. Ibid., 57. Bhabha contends that a space exists "in-between the designations of identity" and that "this interstitial passage between fixed identifications opens up the possibility of a cultural hybridity that entertains difference without an assumed or imposed hierarchy." Homi K. Bhabha, *The Location of Culture* (London: Routledge, 1994), 4.
45. Didier Eribon, *Insult and the Making of the Gay Self*, trans. Michael Lucey (Durham, NC: Duke University Press, 2004), 4, 29.
46. Jacqueline M. Hidalgo, "Reading from No Place: Toward a Hybrid and Ambivalent Study of Scriptures," in *Latino/a Biblical Hermeneutics: Problematics, Objectives, Strategies*, ed. Francisco Lozada Jr. and Fernando F. Segovia (Atlanta: SBL, 2014), 166.

[can] see through serpent and eagle eyes," or that will "cross the border into a wholly new and separate territory."[47]

You will find no clearer articulation of this spatial and psychological vertigo than in W. E. B. Du Bois's 1903 classic, *The Souls of Black Folk*:

> From the double life every American Negro must live, as a Negro and as an American, as swept on by the current of the nineteenth while yet struggling in the eddies of the fifteenth century,—from this must arise a painful self-consciousness, an almost morbid sense of personality and a moral hesitancy which is fatal to self-confidence. . . . Such a double life, with double thoughts, double duties, and double social classes, must give rise to double words and double ideals, and tempt the mind to presence or revolt, to hypocrisy or radicalism.[48]

The psychic pressures that leave African Americans caught between revolt and hypocrisy may produce a "double-consciousness." How can we even begin to speak of identity when systemic and historical injustices militate the very possibility of an identity that is singular or seamless?

Many white Americans are only recently coming to experience the psychic dissonance and troubling sense of self that marginalized Americans have endured for centuries. In his recently published and incisive book *The End of White Christian America*, Robert Jones narrates the

47. Gloria Anzaldúa, "*La Conciencia de la Mestiza*: Towards a New Consciousness," in *Feminisms: An Anthology of Literary Theory and Criticism*, ed. Robyn R. Warhol and Diane Price Herndl (New Brunswick, NJ: Rutgers University Press, 1997), 766. See also Anzaldúa, *Borderlands/La Frontera: The New Mestiza* (San Francisco: Aunt Lute Books, 1987) and Claudio Carvalhaes, *Eucharist and Globalization: Redrawing the Borders of Eucharistic Hospitality* (Eugene, OR: Pickwick, 2013), 19: "However, in spite of the idea of protection and separation that borders convey, they are often made of a porous structure with unattended spaces."

48. W. E. B. Du Bois, *The Souls of Black Folk* (New Haven, CT: Yale University Press, 2015), 152. The psychic pressures of the African-American "double-consciousness" that leave people caught between revolt and hypocrisy is witnessed more recently by Ta-Nehisi Coates in his haunting memoir/indictment of American racial injustice, *Between the World and Me* (New York: Spiegel & Grau, 2015). Coates writes, "Resent the people trying to entrap your body and it can be destroyed . . . And destruction is merely the superlative form of a dominion whose prerogatives include frisking, detaining, beatings, and humiliations. All of this is common to black people. All of this is old for black people" (9). See also Michael Eric Dyson, *Tears We Cannot Stop: A Sermon to White America* (New York: St. Martin's, 2017), who extends this paradox to America itself, writing, "Real American history is the sticky web in which black and white are stuck together. . . . What horrifies many of you [white people] is that America, at its root, has been in part made by blackness. God forbid, but it may in part be black. Slavery made America a slave to black history. As much as white America invented us, the nation can never be free of us now. America doesn't even exist without us" (76).
    Audre Lorde writes, "Growing up, metabolizing hatred like daily bread. Because I am Black, because I am woman, because I am not Black enough, because I am not some particular fantasy of a woman, because I AM. On such a consistent diet, one can eventually come to value the hatred of one's enemies more than one values the love of friends, for that hatred becomes the source of anger, and anger is a powerful fuel." "Eye to Eye," in *Sister Outsider: Essays and Speeches* (Berkeley, CA: Crossing Press, 2007), 152.

decline of the cultural and political dominance that has been maintained by mostly white, mostly protestant American Christians since our nation's founding. Cultural antipathy toward this sense of loss birthed the Tea Party movement and now the farce of a Trump presidency.[49]

From a different angle, in his book *White Like Me*, Tim Wise confesses that "[b]eing a member of the majority, the dominant group, allows one to ignore how race shapes one's life. For those of us called white, whiteness simply is. Whiteness becomes, for us, the unspoken, uninterrogated norm, taken for granted, much as water can be taken for granted by a fish."[50] In keeping with Wise's metaphor, the fish notices the water when someone opens the drain.

Given the clarion call of this cloud of witnesses, it is baffling that so much of mainstream homiletical theology has paid so little attention to the person who preaches: the preacher. I'm not talking about a rare omission perpetrated by a few scholars. No. Homiletics is nearly uniform in overlooking *how* the preacher's identity shapes her preaching. Even in minoritized homiletical traditions (Black preaching, Asian-American preaching, etc.), the preacher's identity has rarely been tested, questioned, or articulated on a level sufficient to the intersectional and diachronic complexities identity demands.[51] There are exceptions, of course; but these homiletical contributions are few and are largely relegated to preaching electives and doctoral seminars.[52]

---

49. Robert P. Jones, *The End of White Christian America* (New York: Simon & Schuster, 2016). See also Carol Anderson, *White Rage: The Unspoken Truth of our Racial Divide* (New York: Bloomsbury, 2016).

50. Tim Wise, *White Like Me: Reflections on Race from a Privileged Son*, 3rd ed. (Berkeley, CA: Soft Skull Press, 2011), 2.

51. Consider, for instance Jennifer Copeland's *Feminine Registers*. In spite of the book's important work in advocating for women in the pulpit, her critique is limited by an essentialized femininity that ignores how race, sexual orientation, gender identity, and class, affect the homiletical "register." In chapter 5, entitled "Listening for the Register," Copeland highlights only the feminist contributions of white women (and John McClure receives honorable mention; but, of course, he too is white). She considers in her "listening" no women of color, no ethnic minorities, and no transgender persons. Even in her section on Christine Smith, Copeland attends exclusively to Smith's femaleness with no mention of how Smith's self-identification as a lesbian disrupts a stable conceptualization of the feminine.

52. See, for instance, Eunjoo Kim's *Preaching in an Age of Globalization* (Louisville: Westminster John Knox, 2010)—especially, her chapters "Transcontextual Hermeneutics" (65–86) and "Negotiating Diversity" (87–109). Kim avers that "the preacher's social location is decisive in how she sees the world, constructs reality, and interprets biblical texts. So it is necessary for the preacher to ask herself how her interpretation is conditioned by her social location and how it serves a political function" (81).

An emerging cohort of homileticians are engaging matters of identity and difference, attending to the ways in which the preacher's "self" shapes the preaching event itself. Scholars like Lisa Thompson, Carolyn Helsel, Amy McCollugh, Geoffrey Schoonmaker, and Melva Sampson are helping the guild with this glaring oversight: preaching bodies. See Lisa L. Thompson, "'Now that's Preaching!' Disruptive and Generative Preaching Practices," *Practical Matters* 8 (April 2015): 73–84;

There's No "I" in Preacher

Determining the self in the preacher that "I am" troubles homiletics. Upon what ground and by what measure might homiletics determine that the "I" whom I understand myself to be can be made known in—or perhaps before—preaching? Historically, as we've witnessed, selfhood arises out of the radical exclusion of otherness. However, as James Baldwin reminds us, "It is a terrible, an inexorable, law that one cannot deny the humanity of another without diminishing one's own: in the face of ones' victim, one sees oneself."[53] How can mainstream homiletics in particular treat the preacher as a unitary subject when so much of our subjecthood arises out of the subjection of others?

Homiletical theologies are further challenged in terms of identity and subjecthood because what the preacher most wants to say is that which only God can say.[54] How might the preacher enter into a stream of discourse that is at once originary (that is, beyond history/origin) and particular (beyond any abstraction from history)? Any proclamation worthy of the name must factor the preacher's irreducible complexity into its homiletical calculus.

Preachers are in trouble. At our core. Like Frankenstein's monster, we are a patchwork of parts, identities implanted on us by our respective cultures and traditions. Our identities emerge out of our dissonance within those very cultures and traditions. So, what are we to do? Ought we throw in the towel? Yes . . . in a sense. We must die to self—but not in the way of self-abnegation, which paradoxically bolsters the self according to the very measures one takes to empty (*kenoó*) oneself. Nor am I advocating a kind of Pauline "crucified with Christ" subjectivity sufficient to mask our particularities under a vague notion of unity in Christ (cf. Gal 3:28).[55]

What I am suggesting is that homiletics ought to reorient itself to

McCullough, "Her Preaching Body"; Carolyn Browning Helsel, "The Hermeneutics of Recognition: A Ricoeurian Interpretive Framework for Whites Preaching on Racism" (PhD diss., Emory University, 2014); Geoffrey Noel Schoonmaker, "Preaching About Race: A Homiletic for Racial Reconciliation" (PhD diss., Vanderbilt University, 2012); and Melva L. Sampson, "Fetching Spiritual Power: Black Women's Preaching Bodies as African-Centered Womanist Oratory" (PhD diss., Emory University, 2016).

53. James Baldwin, *Nobody Knows My Name* (New York: Vintage Books, 1993), 71.

54. Derrida helps us here. He writes, "This becoming-responsible, that is, this becoming-historical of humankind, seems to be tied to the properly Christian event of *another secret*, or more precisely of a mystery, the *mysterium tremendum*: the terrifying mystery, the dread, fear, and trembling of the Christian in the experience of the sacrificial gift. This trembling seizes one at the moment of becoming a person, and the person can only become what it is in being paralyzed [*transie*], in its very singularity, by the gaze of God." Jacques Derrida, *The Gift of Death*, trans. David Wills (Chicago: University of Chicago Press, 1995), 8.

facilitate the death of the preacher as a singular, unified subject. Homiletics ought to help preachers die to our selfhood by embracing the very fiction of selfhood. Homiletics must aid in leading preachers to cross over to the other side of identity, to a shore that is always and forever terra incognita. Scary though this sounds, it need not frighten us. As Judith Butler notes, "To claim that the subject is itself produced in and as a gendered matrix of relations is not to do away with the subject, but only to ask after the conditions of its emergence and operation."[56] It's time for homiletics to ask such questions.

Section Two: The Preacher *as* Trouble

In order to arrive at what you are not you must go through the way in which you are not.

— T. S. Eliot[57]

We've reached the point in our story where I'm supposed to tell homiletics how to help preachers become their fullest, most beautiful, most magnanimous selves. That's what you were hoping for, right? Sadly, I must disappoint you. What I've been describing about the selfhood and identity of the preacher cannot be overcome by moments of existential apophasis, kenosis, or self-abnegation—which diminish only to rally bigger and stronger by the tale's end.[58] This is not a Rocky movie. The troubling of our homiletical identities goes all the way down and does not rest.

There is no "I" in preacher, but this doesn't mean that homiletics ought to give up on preaching. Homiletics can guide the p/reacher to "reach" for something more that simplistic notions of personhood. In such *reaching*, such striving toward and through selfhood and identity, preachers may discover more and better ways of situating ourselves in relation to preaching. The troubling of the preacher as an individual, as a subject, as an "I" in the strong sense, is more than a harbinger of death. It is a *summons* to die.[59] By no means am I suggesting a literal

---

55. See Brad R. Braxton, *No Longer Slaves: Galatians and African American Experience* (Collegeville, MN: Liturgical Press, 2002), 92–95.
56. Butler, *Bodies that Matter*, xvi–ii.
57. T. S. Elliot, "East Coker," in *The Four Quartets* (New York: Houghton Mifflin Harcourt, 1943), 29.
58. See Jacques Derrida's critique along these lines in "How to Avoid Speaking: Denials," in *Languages of the Unsayable: The Play of Negativity in Literature and Literary Theory*, ed. Sanford Budick and Wolfgang Iser, trans. Ken Frieden (Stanford: Stanford University Press, 1987), 3–70.
59. Again, Derrida: "The question of the self: 'who am I?' no longer in the sense of 'who am I' but 'who is this 'I' that can say 'who'? What is the 'I' and what becomes of responsibility once the identity of the 'I' trembles *in secret*?" Derrida, *The Gift of Death*, 92.

death (*Deo volente*), but a metaphysical and existential death in which the preacher is emboldened to cross over to the other side of selfhood, to embrace a non-foundational and polyphonic sense of identity.

The preacher themself, like the Good Shepherd in John's Gospel, is summoned to lay down their life for those entrusted to their care. As Mary Lin Hudson puts it, "not only must we disengage from the word that we preach, we must also let it and the preacher in us die in order for the word to rise to new life in the hearts and voices of the faith community."[60] What I am advancing is a reorientation of our understanding of selfhood and identity that *reaches* into the aporias of selfhood and identity. Upon arriving on this *terra incognita*, without foundation or surety, the preacher exposes themself—along with preaching itself—to a deconstruction always already at work within it and therein discovering (perchance) new ways of dreaming.

Discovering the Self in Identity *and* Difference

In experiencing his death, the preacher is exposed to an alterity always already constitutive of selfhood.[61] In other words, placing himself under erasure allows the preacher to discern the traces of otherness that structure and/or deconstruct his self-understanding. Let's think about this spatially and temporally. In his illuminating text *Speaking From Elsewhere*, philosopher José Medina challenges the spatial orientation of the speaking subject, particularly the dualistic articulation of positionality. Such spatial conceptualizations of our situatedness as speakers, thinkers, and agents offer alternative frameworks for how we make meaning out of the sensory data we encounter, how we come to understand ourselves as subjects, and how we speak and act out of that identity to affect the world around us.

Historically, we have seen two dominant views of identity vis-à-vis discourse. On the one hand, there are those who argue for a *view from nowhere*. By this account, humans possess the capacity to think about the world in objective terms that transcend individual experience or

---

60. Mary Lin Hudson, "To Die and Rise Again: Preaching the Gospel for Liberation," in *Preaching as a Theological Task: World, Gospel, Scripture: In Honor of David Buttrick*, ed. Thomas G. Long and Edward Farley (Louisville: Westminster John Knox, 1996), 119.
61. As Charles Taylor puts it: "This crucial feature of human life is its fundamentally *dialogical* character. We become full human agents, capable of understanding ourselves, and hence of defining our identity, through our acquisition of rich human languages of expression. . . . But we learn these modes of expression through exchanges with others. People do not acquire the languages needed for self-definition on their own. Rather, we are introduced to them through interaction with others who matter to us." "The Politics of Recognition," in *Multiculturalism: Examining the Politics of Recognition*, ed. Amy Gutmann (Princeton, NJ: Princeton University Press, 1994), 32.

interest, that is, to consider the world from a vantage point that is "nowhere in particular."[62] This orientation is labeled *objectivism* or *positivism*. Other scholars stress the finitude and subjectivity of human perception. Such a *view from here* perspective eschews notions of universalism by stressing our positionality as perceivers and speakers. Scholars label this position *contextualism* or *constructivism*.[63] In short, objectivism assumes that anyone can see the world in the same way as anyone else, no matter where they are located. The world is what it is, and we can all see it. Constructivism suggests otherwise, arguing that *where* we stand shapes *what* we see. In this mode of thinking, location is an essential variable in how we understand the world and ourselves.

In critical conversation with these traditions, Medina advances a new kind of contextualism, an "eccentric" contextualism, that can inform the preacher's understanding of identity and selfhood. This *"view from elsewhere"* is constructivist without slipping into epistemic nihilism; this view acknowledges that we construct knowledge and identity without leaving us devoid of any sense of truthfulness or specificity: *"underdetermination does not warrant indeterminacy."*[64] Such positional agnosticism attends to the social construction of selfhood as a dialectic of identity and difference that opens speakers and agents to social responsibility beyond their particular communities. Hereby, Medina overcomes the discursive dilemma of a radical constructionism that would make it impossible to posit any truth claim beyond one's local context. After all, if all knowledge is constructed and tied only to a particular cultural space, then how can a preacher make a prophetic claim to speak God's "Word" to others and other communities? Medina helps us imagine another possibility.

Subjectivity arises out of a *polyphony* of identities. Medina puts it this way: "In order to achieve a unique individuality we do not have to define ourselves negatively with respect to the multiple others we face, or with respect to the multiple selves we develop in our interactions with them." Medina advances a "post conventional identity,"

---

62. See Thomas Nagel, *The View From Nowhere* (Oxford: Oxford University Press, 1986) and Claude Lévi Strauss, *The View From Afar*, trans. Joachim Neugroschel and Phoebe Hoss (Chicago: University of Chicago Press, 1992).
63. Or "sociologism," as it is found following the influence of Peter Winch. See his *The Idea of a Social Science and its Relation to Philosophy*, 2nd ed. (London: Routledge, 1990).
64. José Medina, *Speaking from Elsewhere: A New Contextualist Perspective on Meaning, Identity, and Discursive Agency* (Albany: SUNY Press, 2006), 46–47: "No matter how well consolidated and rigidly structured they may become, discursive contexts are always *unfinished or incomplete*.... [Nevertheless,] a discursive context always has some ties to other contexts; and these ties are not mere accidental connections, but constitutive relations that collectively shape the context in a particular way. Discursive spaces are intrinsically interconnected."

which does not call for an oppositional relation to cultural selves, but for the dialectical integration of this "multiplicity of selves."[65] His spatial reorientation of identity offers preachers a way of embracing our own dissimulation—not as a mode of silence, but as a mode of discourse and action that does not silence otherness. Such a reorientation can help preachers embrace difference within and beyond themselves.

In spite of Medina's theoretical advances, we need some practical support in moving homiletics toward a "post conventional identity" for preaching. We find such in the writings of one of the most prolific and influential philosophers of the twentieth century: Paul Ricoeur. Much of Ricoeur's work focused on the *temporal* capacities of the self to structure meaning out of the world of one's experiences. In one of his most significant books, Ricoeur interrogates the philosophical basis for the permanence of a proper name. Let's take me as an example.

I call myself *Jake*. What is it about my Jakeness that makes me a *proper* self? Ricoeur would respond by pointing to my always-evolving narration of myself to myself in relation to my experiences. The self characterized by self-sameness is *refigured* by the reflective application of narrative configurations.[66] So, the essential quality that constitutes my Jakeness is the story I tell *myself about myself.* This temporal narration bolsters my sense of selfhood.

But, selfhood emerges out of a play of sameness and otherness. In continuously reconfiguring the Jake that I am, I do two things. First, I lift up those aspects of my story by which I am able to identify myself ("That's so like me"). Second, I work to integrate those elements of difference at work *on the inside* of my selfhood that seem at odds with the "I" I understand myself to be ("How does this jive with my self understanding?"). Selfhood, in and according to itself, is a structural impossibility. We cannot know and thereby establish selfhood apart from otherness and difference.[67] Selfhood emerges out of the

---

65. Medina, *Speaking from Elsewhere*, 83. These "selves" are integral to "post conventional identity" but are not collapsible. Patricia Hill Collins brings a crucial critique along these lines. She challenges the way that some feminist philosophies have "colorized" preexisting theories. She writes, "Rather than seeing women of color as fully human individuals, we are treated as the additive sum of our categories." Collins, *On Intellectual Activism* (Philadelphia: Temple University Press, 2013), 224. I am grateful to Teresa Fry Brown for directing me to this book.

66. Paul Ricoeur, *Time and Narrative*, vol. 3 (Chicago: University of Chicago Press, 1988), 246: "The story told tells about the action of the 'who.' And the identity of this 'who' therefore itself must be a narrative identity. Without the recourse to narration, the problem of personal identity would in fact be condemned to an antinomy with no solution."

67. For Hegel—and later, Badiou—selfhood is tethered to a certain theology, whereby the finitude of the self arises as the negation of the Infinite's infinitude. Such emerges, explains Hegel, as a "direct result of the circumstance that the finite remains a determinate being opposed to the infinite, so that there are *two* determinatenesses; *there are* two worlds, one infinite and one finite, and

play of activity and passivity—what Ricoeur labels the *"triad of passivity and hence of otherness."*[68] This "triad of passivity" relates the self to the experience—even alienation—perceived in relation to bodily otherness, worldly otherness, and psychological otherness. Let's unpack each of these in turn.

The "I" signifying my selfhood, the assertion of my individuality—my Iakeness—emerges passively out of the experiences of my body. The psycho-spiritual response to what my body endures or enjoys forms me whether I want it to or not. Ricoeur will call this my *flesh*: the mediator between the self and the world that takes shape in accordance with its variable degrees of practicability and foreignness.[69] If I am differently abled. If I am a person of color. If I am cisgender or transgender, or somewhere in between. If I have been sexually abused—all of these fleshly experiences, experiences over which I have no control, shape my sense of self.

At this fleshly site Ricoeur draws a distinction between the *lived* body and the *objectified* body. The former signifies an otherness independent of relations to others. If I suffer from migraines or asthma, or if I have cerebral palsy, the experience of my neurological, respiratory, or muscular impairment will shape myself in relation to myself. The objectified body—on the other hand, though overlapping with the lived body—is largely cultural. This aspect of passivity is expressed with haunting precision by Frantz Fanon in his book *Black Skin, White Masks*, where he articulates the psychological impact of colonial subjugation upon Black people.[70]

The second passivity relates to *intersubjectivity*, that is, my relationship with that which is foreign: other than self. Ricoeur argues that it is impossible to construct this dialectic between the same and the

---

in their relationship the infinite is only the *limit* of the finite and is thus only a determinate infinite, an *infinite which is itself finite*." G. W. F. Hegel, *Hegel's Science of Logic*, trans. A. V. Miller (New York: Humanity Books, 1991), 139–40.

68. Ricoeur, *Oneself as Another*, 318. The explanation that follows is drawn directly from this text of Ricoeur along with several of his essays.

69. Rivera is instructive here: "My visible body affects which areas of the world I may inhabit and how the world reacts to my approach. The particular ways in which my *flesh* is shaped by the world depends on how my *body* is perceived in society." Rivera, *Poetics of the Flesh*, 114.

70. "Since I realize that the black man is the symbol of sin, I start hating the black man. But I realize that I am a black man. I have two ways of escaping the problem. Either I ask people not to pay attention to the color of my skin; or else, on the contrary, I want people to notice it. I then try to esteem what is bad—since, without thinking, I admitted that the black man was the color of evil. In order to put an end to this neurotic situation where I am forced to choose an unhealthy, conflictual solution, nurtured with fantasies, that is antagonistic—inhuman, in short—there is but one answer: skim over this absurd drama that others have staged around me; rule out these two elements that are equally unacceptable; and through the particular, reach out of the universal." Frantz Fanon, *Black Skin, White Masks*, trans. Richard Philcox (New York: Grove, 2008), 174.

other in a unilateral manner.[71] In other words, I can neither come to self-understanding all by myself nor by completely forgetting myself. We go awry when we attempt to derive our understanding of the other purely from the self *and* when we try to establish the self purely on the basis of the other. Ricoeur's notion of intersubjectivity—the "fundamental distinction" between two kinds of sameness always already at work on the inside of selfhood—is born out of epistemic awareness of the other over time *and* moral responsibility in response to the other. The two are inseparable. I come to understand myself when I encounter that which is other than myself. This otherness affects me in a fundamental way.

To unpack this, Ricoeur draws an important distinction between sameness and identity. The polysemy at work on the inside of selfhood is largely temporal. On the one hand, we have the sense of selfhood as *being* the same through time (*idem* in Latin), which accounts for why I will be recognizable at my twenty-year high school reunion; this is the constancy of selfhood that endures through time, unaffected by particular experiences. On the other hand, there is a selfhood that allows for difference at work on the inside of identity (*ipse* in Latin). The self marked by self-sameness expressed as constancy, which Ricoeur labels "ipse-identity," can include change and mutability within the cohesion of one's self—this is why, in spite of my relative sameness in terms of skin color, height, and voice, at my high school reunion my former classmates will experience me as quite different from the boy they knew. The self-constancy at the heart of ipse-identity provides a means for Ricoeur to tether identity to responsibility. Self-constancy means that we are accountable to others for ourselves and responsible to their summons. Narrative identity mediates between ipse-identity and idem-identity.

Thirdly, there is for Ricoeur an undeniable aspect of my selfhood, the "most deeply hidden passivity," arising out of the relation of the self to itself: namely, *conscience*. In spite of its fraught philosophical history, Ricoeur insists on the importance of conscience because it highlights a relation to the other experienced through time as a summons to responsibility. This summons establishes the self as one always already in debt. Elsewhere Ricoeur explains that conscience, which "is barely

---

71. Ricoeur, *Oneself as Another*, 331. Irigaray captures this dynamic, writing, "You are moving. You never stay still. You never stay. You never 'are.' How can I say 'you,' when you are always other?" "When Our Lips Speak Together," in *This Sex Which is Not One*, trans. Catherine Porter (Ithaca, NY: Cornell University Press, 1985), 214.

discernible from conviction," constitutes the self as *attestation:* "In this sense, conscience is nothing other than the attestation by which a self affects itself." Said differently, selfhood as conscience appears as the "inner assurance" that overcomes doubt, hesitation, the suspicion of inauthenticity, hypocrisy, self-compliance, and self-deception. I perceive in my soul that I am responsible for the other. To this the only response is at one with the Hebrew prophets: "Here I am."[72] Selfhood arises out of *action* rather than Truth or Being.

With the philosophical support of Medina and Ricoeur, we are able to reimagine the preacher in her crossing over to the other side of selfhood. Such is not far from death. Homiletical selfhood and identity *are* nothing, ontologically speaking. However, as a kind of *reaching* toward (the) other(ness) in space and through time, the preacher leans into a mode of self-understanding that is constituted by sameness and difference. These need not constrain the preacher to identity politics or self-abnegation; rather, in embracing death through discursive modes of attestation, a striving toward and on behalf of the other, the preacher *becomes a self* (perchance).

The Homiletical Path Beyond Selfhood and Identity: Erotic Preaching

I want us to move now from theory to practice, not because these are radically separate but precisely because they are radically connected. How, we must ask, may the preacher participate in the trouble always already at work with/in their identity? What does this look like? What does this sound like?

bell hooks, a tireless advocate against racism, sexism, heterosexism, and classism, offers practical wisdom for how we might live into the death of the preacher in and beyond preaching. She does so under the banner of *eros.* In her books, *Teaching to Transgress: Education as the Practice of Freedom* and *Outlaw Culture: Resisting Representations,* hooks guides us with an intersubjective vision of selfhood and identity that offers much for homiletical consideration.

First, she articulates selfhood as a summons to sociopolitical activism for radical social change. This vision of intellectual and political engagement ramifies according to a kind of prophetic desire that risks the self on behalf of the other. In *Teaching to Transgress,* hooks

---

72. Paul Ricoeur, "From Metaphysics to Moral Philosophy," trans. David Pellauer, *Philosophy Today* 40 (1996): 454.

imagines the classroom as a "dynamic place where transformations in social relations are concretely actualized and the false dichotomy between the world outside and the inside world of academia disappears."[73] This is achieved through *transgression*, that is, a willingness of the teacher—and, mutatis mutandis, the preacher—to break through ideological, disciplinary, and cultural boundaries out of a desire for embodied knowledge.

Historically, both classrooms and pulpits have erased the body.[74] Passion, desire, yearning—the bodily movement of *eros*—ought to guide teaching and preaching alike. Transposing hooks into a homiletical key, "To restore passion to the [pulpit] or to excite it in [congregations] where it has never been, [preachers] must find again the place of *eros* within ourselves and together allow the mind and body to feel and know desire."[75] The preacher discovers himself through the prophetic vocation, becoming a "summoned subject."[76] In loving, ontology is replaced with something that transcends Being. If the preacher can embrace an erotic vocation, then this will redefine him; it will reorient every aspect of the constitutive tasks that constitute the preaching life.

Second, in *Outlaw Culture*, hooks argues that "[w]ithout an ethic of love shaping the direction of our political vision and our radical aspirations, we are often seduced, in one way or the other, into continued allegiance to systems of domination—imperialism, sexism, racism, classism."[77] The erotic structures a ground of becoming that purges the apathy of "imperial consciousness," to borrow Brueggemann's phrase, *and* critically interrogates cultural forces that militate against self-love. In short, erotic preaching situates the preacher's identity as a host, welcoming the other and the otherness of the self who never quite exists.

In extending hospitality to the other—other bodies, other interpretations, other politics—the preacher redefines herself to herself and

73. bell hooks, *Teaching to Transgress: Education as the Practice of Freedom* (New York: Routledge, 1994), 195.
74. And with this erasure corresponds a certain silencing which is rightly challenged by Mary Donovan Turner and Mary Lin Hudson in their book, *Saved from Silence: Finding Women's Voice in Preaching* (St. Louis: Chalice, 1999). Herein, they employ the metaphor of "finding voice" to help women (and men) lean into their selfhood "in relation to particular contexts, allowing authentic dimensions of the self to arise to expression rather than be submerged in a sea of competing expectations and roles" (11).
75. hooks, *Teaching to Transgress*, 199.
76. See Paul Ricoeur, "The Summoned Subject in the School of the Narratives of the Prophetic Vocation," in *Figuring the Sacred: Religion, Narrative, and Imagination*, ed. Mark I. Wallace, trans. David Pellauer (Minneapolis: Augsburg Fortress, 1995), 262–77. Cf. Taylor, *Sources of the Self*, and particularly his argument in chapter 4 on behalf of a "moral ontology" grounded in religious community.
77. bell hooks, *Outlaw Culture: Resisting Representations* (New York: Routledge, 1994), 243.

to her congregation. Playing host to otherness in oneself and in one's words need not be passive; in fact, it must not be. Where the preacher-as-subject hosts the other—even the *Word* of God, which "is" absolutely other, if it "is" anything at all—he is transformed in direct proportion to the degree that he gives himself to this otherness, as Jean-Luc Marion argues.[78] He is no longer a self, an ego in the strong sense, but a "gifted" who receives a selfhood and an identity in the act of giving.

The Preacher as Summoned Subject: Listening to/for the Other

Love is a summons. It is not (only) a feeling; it is a call to action. Philosopher and oftentimes theologian John D. Caputo offers us a framework for reimagining the preacher's subjecthood according to the vocation of the prophet. He argues that the prophet does not belong to the order of *being* but to the order of the *event*. In responding to the call—of God, of the other, to justice—the preacher as prophet is summoned not to presence but to provocation: "as one who speaks for (*prophetes*) justice, who calls for justice, who warns about ignoring justice."

The prophet's subjecthood is reconstituted by God and the community that has called her to conjoin her selfhood with the *event* of preaching—not preaching as such (see chapter 1), but what is happening or *wants* to happen in preaching. To the degree that the preacher *is* anything, she is a "functionary of the event."[79] The erotic preacher finds herself not in *being* but in *doing*, in performing her being by her doing.[80] It is ontologically impossible to declare, "I am a preacher."

<hr/>

78. The subject is not eviscerated under Marion's phenomenology of givenness; rather, the subject is displaced. Marion writes, "I will contest the claim that [the I] occupies this center as an origin, an ego or first person, in transcendental 'mineness.' I will oppose to it the claim that it does not hold this center but is instead held there as a recipient where what gives itself shows itself, and that it discloses itself given to and as a pole of givenness, where all the givens come forward incessantly. At the center stands no 'subject,' but a gifted, he whose function consists in receiving what is immeasurably given to him, and whose privilege is confined to the fact that he is himself received from what he receives." Jean-Luc Marion, *Being Given: Toward a Phenomenology of Givenness*, trans. Jeffrey L. Kosky (Stanford: Stanford University Press, 2002), 322.
79. John D. Caputo, *The Weakness of God: A Theology of the Event* (Bloomington: Indiana University Press, 2006), 31.
80. Accordingly, philosopher Judith Butler argues that subjectivity is not given, but *performed* through discourse. In her words: "For discourse to materialize a set of *effects*, 'discourse' itself must be understood as complex and convergent chains in which 'effects' are vectors of power. In this sense, what is constituted in discourse is not fixed in or by discourse, but becomes the condition and occasion for further action. This does not mean that any action is possible on the basis of a discursive effect. On the contrary, certain reiterative chains of discursive production are barely legible as reiterations, for the effects they have materialized are those without which no bearing in discourse can be taken. The power of discourse to materialize its effects is thus consonant with the power of discourse to circumscribe the domain of intelligibility." *Bodies That Matter*, 139.

Such a declaration implies a static condition of being that cannot be sustained through preaching. Rather, according to a kind of *love as strong as death*, a desire for and according to the *event* of proclamation, the preacher discovers herself in the summons to preach. Herein she submits to death. She *is* nothing. She *becomes* more than nothing. But submitting herself to erasure before a summons that transfigures and transgresses selfhood, the preacher harmonizes with a calling, a summons, which she does not possess but is nevertheless particular to her.

Theologian Mayra Rivera reminds us of the risks inherent in such a summons. We do not all possess the same degree of agency in shaping our bodies and our worlds. Power dynamics abide. The discourses that structure social institutions shape our ways of knowing and foster cultural practices that shape our material realities. How we employ our discursive agency makes all the difference: "words weave the flesh of the world."[81] Accordingly, the coming to selfhood of the preacher takes shape between agency and passivity. Even as words delimit our capacity for action, we preachers get to decide how we will preach—whether or not we will cry out (*proclamare*) for justice and the righteousness of God. Our agency places a tremendous responsibility on preachers and presents a number of challenges for teachers of preaching.

In their book *Saved from Silence: Finding Women's Voice in Preaching*, Mary Donovan Turner and Mary Lin Hudson teach preachers to nurture what I have labeled elsewhere an "erotic epistemology."[82] Through a process that they call "prophetic listening," they help their students to consider their theological identity and modes of biblical interpretation by forcing them to take on the identity of another. Herein, students must draw an identity from a hat, identities designed by the professor in advance to reflect marks of difference and sameness along lines of race, gender, age, ability, sexual orientation, and economic level. Then the students are asked to articulate this person's most pressing issue, as well as his/her/their understanding of God. Lastly, the students have to interpret a biblical text and begin the process of sermon development, all from this *other person's* point of view. Hudson and Turner observe, "We are accustomed to thinking about the prophet as the one who speaks. . . . But this one who speaks is also called to a process of prophetic listening."[83] Accordingly, they

81. Rivera, *Poetics of the Flesh*, 113.
82. See Jacob D. Myers, "Toward an Erotic Liturgical Theology: Schmemann in Conversation with Contemporary Philosophy" *Worship* 87, no. 5 (September 2013): 387–413 and Myers, "The Erotic Approach: Homiletical Insights form the Work of Georges Bataille," *Theology and Sexuality* 19, no. 1 (2013): 26–37.

report that what students glean from this exercise is not a total understanding of the other's point of view, which would be impossible; rather, the students learn how much their own stereotypes and prejudices shape *their* world and the need to listen in different and nuanced ways to others.

As a summoned subject, the preacher receives selfhood from beyond himself, and, at the same time, he decides how and to what degree he will heed this summons in his preaching. Preachers possess what Medina, following Butler, labels an "echoing responsibility," which takes shape as the "mobilization of our discursive powers" to tackle issues of systemic injustice.[84] Words are not neutral. They posses a legacy that preachers must know and exploit if they are to dismantle ways of knowing, speaking, and behaving that militate against justice. We must find words that *echo* our *respons*-ibility for the other. The eminent Jewish philosopher Emmanuel Levinas once remarked, "It is often said 'God is love.' God is the commandment of love. 'God is love' means that He loves you. But this implies that the primary thing is your own salvation. In my opinion, God is a commandment to love. God is the one who says that one must love the other."[85] This is the prophetic summons, to echo God's love for the world—that is, unto death.

The Preacher as Host: Identity with the World

To be a self is to be a subject. Much as the protagonist of a story is free to affect change, to act upon her storied world, to be the main character in her story, the self is the agent of her own life. From liberation theologians we have learned, however, that not every self has been granted equal access to selfhood. Ethnic, gender, class, and sexual minorities, as well as the environment, have all been denied selfhood to varying degrees. How can we love with a Jesus kind of love if the structures of inequity and injustice at work in our world deny us the agency to love ourselves?

Or consider the situation of those who do not experience marginalization on account of demographic markers (e.g., mostly white, mostly educated, mostly straight men), but who nevertheless recognize a certain intellectual bondage at work within and upon them.[86] Are such

---

83. Turner and Hudson, *Saved from Silence*, 105–6.
84. Medina, *Speaking From Elsewhere*, 140.
85. Levinas, "The Paradox of Morality: An Interview with Emmanuel Levinas," trans. Andrew Benjamin and Tamra Wright, in *The Provocation of Levinas: Rethinking the Other*, ed. Robert Bernasconi and David Wood (London: Routledge, 1988), 177.

persons so firmly entrenched in oppressive power systems that they too are incapable of loving beyond objectification? Can a self who is already defined as an oppressor actually love himself?

In opposition to the Cartesian subject, whose subjectivity is tethered to knowledge of human and non-human others as *objects* of knowledge, I want to suggest an erotic way of conceptualizing the self: as *host*.[87] The self-as-host participates in the erotic approach to the o/Other manifested in liberationist and radical theologies. This modality of selfhood facilitates movement toward the other beyond objectification. Furthermore, this approach instantiates a mode of relating to the self in and according to love. Homiletically, this reorientation resonates with Campbell's notion of "preaching among friends."[88]

The word *host* is semantically rich. The word diverges in English from its Latin root to structure two very different meanings. The one is linked with *hospitality* (*hospes*) and the other is linked with *hostility* (*hostis*), both of which remain alive and active within the term *host*. This internal tension always in play within the concept of host must not be dismissed or overlooked.

Hospitality, strictly speaking, is impossible. To show hospitality—to play host to the other—one must first be "master" to some extent. How can I invite another into a house, country, or field of knowledge that is not to some degree mine? The self-as-host is first and foremost a self endowed with power. Furthermore, to maintain hospitality, to remain host, one must remain in power over the other to a certain extent. If a robber breaks into my home, I am not his host. He has seized that possibility from me; it's the first thing that he steals from me. He cannot be

86. See Cone, "Theology's Great Sin," 3: "Physical death is only one aspect of racism that raises serious theological questions. Spiritual death is another, and it is just as destructive, if not more so, for it destroys the soul of both the racists and their victims."
87. I am indebted to Derrida's thinking in this regard. See Jacques Derrida and Anne Dufourmantelle, *Of Hospitality*, trans. Rachel Bowlby (Stanford: Stanford University Press, 2000); Derrida, *The Gift of Death*; and Derrida, *Adieu to Emmanuel Lévinas*, trans. Pascale-Anne Brault and Michael Naas (Stanford, CA: Stanford University Press, 1999).
88. See Charles L. Campbell, *The Word Before the Powers: An Ethic of Preaching* (Louisville: Westminster John Knox, 2002), 161–64. However, it is in relation to hostility that I believe that my notion of preacher-as-host does more work for us homiletically and theologically than Campbell's notion of the preacher-as-a-friend-among-friends. Even as Campbell's friendly preacher resists the false choice between an "open-ended" homiletic that may be reluctant to make authoritative claims for fear of silencing the voice of the other and a homiletic that participates in the power of the "Domination system" but speaks boldly against injustice, Campbell's preacher-as-friend erases the animosity toward the other presumed by the preacher-friend. This is ironic because Campbell notes without equivocation that "preaching *inevitably* involves power and *always* runs the risk of becoming the voice that silences all other voices; one person speaks, telling others what to think and do, while everyone else remains silent and passive" (161–62, emphasis added). It is precisely this inevitable/always of hostility that I wish to retain, reminding—even haunting—the preacher's self-conceptualization.

my guest because he has already asserted himself according to a different relation: as an intruder. This internal tension is why hospitality is simultaneously possible and impossible. Genuine hospitality demands a certain non-mastery, a certain divestment of all claims to property, power, or ownership. At the same time, hospitality requires a certain level of control, forcing me to place limits on the other. No matter how you slice it, a certain hostility coincides with hospitality.

The erotic approach to the homiletical vocation proceeds by love, of preacher-as-host, in this ambiguous, tenuous sense. The homiletical self whom we are called to love is wrought with complexities. The preacher-as-host blurs the lines between slave and master, colonizer and colonized, subject and object. As we've seen, identities are always in flux; identity is constantly being renegotiated in the play of sameness and otherness. As I put it elsewhere, the erotic approach opens by the double movement of divestment and boldness in response to the wor(l)d of God.[89] Such "bold humility" is an existential and spiritual attitude whereby the preacher simultaneously wills to love the other beyond objectification and in the process asserts themself boldly and bodily before the other as one relating to particular cultures and ways of being in the world.[90]

The space of love participates in the ambiguities and richness of the preacher-as-host because it clears a space of hospitality within the self for the other (divestment) and *at the same time*, by asserting the self not as knower but as lover (boldness) it draws a line, a mark of hostility, at the threshold of encounter beyond which the other may not cross.[91] The preacher-as-host opens the movement of love toward the o/Other without encroaching upon the world of the other. It is at once a site of power and powerlessness. Indeed, it leads us into a third space beyond such dualisms. Such is a world of "interdependence," which poet Audre Lorde defines as a site of "freedom which allows the *I* to *be*, not to be used, but in order to be creative."[92] The preacher-as-host fosters a sense of self that is at once capable of love and worthy of love.

Most concretely, the preacher-as-host is affected by a kind of double

89. See Jacob D. Myers, *Making Love with Scripture: Why the Bible Doesn't Mean How You Think It Means* (Minneapolis: Fortress Press, 2015), 119–32.
90. I find a helpful parallel here with the work of Gilbert, *Journey and Promise*, 61: "Only a reciprocally enriching prophetic and priestly conception of a practical theology for homiletics can bolster the health of the church's proclamation and through wisdom keep in motion the community's story."
91. See Anna Mercedes, *Power For: Feminism and Christ's Self-Giving* (London: T & T Clark, 2011).
92. Lorde, "The Master's Tools Will Never Dismantle the Master's House," in *Sister Outsider*, 110.

death: the death of the ego and the death of objectification. The first, as Levinas puts it, appears thusly:

> The [homiletical] ego stripped . . . of its scornful and imperialist subjectivity, is reduced to the "here I am," in transparency without opaqueness, without heavy zones propitious for evasion. "Here I am" as a witness of the Infinite, but a witness that does not thematize what it bears witness of, and whose truth is not the truth of representation, is not evidence.[93]

Note here that the homiletical "I" relinquishes opacity, exposes himself completely in the act of bearing witness. The obverse side of this coin, the side of the other encountered in and according to hospitality, remains opaque. This is where Glissant's thinking according to relational-identity, as opposed to root-identity, is instructive. He writes, "The poetics of relation presuppose that each of us encounters the density (the opacity) of the Other. The more the Other resists in his thickness or his fluidity (without restricting himself to this), the more expressive his reality becomes, and the more fruitful the relation becomes."[94] Relation and opacity work in tandem to resist totalization and reductive assimilation of otherness: the possibility of resurrection.

Preaching: From Dogma to Cosmopoetics

A second feature arising within the self through the erotic approach revealed in and through preaching is the shift from dogma to cosmopoetics, from words about God to a burning desire to see God's love made manifest in the world.[95] The erotic approach teaches homiletics that preaching does not exist to teach us *about* God—as if God could be grasped intellectually. Preaching exists, to borrow a phrase from Caputo, so that God may "insist."[96] The preacher is not here to teach us about God but to draw us *into* God. As a mother draws a child to

93. Levinas, *Otherwise than Being*, 146–47. Cf. Taylor's notion of the self as "respondent": "A person is a being who can be addressed, and who can reply. . . . Any philosophical theory of the person must address the question of what it is to be a respondent." Charles Taylor, "The Concept of a Person," in *Human Agency and Language: Philosophical Papers I* (Cambridge: Cambridge University Press, 1989), 97.

94. Glissant, *Introduction à une poétique du divers*, 24. Unfortunately, this work has not yet been translated into English.

95. This is a nuanced reading of Caputo's term "cosmo-theopoetics." Inasmuch as I regard God's "insistence," to use Caputo's term, according to God's radical otherness, I do not see the world "insisting" on its own. Rather, the world, too, is other: it too cries out for justice. Listening to the other is also a listening to the world as other.

96. See John D. Caputo, *The Insistence of God: A Theology of Perhaps* (Bloomington: Indiana University Press, 2013).

her breast or as a father holds his child in a swaddling embrace, erotic preaching draws us into the insistence of God so that we may join in God's liberative, life-giving work in the world. Herein we discover our identity.

The (possible) gift given by and according to an erotic homiletic transcends ethics.[97] This is so because ethics attends to the logic of obligation: doing one's duty. The gift, if there is such a thing, operates according to a different economy. It shifts the ethical imperative to do to others what you wish they would do for you (Luke 6:31): *Since it has been given to you, give.* The logic of love is the logic of "superabundance," beyond a tit-for-tat equivalence.[98]

I understand preaching as *poetics*—not ethics or church dogmatics—as a complex compendium of narratives, parables, and paradoxes. Caputo explains, "We might say that a poetics is a discourse with a heart, supplying the heart of a heartless world. Unlike logic, it is a discourse with *pathos*, with a passion and a desire, with an imaginative sweep and a flare, touched by that of madness, hence more of an a-logic or even a patho-logic, one that is, however, not sick but healing and salvific."[99] Poetics moves us to concrete action in the world, not by our own will or what we think the world needs us to do, but according to God's summons made manifest in and through preaching.[100]

Erotic preaching aims at the world God loves *through* us. In this way, the "Word" of God, which is always the *secret* of God (see chapter 4), is an arrow fired by the bow of the preacher, who discovers himself in bending himself toward the world of God. The congregation's task is to fire this arrow and to follow this arrow where it is aimed: toward human and non-human flourishing.[101] In attending to the cries of the

---

97. The difference between an *ethic* and *ethics* is misunderstood by Paul Scott Wilson vis-à-vis McClure and other "radical postmodern" homileticians. See Wilson, *Preaching and Homiletical Theory* (St. Louis: Chalice, 2004), 135–58. Because Wilson is blinded by the very homiletical and theological logocentrism these so-called "radical postmoderns" challenge (see my chapter 4 below), he is incapable of conceiving of an a priori ethic (as "first philosophy," in Levinas's parlance) that subverts ontology and the binary logic Wilson's homiletical theory sustains.
98. Ricoeur, "The Logic of Jesus, The Logic of God," in *Figuring the Sacred*, 282.
99. Caputo, *The Weakness of God*, 104.
100. Thus, I share an appreciation for theological language *as* deconstructive theopoetics that is highlighted by Laurel Kearns and Catherine Keller, "Preface," in *Ecospirit: Religions and Philosophies for the Earth* (New York: Fordham University Press, 2007), which "takes responsibility for its own constructions. It recognizes its shifting and overlapping historical contexts as the basis for an eco-hermeneutics, a textuality that cannot be abstracted from the spirited materiality of the earth" (viii).
101. Again, Caputo is helpful. He writes of the poetics of obligation, as opposed to capital-E Ethics. "To follow the way of obligation means to be stirred by the appeals, to answer the call of lowly proper names, of what is laid low. The right response to what is laid low is not the invocation of a sacred name but offering relief, lending a hand. Without why." John D. Caputo, *Against Ethics: Contribu-*

marginalized and oppressed, erotic preaching participates in a cosmopoetics of obligation, responding to the cry of human and non-human others to make love happen in the world in and beyond our cultures. Only here may any name worthy of the name p/reacher be uttered—and only in the mo(ve)ment of p/reaching.

Cosmopoetics signifies the call made manifest through the world, which thereby solicits our words and our actions. The death of preaching is a way of hearing this call as trouble for the preacher. Such "always calls in and as the world" to drive us to material engagement in pursuit of liberation.[102] We may understand the "Word" of God to be revealed to us in and through preaching precisely where the "Word" moves through the preacher toward the world God loves. The erotic approach enables us to hear this call and to take a stand against forces that militate against God's restorative work in and for the world.

Queering the Pulpit

The preacher is only in trouble when they resist the trouble that abides alongside their homiletical identity. This is not something that should be ignored or can be rectified through homiletical *technes*. Instead, we who have been summoned to proclaim the "Word" of God for the people of God must embrace a discursive agency that is at once hybrid and relational. Our speaking is at once determined and indeterminable, free and bound; it is creative but limited.

All of what we've been discussing in this chapter is instructed by a certain "queering" of the pulpit. Drawing both from queer theory and queer theologies, the conceptualization and articulation of kerygmatic identity I envision makes room for a difference beyond the confines of dominant discourses and identity politics. Thelathia Nikki Young parses the nuance at work in this critical stance:

A queer critical stance disrupts the norms of categorization by illuminating the processes by which they are constructed and implications of their presence. If a potentially infinite coalition of sexual identities, practices, discourses, and sites might be identified as queer, it is not a token of liberal pluralism, but rather a negotiation of the concept of identity itself. Queerness shakes up the foundations of identity by destabilizing

tions to a Poetics of Obligation with Constant Reference to Deconstruction (Bloomington: Indiana University Press, 1993), 237. On human flourishing as the aim of philosophies of religion, see Grace M. Jantzen, *Becoming Divine: Towards a Feminist Philosophy of Religion* (Bloomington and Indianapolis: Indiana University Press, 1999), 156–70.
102. Caputo, *The Insistence of God*, 177.

the organizing rubrics around which those identities (and relevant practices) are understood. As such, the act of affirming queer identities is an appropriate response to the constructive limits of multiplying discursive categories in society and particularly in the liberationist movements and identity-conscious politics of the racial civil rights, feminist rights, and "gay" rights movements. The rhetoric of these movements has been structured predominantly around self-recognition, community, and shared identity—though inadvertently resulting in some modicum of exclusion, delegitimation, a false sense of universality, or, erasure through assimilation—which has often been shaped by imputed labels of sexual personhood.[103]

Such an opening up of discursive spaces may take shape as a radical critique and radical echoing, which Medina labels "the practice of infelicity."

An example of such infelicity in practice is embodied by Phil Snider. Snider serves as the Senior Minister of Brentwood Christian Church in Springfield, Missouri. In 2012, the Springfield City Council was considering Council Bill 2012-226. Also known as the Sexual Orientation and Gender Identity Bill, it included language that added sexual orientation and gender identity to the list of categories of persons protected from discrimination in areas of employment, housing and public accommodations. Before the City Council, Snider identified himself as supporting this piece of legislation. His speech, however, lambasted LGBTQ-identifying persons and decried the horrors of such ways of being.[104]

Snider's speech takes a turn, however, when he appears to trip over his words. He *accidentally* mentions racial segregation. Following this failed performance, this feigned slip of the tongue, Snider informs his audience that all of his words against the inclusion of LGBTQ-identifying persons were direct quotes lifted from white preachers in the 1950s in opposition to racial integration. In his "performative failure," to borrow Medina's terminology, Snider destabilizes the underlying epistemological commitments that bolster the structural discrimination against LGBTQ-identifying persons.[105]

103. Thelathia Nikki Young, *Black Queer Ethics, Family, and Philosophical Imagination* (New York: Palgrave Macmillan, 2016), 191.
104. Phil Snider, "Speech In Support of Council Bill 2012-226," August 20, 2012, https://tinyurl.com/aybckj4.
105. "It is impossible to overemphasize the crucial importance of the norms that structure our linguistic practices and shape what in them counts as a performative success and a performative failure." (Medina, *Speaking From Elsewhere*, 168). Here, Medina is drawing on the work of J. L. Austin. See also José Medina, *Language: Key Concepts* (London: Continuum, 2005), chapter one. See also the

More overtly, in the work and witness of Robyn Henderson-Espinoza we discover the linguistic and material constraints of our (homiletical) cultures taken to task. Self-describing themself as a "Latin@ queer Trans*gressive gender queer," Henderson-Espinoza models a path of resistance that can inform homiletical theologies beyond static conceptualizations of identity and selfhood. Henderson-Espinoza resists, for instance, the assimilationist politics undergirding the marriage equality movement. They teach us how this and similar liberation movements surreptitiously rely upon structures and tactics that reinscribe the logics of white supremacy and heterosexism.

Accordingly, queering the pulpit will participate in a "politics of radical difference" that embraces multiplicity through *diffraction*. Drawing from the parlance of quantum theory, Henderson-Espinoza explains that diffraction is "that particular method of combining disparate strands of thinking and being (and becoming) and finding a particular style of relationality in the in/betweenness of difference."[106] What if our homiletics classrooms were reconfigured—linguistically, pedagogically, materially—to aid preaching students to *stimulate* difference and multiplicity? What if the preacher were not regarded as a homiletical a priori but as one who is always becoming through diffuse modes of p/reaching and inter-relating with human and non-human others, who are also becoming through moments of kerygmatic diffraction?

Even as it works materially to undercut epistemologies of dominance and marginalization, queering the pulpit also works temporally. In his book *Cruising Utopia: The Then and There of Queer Futurity*, José Esteban Muñoz contends that queerness is not a thing that exists in the present. Instead, queerness is a "futurity bound phenomenon," a "not yet here" that critically engages pragmatic presentism. He argues that "queerness is not yet here but it approaches like a crashing wave of potentiality. And we must give in to its propulsions, its status as a destination."[107] Be leaning into a certain queerness, the Christian preacher embraces an identity and a subjecthood that is aspirational. Queerness, like subjecthood, is pursued.

reflections on the fruitfulness of failed performatives in Otis Moss III, *Blue Note Preaching in a Post-Soul World: Finding Hope in an Age of Despair* (Louisville: Westminster John Knox, 2015), 60–61.
106. Robyn Henderson-Espinoza, "Difference, Becoming, and Interrelatedness: A Material Resistance Becoming," *Cross Currents* 66, no. 2 (Jun 2016): 282–83.
107. José Esteban Muñoz, *Cruising Utopia: The Then and There of Queer Futurity* (New York: NYU Press, 2009), 185.

Conclusion: To Be(for)e the Other

So this territory between us feels new and frightening as well as urgent, rigged with detonating pieces of our own individual racial histories which neither of us chose but which each of us bears the scars from.

— Audre Lorde[108]

In this chapter, I've argued that preaching shares no ground with ontology.[109] The preacher is otherwise than Being. To the degree that she "is" anything (a subject, an individual, an ego), she exists according to death. That is the kerygmatic summons that homiletics forgot to mention: *to preach is to die for those whom we love.* This need not lead homiletics to anxiety or fear. As Luce Irigaray notes, "Our all will come. But you can't anticipate it, force it, program it. Our all cannot be projected, or mastered."[110] Who, then, is this preacher to come? And how might homiletics aid in the preacher's coming identity and selfhood in and through preaching?

Homiletics can nudge and nurture p/reachers to *cross over to the other side*, to enact and affect in their personhood a mode of *transgression.* Such is to die to norms of identity and subjecthood, as well as normative discursive practices. This is performed through the voice—not because the voice is somehow *purer,* or because it opens up onto a presence devoid of absence (we'll look more closely at this in chapter 4); rather, because it is through enunciation that the practice of transgression troubles the very foundations of selfhood and speech as selfhood.

Medina situates "infelicitous subjects" on the normative margins of our practices. Accordingly, homiletics must learn from those "border people," who haunt the normative frontiers of homiletical discourse. Medina writes, "Speaking from elsewhere can be negatively characterized as speaking from a not-yet recognized discursive context and with a not-yet recognizable voice. But it implicitly involves a struggle for recognition; and it can be positively characterized as contributing to the creation of new discursive contexts and opening up spaces for new voices that have not been heard yet."[111] Such a *crossing over* of iden-

---

108. Lorde, "Eye to Eye," in *Sister Outsider,* 162.
109. Even beyond a "moral ontology," which remains within an immanent frame of moral intuitions that is decidedly anthropocentric and thus less than the Divine summons that casts preaching within a different frame. See Taylor, *Sources of the Self,* 72–75.
110. Irigaray, "When Our Lips Speak Together," 212.
111. Medina, *Speaking from Elsewhere,* 179. See also Medina, *The Epistemology of Resistance: Gender and Racial Oppression, Epistemic Injustice, and Resistant Imaginations* (Oxford: Oxford University Press, 2012). For example: "To avoid epistemic injustices and to become epistemically virtuous, agents

tity and subjecthood in relation and response to the other is akin to an embrace of death in hope of resurrection—sentencing Being to death without guarantee of resurrection.

But such a challenge to homiletics goes all the way down. The *being-ness* of a preacher is made manifest through a certain death. Homiletics must alert the preacher—if there is one—to what is at stake in this preaching business: in saving her life, the preacher will lose it; in transgressing discursive norms and subverting expectations, she will die. But we are getting ahead of ourselves. Homiletics ought first to help her understand that the very idea of a *self*, understood as a unified center of consciousness, is a myth perpetuated by phallogocentrism. Homiletics must find ways to help the preacher lean into her pluriformity and the possibility of her becoming.[112] This can only take place (perhaps, perchance) according to the epistemic and ontological unraveling of selfhood in p/reaching be(for)e the other: that is, in striving to position oneself *before* the other *for* the other's flourishing.

The preacher-to-come *is performed* in the undoing of the preacher's identity according to a kind of "epistemic resistance," as a challenge to those discursive practices that are always already privileging certain ways of knowing and speaking over others. Such a challenge is at work in Lorde's concept of the erotic as an alternative path toward self-understanding.

The erotic, Lorde explains, "comes from sharing deeply any pursuit with another person." At the same time, the erotic emerges from within oneself. She writes, "In touch with the erotic, I become less willing to accept powerlessness, or those other supplied states of being which are not native to me, such as resignation, despair, self-effacement, depression, self-denial."[113] According to such a mode of epistemic deconstruction, at once before without being against the other (including oneself-as-other)—homiletical theologies may help the preacher to discover the possibility of selfhood in and against relationality; the potential for homiletical identity forms at the confluence of passivity and agency.

---

need to understand (if only intuitively) how identity power functions in their society, and how epistemic appraisals (such as credibility assessments) and testimonial exchanges are mediated and colored by social perceptions and stereotypes. . . . Those who are not critically aware of their own social identity and that of others, those who are not sensitive and responsive to the epistemic consequences of social positionality and relationality, cannot correct biases and achieve (or contribute to the achievement of) epistemic justice" (54).

112. See Irigaray, "When Our Lips Speak Together," 214–15.
113. Lorde, "Uses of the Erotic," in *Sister Outsider*, 56, 58.

3

The Gift of Death: Troubling Scripture

Everyone knows that a place exists which is not economically or politically indebted to all the vileness and compromise. That is not obliged to reproduce the system. That is writing. If there is somewhere else that can escape the infernal repetition, it lies in that direction, where it writes itself, where it dreams, where it invents new worlds.

— Hélène Cixous.[1]

Moana follows a narrative arc on par with the best Disney films: facing impossible odds, the heroine must deliver her people (and herself) from peril. As the title suggests, this heroine is named Moana, a teenage girl next in line to rule her Pacific island village. When the villagers discover that the island is dying and the fish have left the surrounding waters, Moana ventures into the tempestuous sea in search of a mythical demigod named Maui to save her people.

The cosmogony underlying *Moana* is plot critical. Moana's people believe that there was only ocean before the Mother island Te Fiti emerged. In her heart was the power to create life; the world exists because Te Fiti shared this gift. In time, men began to covet Te Fiti's gift. They believed that if they could posses Te Fiti's heart, her creative powers became theirs. One day, a shape-shifting demigod named Maui

1. Hélène Cixous, "Sorties," in Hélène Cixous and Catherine Clément, *The Newly Born Woman*, trans. Betsy Wing (Minneapolis: University of Minnesota Press, 2001), 72.

succeeded in stealing Te Fiti's heart, intending to give it to humankind. But without her heart Te Fiti withered—along with her procreative powers. In her wake emerged Te Ka, a lava monster bent on turning all of creation into lifeless stone.

Moana's quest is simple: find Maui the demigod and force him to return the heart to Te Fiti—all while trying not to drown, lose her way in the vast sea, die at the hands of marauding pirates, or melt in the magma clutches of Te Ka, who stands sentry before Te Fiti's island. Eventually, Moana finds Maui and, having helped him retrieve his magical fishhook (the source of his power), they arrive at last before the foreboding lava monster, Te Ka.

With equal parts temerity and luck, Moana and Maui make it past Te Ka only to discover that the body of Te Fiti is missing. As Maui continues to fight Te Ka, Moana spots a hole in Te Ka's chest, which is the exact shape and size of Te Fiti's heart. Just as Te Ka is about to strike Maui with a deathblow, Moana places the heart into the monster's chest. Te Ka transforms from fire and ash into the lush, green island goddess Te Fiti. Moana returns home. Order is restored.

Preachers are much like Moana. We are hermeneutical wayfarers. We leave our people for a strange and perilous land (the *world of the text*) in pursuit of the "heart" of God's revelation (gospel, truth, etc.). But we are also like Maui. We yearn to give the gift of life to our congregants; but in so doing, we *take hold* of scripture. We sneak. We shapeshift. We wrestle. We subdue. None of this is for *our* glory or power; we don't want to keep the heart (of God) for ourselves, but to give its lifegiving power to our people who are besieged by death.[2]

But here's the rub: we cannot give that which we can never possess. We must not turn *God's* "Word" revealed in and through scripture into a commodity. For such is a *gift*, as Pope Francis teaches us.[3] Preachers struggle because the very thing we want to give is precisely that which we can never give. Because it is not *our* "Word" but God's, we may (like Maui) only ever give it by taking it. But in our taking we destroy the possibility of gift as such.[4] Homiletical theologies have bought into economic assumptions perpetuated by Western thought. This *homiletical*

---

2. It is debatable whether certain megachurch pastors take from scripture for such magnanimous ends. Apropos, see Luke Powery, *Dem Dry Bones: Preaching, Death and Hope* (Minneapolis: Fortress Press, 2012), 8.

3. Francis, *The Joy of the Bishops: Evangelii Gaudium* (Dublin: Veritas, 2013), 75.

4. This is innate to the structure of the gift as such, but it also informs what we do with scripture as texts: whether we allow the ineradicable undecidability of the text to proliferate and disseminate (itself) or whether we will silence the text's Saying according to the Said of our knowledge/reason: to force it to come to a *full stop*. Derrida identifies this dilemma as "the trial of undecid-

logos economy makes the *giving* of God's "Word" impossible by its very operations.

In this chapter, I seek to interrogate how we've been taught to give the "Word" of God to the people of God through preaching. Economies—all economies—deal with the *valuation* and *circulation* of available resources. Economies *govern* the factors of production and consumption. Herein, I want us to consider the modes and structures of exchange at work within and between preaching and scripture.[5] I trouble the (economic) assumptions that bolster various homiletical theologies in hope of opening preaching to the trouble always already at work within them.

Section One: Scripture *in* Trouble

> The presence of the all-powerful Word in the book that is the Bible is a humbled presence, and it is as if a perpetual descent of God toward us.
> — Jean-Louis Chrétien[6]

What is the function of scripture for preaching? How does scripture generate theological value in and through preaching? What role does scripture play within the kerygmatic economy: the *movement* between God and the created order that makes preaching *valuable*? What risks and rewards coincide with our preaching economies? These are the questions that govern my thinking here. At base, I want us to think together about how we *handle* scripture homiletically.

The Bible, to borrow Kant's language, is a *necessary condition for the possibility* of Christian preaching. Few will challenge this claim. Preaching that fails to draw upon scripture *in some way* is just a speech.[7] *How* scripture functions within particular homiletical economies constitutes those economies as such. Said differently, the *manner* in which preachers engage scripture is the single greatest factor in determining the *kind* of preaching being enacted.[8] It is not too far afield to assert

---

ability." Jacques Derrida, "Afterword: Toward an Ethic of Discussion," in *Limited Inc.*, trans. Samuel Weber (Evanston, IL: Northwestern University Press, 1998), 210.

5. The boundary is blurred between preaching and scripture because the *written* word was always already a *spoken* word. As Ricoeur puts it, "There has always been a hermeneutic problem in Christianity because Christianity proceeds from a proclamation." Paul Ricoeur, "Preface to Bultmann," in *The Conflict of Interpretations: Essays in Hermeneutics*, ed. Don Ihde, trans. Peter McCormick (Evanston, IL: Northwestern University Press, 1974), 382.

6. Jean-Louis Chrétien, *Under the Gaze of the Bible*, trans. John Marson Dunaway (New York: Fordham University Press, 2015), 7.

7. Ruthanna B. Hooke, *Transforming Preaching* (New York: Church Publishing, 2010), 26–27; James H. Harris, *Preaching Liberation* (Minneapolis: Fortress Press, 1995), 7; William H. Willimon, *Proclamation and Theology* (Nashville: Abingdon, 2005), 15, 23.

that biblical content is the *dominant currency* of the homiletical realm. And yet, no two homiletical theologies valuate scripture per the same weights and measures.

Some would argue that we are in the midst of a Great Homiletical Recession.[9] If this is so, it is incumbent upon homiletical theologians to get out the balance sheets and do some basic accounting. This, precisely, is what I attempt below. I contend that scripture, along with preaching, is in trouble because our current preaching practices are locked in a homiletical logos economy. What I seek is a way beyond economy that is able to give the gift (of God) without taking.

Homiletical Econometrics: The Value and Circulation of Biblical Currency

Every homiletical theology is economic.[10] This is no aspersion. It's a matter of fact. Decisions must be made: What's the "market value" of scripture for *this* community? Who gets to set that value? Is scripture itself the product, or is it the raw material from which consumables are made? Who has access to the materials of production? What credentials are necessary for this work?

To state that all homiletical theologies are economic is to assert that one of their central tasks is to *valuate* and *regulate* the deployment of scripture vis-à-vis congregational contexts.[11] My work here is not to

8. As Paul Scott Wilson reminds us, how we choose to employ the Bible in preaching is "a small step in the sermon process, but in other ways this is the most important step a preacher can make." *Preaching and Homiletical Theory* (St. Louis: Chalice, 2004), 8. His own view, as he puts it later in this book, is that "[t]he Bible becomes scripture because it has the capacity to reveal God's actions and human identity in history and in the present" (152).

9. "At the beginning of the twenty-first century, the art of preaching is in peril." Michael A. Turner, *A Peculiar Prophet: William H. Willimon and the Art of Preaching* (Nashville: Abingdon, 2010), 1.

10. This has always been a feature of homiletics. In what is largely recognized as the first homiletics textbook, St. Augustine argues that scripture is to be valued qualitatively or quantitatively in proportion to the perspicacity of the preacher: "Those who remember the word [of scripture] closely but penetrate to the heart of scripture with the eyes of their own heart are much to be preferred, but better than either is the person who not only quotes scripture when he chooses but also understands it as he should. For a person who has to speak wisely on matters which he cannot treat eloquently, close adherence to the words of scripture is particularly necessary. The poorer he sees himself to be in his own resources, the richer he must be in those of scripture, using them to confirm what he says in his own words; so that although once deficient in words of his own he can grow in stature, as it were, by the testimony of something really important. A preacher who cannot give pleasure with his words may give pleasure with his texts." St. Augustine, *On Christian Teaching*, trans. R. P. H. Green (Oxford: Oxford University Press, 2008), Bk 4, V7–VI 9, p. 105.

11. One may counter that preaching is an-economic because it orients itself to the gift of God that is not about exchange as such; doesn't the very act of *giving* a sermon remove it from economic calculation? In his famous study of so-called archaic societies, which abstain from modern economic practices of payment for goods and service, Marcel Mauss discovered something that addresses this query. Mauss found that the "voluntary character" of gift-giving, which is "apparently free

privilege one homiletical economy over others or to denigrate how different traditions value scripture for preaching; rather, I aim to help us better understand what's going on homiletically between text and context and what that commits us to theologically.

Econometric analyses help us assess the *valuation* and *circulation* of biblical currency in the homiletical marketplace. Such a mode of inquiry attends to the role (value) of scripture in preaching and the methodologies (circulation) that keep our homiletical houses in working order. To enter into this or that homiletical economy is to abide by its laws, which are compulsory; to do otherwise is to do wrongly. Two points of clarification are necessary before we proceed. These are not so much two distinct and separate points as they are two sides of the same coin.

On the one hand, I'm invoking economics metaphorically. It provides a framework for homiletical analysis. As with all metaphors, however, if we force it to do too much work for us it will break.[12] My goal in the following econometric assessments of homiletical theories is not to assign a label to every homiletical proposal, which would inevitably rarify if not misconstrue said proposals. I seek merely to help us think more critically about how we adjudicate biblical value for preaching and how the Bible is employed (or ought to be employed) in sermons and to what end. Economic concepts help us here.

On the other hand and at the same time, economics is literal. As

and disinterested" is "nevertheless constrained and self-interested." Mauss concludes, "Almost always such services have taken the form of the gift, the present generously given even when, in the gesture accompanying transaction, there is only a polite fiction, formalism, and social deceit, and when really there is obligation and economic self interest." *The Gift: The Form and Reason for Exchange in Archaic Societies*, trans. W. D. Halls (London: Routledge, 1990), 3.

Jacques Derrida, drawing upon Mauss's insights would later write, "Now the gift, *if there is any*, would no doubt be related to economy. One cannot treat the gift, this goes without saying, without treating this relation to economy, even to the money economy. But is not the gift, if there is any, also that which interrupts economy? That which, in suspending economic calculation, no longer gives rise to exchange? That which opens the circle so as to defy reciprocity or symmetry . . . If the figure of the circle is essential to economics, the gift must remain *aneconomic*. Not that it remains foreign to the circle, but it must *keep* a relation of foreignness to the circle, a relation without relation of familiar foreignness. It is perhaps in this sense that the gift is impossible." *Given Time I: Counterfeit Money*, trans. Peggy Kamuf (Chicago: University of Chicago Press, 1994), 7.

12. Ricoeur helpfully articulates the dual and necessary features of metaphor as being both consonant and dissonant. He writes, "The *maker* of metaphors is this craftsman with verbal skill *who*, from an inconsistent utterance for a literal interpretation, draws a significant utterance for a new interpretation which deserves to be called metaphorical because it generates the metaphor not only as deviant but as acceptable. In other words, metaphorical meaning does not merely consist of a semantic clash but of the *new* predicative meaning which emerges from the collapse of the literal meaning, that is, from the collapse of the meaning which obtains if we rely only on the common or usual lexical values of our words. The metaphor is not the enigma but the solution of the enigma." Paul Ricoeur, "The Metaphorical Process as Cognition, Imagination, and Feeling," *Critical Inquiry* 5, no. 1 (Autumn 1978): 146.

Fred Craddock puts it, "All serious preachers are bound by fear that, in the responsible transaction of changing coinage [between text and sermon], there may be a reduction of value."[13] He's right. There is an *actual* and *quantifiable* value assigned to scripture in every homiletical theology. There is also a *particular* way in which scripture is purported to function contextually in various approaches to preaching. Even though homiletics scholars do not articulate our proposals explicitly in terms of exchange, transactional assumptions bolster our methods nevertheless. By drawing such economic matters to the surface, we are better able to understand the Bible's role in preaching.

Equivocatory Economies of Scripture

Equivocatory economies of scripture operate per an awareness of the Bible's *ambivalence* regarding its central claims. Such economies value the Bible as authoritative only to the extent that it forwards a message of God's "unconditional concern" for emancipation of the oppressed. To the degree that the biblical witness seems to bear witness *against* its own claims to announce liberation, the Bible fails to live up to its status as *holy* scripture. Feminist homiletician Christine Smith engages scripture along such lines. She does not regard scripture as a "slate of norms" but as a means of deliverance from oppressive systems. Smith advances a way with scripture that at once recognizes the Bible's complicity in perpetuating oppression and injustice and sees therein a means to challenge theological and ecclesiological evils. In short, a text's "ultimate authority" for preaching lies in its capacity for liberation and redemption.[14]

Smith writes, "All who preach from a feminist perspective must strip away years of patriarchal interpretations and a pervasive androcentric worldview within the biblical narratives themselves in order to recover the voice of the powerless and oppressed."[15] She employs the metaphor

---

13. Fred B. Craddock, *As One Without Authority*, rev. ed. (St. Louis: Chalice, 2001), 98.
14. Christine M. Smith, "Preaching as an Act of Resistance," in *The Arts of Ministry: Feminist-Womanist Approaches*, ed. Christie Cozad Neuger (Louisville: Westminster John Knox, 1996), 39–59, and Smith, *Preaching as Weeping, Confession, and Resistance: Radical Responses to Radical Evil* (Louisville: Westminster John Knox, 1992); Smith, *Weaving the Sermon: Preaching in a Feminist Perspective* (Louisville: Westminster John Knox, 1989), 98. See also Mary Donovan Turner, "Disrupting a Ruptured World," in *Purposes of Preaching*, ed. Jana Childers (St. Louis: Chalice, 2004), 137.
15. Smith, *Weaving the Sermon*, 65. This is not without its challenges: "The unrelenting conviction to move beyond the boundaries of the tradition toward a transforming vision is also a painful and uncompromising given. For feminist preachers, the intimate weaving of our lives within the lives of those who are in community with us is of paramount concern, and the nonauthoritarian empowerment of all is of *ultimate value*" (140, emphasis added).

of *weaving* to articulate how a certain reading of scripture and lived experience may come together to form a beautiful, liberating, and life-giving tapestry. She concludes, "When sermons are interwoven witnesses to the vision and radical power of the Christian faith in all its confrontation and hope, those proclaimed words are also the best the craft can offer."[16]

Another excellent example of an equivocatory economy of scripture is articulated by Sarah Travis in her book *Decolonizing Preaching*. Like Smith, Travis not only acknowledges but laments the Bible's ambiguous relationship to colonial power. Scripture has been used as a "weapon of colonial/imperial power," *and yet*, it has also been a "source of positive and redemptive transformation for colonized persons" in and beyond ecclesial contexts. The tasks of a decolonizing homiletic are thus threefold: 1) to help preachers recognize the ways in which texts and people are "vulnerable to the lure of empire"; 2) to interpret texts and contexts for preaching that aid in the "decolonizing of the mind"; and 3) to proclaim a gospel that "transforms and transcends discourses of power" in view of epistemological-spiritual deliverance.[17]

In their groundbreaking book *Liberation Preaching*, Justo and Catherine González make a similar claim. They write, "In the act of preaching, the social and political situation of speaker and hearer are part of the context that gives meaning to the words that are spoken."[18] An *ideological suspicion* governs biblical interpretation within their homiletical economy. Accordingly, preaching from such an emancipatory perspective holds the words of scripture in tension with what González and González label the "political question" and advance a hermeneutic by which "the entire Bible must be read in light of that question."[19] The political question inquires into the interplay of power, authority, and inclusion/exclusion *and* the ways in which God intervenes in such inequitable circumstances. It is this political question that governs the

---

16. Ibid., 140.
17. Sarah Travis, *Decolonizing Preaching: The Pulpit as Postcolonial* Space (Eugene, OR: Cascade Books, 2014), 109, 47–48. See also Travis, "Troubled Gospel: Postcolonial Preaching for the Colonized, Colonizer, and Everyone in Between," *Homiletic* 40, no. 1 (2015): 46–54.
18. Justo L. González and Catherine Gunsalus González, *Liberation Preaching: The Pulpit and the Oppressed* (Nashville: Abingdon, 1980), 95. The central questions become, "[W]hat are the oppressive biases which find subtle expression in this writing?" and "What view of reality and of God's purposes does this writing espouse, perhaps without even being aware of it?" (46).
19. Ibid., 73. "If the major portion of the Bible is written by those who, in their own social situation, are the powerless and oppressed, if it is their perspective on the activity of God that is given us by Scripture, then surely a more accurate interpretation of the biblical word can be gained by those who currently stand in a parallel place in our own societies than by those who are powerful" (16).

circulation between text and context within their homiletical economy.

Ideational Economies of Scripture

Ideational economies of scripture aim to refine a biblical concept into a homiletical idea and to validate and apply it to the lives of congregants. Such value most highly the *concepts* or *ideas* that reside in the minds of the biblical writers and tend to privilege the technique of exposition to govern the circulation of these ideas. Haddon Robinson, a leading proponent of this approach, asserts that "God speaks through the Bible." It is the *medium* through which God encounters and confronts humans and "seizes them by the soul." Robinson clarifies that his homiletical method is irreducible to historical or doctrinal explication and that many who operate under the banner of expository preaching are actually doing something else entirely. Interestingly, Robinson notes that the Bureau of Weights and Measures holds no "standard expository sermon encased in glass against which to compare other messages." Robinson insists that "genuine expository preaching" is the type of preaching that "best carries the force of divine authority."[20] In short, exposition circulates biblical concepts most effectively.

Robinson articulates an ideational approach as the communication of a "biblical concept" that is "derived from and transmitted through a historical, grammatical, and literary study of a passage in context."[21] What is central for Robinson is that the preacher attends to the *thought* of the biblical writer, for only this is sufficient to determine the *substance* of the sermon. Bryan Chapell agrees, writing, "Expository preaching solemnly binds a preacher to the task of representing the precise meaning of a text as intended by the original author or as illumined by another inspired source within the Bible."[22] The ideational truth of the text is what the preacher seeks. Thus, exposition is proffered as the most effective method of obtaining the biblical idea and

---

20. Haddon Robinson, *Biblical Preaching: The Development and Delivery of Expository Messages*, 3rd ed. (Grand Rapids, MI: Baker Academic, 2014), 4. Robinson writes, "While an orthodox doctrine of inspiration may be a necessary plank in the evangelical platform on biblical authority, this sometimes gets in the way of expository preaching. . . . In our approach to the Bible, therefore, we are primarily concerned not with what individual words mean but with what the biblical writers mean through their use of words. . . . If we desire to understand the Bible in order to communicate its message, we must grapple with it on the level of ideas" (6).
21. Ibid., 5. This is also the case in much Roman Catholic preaching. See Pontifical Bible Commission, *The Interpretation of the Bible in the Church* (Rome: Liberia Editrice Vaticana, 1993), 34.
22. Bryan Chapell, *Christ-Centered Preaching: Redeeming the Expository Sermon*, 2nd ed. (Grand Rapids, MI: Baker Academic, 2005), 75.

the goal of preaching is to apply its concepts to the lives of the preacher and congregants: "Application gives expository preaching its purpose."[23]

Ideational homiletical economies approach scripture from a propositional frame. They value ideas because it is through ideas that God communicates with us through scripture. Many such homileticians maintain that the *only* viable method for preaching is exposition, the presentation and application of biblical truths.[24] The goal here is to extract some biblical idea sufficient for congregational direction. Chapell puts it this way: "As expository preachers, our ultimate goal is not to communicate the value of our opinions, others' philosophies, or speculative mediations but rather to show how God's Word discloses his will for those united to him through his Son." Note the role of validation in what comes next. "Truths of God proclaimed in such a way that people can see that concepts derive from Scripture and apply to their lives preoccupy the expository preacher's efforts."[25] For Chapell, sermons ought to excavate and refine the raw material of God's "Word" in the Bible.

Not all ideational economies of scripture insist on exposition as the privileged mode of ascertaining and communicating the Bible's concepts. This does not make these homiletics any less biblical. Paul Scott Wilson, for instance, argues, "Preaching needs to be biblical, and one of the best ways for us as preachers to produce stronger sermons is to pay

---

23. Robinson, *Biblical Preaching*, 10. Later, he writes, "No matter how brilliant or biblical a sermon is, without a definite purpose it is not worth preaching" (71).

24. In addition to Robinson and Chapell, see John Stott, *Between Two Worlds: The Challenge of Preaching Today* (Grand Rapids, MI: Eerdmans, 1982) and Hershael W. York and Bert Decker, *Preaching with Bold Assurance: A Solid and Enduring Approach to Engaging Exposition* (Nashville: B & H, 2003).

25. Chapell, *Christ-Centered Preaching*, 31. The theological justification for this approach is purportedly contained within scripture itself (2 Tim 3:16-17). Chapell avers, "God uses his [sic] Word to make us what we could not be on our own. In this sense, God's word acts as an instrument of his redeeming work. Scripture continually aims to restore aspects of our brokenness to spiritual wholeness so that we might reflect and rejoice in God's glory" (269–70).

Even as she pushes against a certain fundamentalism at work in Asian American appropriations of the Bible for preaching, Eunjoo Kim's early work on a "spiritual homiletic" continues to operate within a transactional mode of exchange. She writes, "The preacher as interpreter [of scripture] is sent to the text as the representative of the congregation *in order to gain spiritual guidelines* for the community of faith . . ." Eunjoo Mary Kim, *Preaching the Presence of God: A Homiletic from an Asian American Perspective* (Valley Forge, PA: Judson, 1999), 96. Emphasis added. Later, she writes that "the Bible functions as the manual of spirituality of the congregation by mediating the relationship between them and the living God" (97). Likewise, in arguing, among other things, for the "preacher as sage," Alyce McKenzie advances a way with scripture that puts divine wisdom "into circulation among the people" and asserts that preaching is only relevant and useful when it expresses God's will for daily living. Alyce M. McKenzie, *Preaching Proverbs: Wisdom for the Pulpit* (Louisville: Westminster John Knox, 1996), xxii. See also McKenzie, "Wisdom as a Resource for Preaching in a Time of War," *Journal for Preachers* 28, no. 1 (2004): 21–27, and McKenzie, "Out of Character! Preaching Biblical Wisdom in a Secular Age," *Journal for Preachers* 22, no. 4 (1999): 44–50.

better attention to what we do with the Bible in preaching."[26] Arguing that God is absent from many sermons, Wilson posits a "four-pages" approach to preaching that aims to help preachers move between the conceptual richness of scripture and the contemporary reality of sin and brokenness that blind us to God's grace and hope. "We preach from the Bible to ensure that God's Word is proclaimed," writes Wilson, but preaching the text is not enough. Preachers must get a "handle" on the text so that the "heart of the text" may be proclaimed.[27] Further-more, and like Chapell and Robinson, Wilson argues for the primacy of conceptual transference in the form of a thesis sentence, which he labels "the listener's best friend" and the absence of which is a "form of tyranny."[28]

When we attend closely to the homiletical metaphors employed by those who commend an ideational economy of scripture, we discern what they most highly value. Robinson writes, "All [the text's] diamonds do not lie exposed on the surface. Its richness is *mined* only through hard intellectual and spiritual spadework."[29] Chapell, too, describes his approach to preaching along the lines of excavation and digging.[30] And Wilson writes, "We maintain that theological meanings genuinely reside in the text and only by their presence does the Bible function as Scripture. We need to determine what method best *extracts* them."[31] This suggests to me that what God wants to give through the text, the concept or idea, is not immediately or easily given but depends instead upon the preacher to force it out of the biblical ground, as it were.

These homileticians also employ images of light and darkness to explain their approach. For Chapell, "Expository preaching sheds ordi-nary light on the path that leads to understanding a text. . . . The right amount of light not only *exposes* the path but also helps those on the path find their own way in the future."[32] Robinson contends that when

---

26. Paul Scott Wilson, *God Sense: Reading the Bible for Preaching* (Nashville: Abingdon, 2001), 9. See also Paul Scott Wilson, *The Four Pages of the Sermon: A Guide to Biblical Preaching* (Nashville: Abingdon, 1999), 17: "the Bible is our authority to preach and cannot be wisely by-passed."
27. Wilson, *The Four Pages of the Sermon,* 37–39. Wilson labels this a "theme statement," but he is quick to note, "Even a theme statement is not enough, although in homiletics in the last few centuries often this was all that was required. A sermon is not about anything you feel like talking about; it should be about God . . . For the text to be functioning at a theological level, and for it to lead into good news that casts listeners upon God's resources as well as their own, the actual starting place must be a theme statement that answers: What is God doing in or behind this text?" (39).
28. Wilson, *Preaching and Homiletical Theory*, 23.
29. Robinson, *Biblical Preaching*, 6. Emphasis added.
30. Chapell, *Christ-Centered Preaching*, 69: "In my earliest years of ministry, I most valued *mining* obscure texts." Emphasis added.
31. Wilson, *God Sense*, 69. Emphasis added.

a proposed subject "accurately describes what the writer is talking about, it *illuminates* the details of the passage; and the subject, in turn, will be illuminated by the details."[33] Observe here that the expository preacher is the one who performs the illumination. For Wilson, illumination is a predicate of the gospel itself. The preacher can occlude this light; however, "one also allows the light of the gospel to shine through the text to illuminate the listener's life in front of the text."[34] Ideational economies of scripture value most highly the propositional "truths" of scripture and preaching, properly executed, delivers said "truths" to congregants and parishioners in the distilled and refined form of a sermonic idea.

Figurative Economies of Scripture

A significant and influential homiletical economy of scripture centers on a trifold understanding of the Bible's value for preaching. Such a homiletic ramifies according to scripture's *figurative* capacities, that is, its power to re-present *forms* of life. As Lance Pape puts it, preaching is obliged to "pay against three debts": 1) the *prefigured* realities of the congregation; 2) the *configuring* power of scripture to disorient and reorient us in relation to God's revealed reality; and 3) the *reconfiguration* of the church's reality in light of God's reality.[35] In other words, scripture's value for preaching is grounded in its ability to help us *figure* the world otherwise.

Thomas Long is one of the most passionate defenders and effective exemplars of this homiletical economy. Long stresses the Bible's value for preaching as a way to *configure* and *refigure* life into a "meaningful world of action and purpose."[36] Accordingly, much of Long's scholarly

32. Ibid., 103. Emphasis added.
33. Robinson, *Biblical Preaching*, 41. Emphasis added.
34. Paul Scott Wilson, *The Practice of Preaching*, rev. ed. (Nashville: Abingdon, 2007), 251.
35. Lance B. Pape, *The Scandal of Having Something to Say: Ricoeur and the Possibility of Postliberal Preaching* (Waco, TX: Baylor University Press, 2013), 144.
36. Thomas G. Long, *Preaching From Memory to Hope* (Louisville: Westminster John Knox, 2009), 24. Herein, Long accepts the critique leveled against forms of narrative preaching that have trivialized the gospel in service of making it relevant to human experience. He stands his ground, however, defending narrative as a privileged medium for preaching. Long writes, "At its best the narrative impulse in preaching grows out of a deep sense of the character, shape, and epistemology of the gospel. If preaching is a sacramental meeting place between the church and the word, the hearers of the gospel, then the substance of preaching is shaped by scripture and by human experience under the sign of grace, and both of these aspects call for narration" (25). See also Stephen Farris, *Preaching That Matters: The Bible and Our Lives* (Louisville: Westminster John Knox, 1997), 24: "there is a spoken or unspoken analogy between something in or behind the text and something in the contemporary world. Preachers of biblical texts must always make or suggest connections of relevance to the lives of their hearers."

work takes place at the intersection of biblical meaning-making and congregational experience: the locus of preaching-as-witness. In one of his earlier books, Long puts it this way:

> The preacher's task is not to *replicate* the biblical text but to *regenerate* the impact of some portion of that text. In this sense the biblical text is like a stone tossed into a pond. The immediate impact is felt where it falls—the historical situation into which it originally landed—this impact creates ripples which flow in time across the surface. As the ripples move away from the center in ever-expanding circles, their motion is impelled by the original events of the text, but their shape is altered as they strike objects in the water and blend with other waves. The task of preaching is not merely to recover the text's original breaking of the surface but to express what happens when one of the ripples sent forth by that text crosses our spot in the pond.[37]

Likewise, Pape affirms the centrality of the Bible's capacity for *interaction*, which arises most acutely in the form of story. He writes that "narrative succeeds in moving along the conversation about what it means to be human in time because it neither unilaterally constructs, nor completely absorbs, nor sluggishly reflects, nor irresponsibly escapes the real world of our doing and suffering; it interacts with it."[38] Stories are not something we add to our preaching to make it more entertaining or compelling; narrative is a privileged biblical *and* experiential medium.

At work behind both Long's and Pape's homiletics is the hermeneutical philosophy of Paul Ricoeur.[39] Following Ricoeur's mimetic theory, Long avers, "In biblical exegesis for preaching, instead of searching for obvious analogies between the text and the contemporary context, or drawing 'lessons' from the text, the preacher-exegete seeks to chart the arc of divine action in the text."[40] For Long, preaching is not about submitting to scriptural authority at the expense of the authority of

---

37. Thomas G. Long, *Preaching and the Literary Forms of the Bible* (Philadelphia: Fortress Press, 1988), 127.

38. Pape, *Scandal of Having Something to Say*, 105.

39. See Jacob D. Myers, "Preaching Philosophy: The Kerygmatic Thrust of Paul Ricoeur's Philosophy and its Contribution to Homiletics," *Literature and Theology* 27, no. 2 (May 2013): 208–26.

40. Long, *Preaching From Memory to Hope*, 50. As he puts it elsewhere, "In the end, I agree with many of those who say that preaching today is malnourished biblically, theologically, and didactically, but the real dilemma, I would argue lies elsewhere. Getting right to the point: the main problem with much of today's preaching is that it is simply not newsworthy. . . . What is often lacking from our proclamation of the 'good news' is a deep sense of the gospel itself as 'news.'" Thomas G. Long, "No News is Bad News," in *What's the Matter with Preaching Today?* ed. Mike Graves (Louisville: Westminster John Knox, 2004), 149. To clarify, Long is writing of "news" in the theological sense: "preaching is about something that God has done."

lived-experience; but neither does he espouse an equivocatory view. He commends scripture as a starting point for preaching because he regards much of scripture already to be oriented toward our lived experiences. He notes, "Often the biblical text itself can provide a pattern for shaping the sermon, since texts are themselves fashioned in such a way as to make their claims heard."[41]

In a similar way, Pape argues that the purpose of preaching is "to join the preacher's own voice to the text's work of displaying a particular world."[42] This focus on a *world*, which Pape situates *in front of the text* (à la Ricoeur), is the true referent of biblical preaching. Scripture projects a textual world, which is the site of God's "Word." That is why, for Long, preachers must not "filter out" congregational realities. "The whole aim of a preacher's study of a biblical text," Long argues, "is to hear in that text a specific word for us, and who 'we' happen to be at this moment makes a considerable difference in how the preacher approaches the text."[43] At base, figurative economies value the Bible's capacity to mirror and then reconfigure reality.

Cathartic Economies of Scripture

Cathartic economies of scripture stress the psychological impact of sermons. This homiletical approach aims to help preachers engage scripture with an eye to emotional and intellectual *release*. Accordingly, life's woes set the stage on which the "homiletical plot" might unfold, to which the good news revealed in scripture provides the denouement. As Eugene Lowry argues, all sermons ought to create a "homiletical bind," a sensed discrepancy between the world of our collective experience and the world borne out of scripture. Lowry writes, "The question of the human condition is, I believe, the most fundamental and consequential question of all." Thus, "The particularized problem, discrepancy, or bind provides the problem of every sermon. It constitutes the central ambiguity the sermon seeks to resolve. The analysis of that discrepancy determines the entire shape of the sermon, including the form of the good news proclaimed."[44] In other words, the problems of life create an "itch" that only the gospel can "scratch."

41. Thomas G. Long, "Shaping Sermons by Plotting the Text's Claim Upon Us," in *Preaching Biblically: Creating Sermons in the Shape of Scripture*, ed. Don M. Wardlaw (Philadelphia: Westminster, 1983), 90.
42. Pape, *Scandal of Having Something to Say*, 118.
43. Thomas G. Long, *The Witness of Preaching*, 3rd ed. (Louisville: Westminster John Knox, 2016), 77.
44. Eugene Lowry, *The Homiletical Plot: The Sermon as Narrated Art Form*, exp. ed. (Louisville: Westminster John Knox, 2001), 40–41.

In his seminal text, *Black Preaching*, Henry Mitchell writes, "No matter how creative or inventive Black preachers may be, in the culture of the Black church they must appear to exercise their freedom within the limits of that vast and profound reservoir of truth called the Bible."[45] For Mitchell, scripture is an "inexhaustible source" for preaching, but exposition is not the end goal of preaching. The purpose of preaching is an "*experience* of the Word, which plants the Word deep in human consciousness."[46] Mitchell's protégé, Frank Thomas, also proceeds out of an experiential orientation to sermon preparation that looks to the point at which a biblical text may enliven congregational consciousness. This theological conviction arises out of an understanding of preaching as an experiential "text-event" that is transformative—both emotionally and intellectual.[47]

For "celebration style" homileticians like Mitchell and Thomas, biblical value and its circulation via preaching hold scripture and experience in creative tension. Thomas illustrates this homiletic in stressing the importance of sermonic language to draw congregants into an experience with scripture:

> When people become a part of and invest in the sermon, they move more easily at the level of emotional process and experience the gospel more deeply and profoundly. In the classical rationalistic deductive method, it was as if the minister had come down from Mt. Sinai with a message from God, while the people waited passively for the revelation. But when dialogical language is used effectively, the people and the minister go up to the mountain of God *together* and encounter the word of God. If we are concerned about emotional process, we must use language that includes people.[48]

I hasten to add that even as creating a cathartic experience of the "Word" is the *telos* of this iteration of Black preaching, such collaborates with scholarly inquiry and elucidation. Mitchel makes a strong

---

45. Henry H. Mitchell, *Black Preaching: The Recovery of a Powerful Art* (Nashville: Abingdon, 1990), 56. Note that Mitchell distances this core conviction from bibliolatry and inerrancy, rejecting religious truth as either science or history (57).

46. Ibid., 59. See also David Buttrick, *Homiletic: Moves and Structures* (Philadelphia: Fortress Press, 1987).

47. Thomas writes, "Experiential orientation in the preparation means that we prepare the sermon from the cognitive, emotive, and intuitive aspects of human awareness. . . . Exegesis and rational inquiry are absolutely essential to quality preaching, but when exegesis is opened to include the emotive and intuitive, the preacher is able to generate images that shape and order experience." Frank Thomas, *They Like to Never Quit Praisin' God*, rev. and exp. ed. (Cleveland: Pilgrim, 2013), 84. When it comes to engaging texts, Thomas advocates a certain "homiletical exegesis," which situates biblical meaning in the "existential human condition of suffering" (89).

48. Thomas, *They Like to Never Quit Praisin' God*, 23.

case for engaging biblical scholarship, but not as an end it itself. He encourages the use of scholarship as "a small part of a much broader use of imagination to put flesh on the often skeletal narratives of the Bible—to breathe life into both the story and the truth it teaches." The end of historical and theological scholarship is to allow the hearer to be "caught up in the experience being narrated," which leads to deeper understanding and application in one's life.[49]

Cathartic preaching in the Black homiletic tradition necessitates a biblical approach that is ever aware of the experiences of African Americans. Here is where Luke Powery's work is particularly instructive. In his books *Spirit Speech* and *Dem Dry Bones*, Powery helps preachers better attend to the pervasive realities of suffering and pain—experienced most poignantly in African-American communities but extending to all church traditions and peoples. While affirming the importance of celebration for its cathartic qualities, Powery proffers lament as an alternative "depth expression," a "homiletical posture" that fosters individual and communal experiences of grace, unity, and fellowship.[50]

Lament and celebration are not actually alternatives; rather, they are two sides of the same homiletical coin. For Powery, lament is the proper "foundation" for celebration, and its homiletical method is that of *naming* human realities of pain and suffering concretely. He writes, "In preaching lament, one does not back away from dealing with tough issues in the 'light of day' but names them directly and firmly within the listening community."[51] "Spirit speech," Powery, Mitchell, and Thomas concur, must do more than merely name these insidious realities. Powery argues, "Expressions of lament go beyond mere description of the trouble to an attempt to move all hearers to experience the immensity of trouble and lament such that the voice of lament becomes their own."[52] Rhetoric *generates* the "deep feeling" that Powery identifies with the Spirit; this does not, however, preclude the Spirit's agency through scripture:

49. Mitchell, *Black Preaching*, 63.
50. Luke A. Powery, *Spirit Speech: Lament and Celebration in Preaching* (Nashville: Abingdon, 2009), xv.
51. Ibid., 119, 120. Or, as he puts it elsewhere, "One needs sermons fueled and powered by the Holy Spirit to create life and destroy death. . . . Death may be successful at times, causing sermons to die before they even reach the ears and hearts of the listeners due to the fear of preachers. However, reimagining preaching through the lens of Ezekiel and the valley of dry bones may help preachers face death with more courage, just like those musical sermons, the African American spirituals." Powery, *Dem Dry Bones*, 19–20.
52. Powery, *Spirit Speech*, 122.

Despite the ambivalent relationship between black peoples and the Bible historically, the Bible plays an important role in the ministry of preaching, as the spirituals demonstrate. Spiritual preaching necessitates conversation with Scripture, even if one eventually closes it as did the old-time preachers. . . . A preacher *wrestles* with the biblical text until God pours out a blessing. . . . Once a preacher *encounters* Scripture, the question becomes, "What will I do with it?" and "How will I read it for preaching hope?"[53]

Powery advances a "hermeneutic of hope" that seeks in scripture a cathartic and life-giving word for those living under the shadow of death.

Thomas asserts much the same thing, writing that "the persuasive task of the African American preacher is to interest their hearers and speak to the basic reality that the daily existence of black people must be lived in an often hostile world dominated by structures of white supremacy. . . ."[54] Or, as he puts it elsewhere, "If you are traveling north on the street of life, and God stops you with a sermon idea, take the idea and keep traveling north until you intersect the street of the biblical text." Likewise, he suggests that "if you are traveling east on the street of the biblical text (perhaps in the lectionary), and God stops you with a text, take it, and keep traveling east until you intersect the street of life." Thomas concludes: "*Sermons that order and shape experience only happen at the intersection of the streets of life and the biblical text.*"[55] Mitchell, too, declares, "Black illustrations [from scripture] tend to stick very close to the gut issues of life and death, of struggle and frustration. And Black preachers tend to illustrate passages already chosen from the Bible on the basis of the same criteria."[56]

Black preaching that aims at emotional and epistemological catharsis engages scripture in such a way that the "Word" at work within scripture resonates in congregational consciousness. Always there is a homiletical intentionality "beyond the teller to the Source of the message—to God's will for the worshiper."[57] For homileticians as diverse as Lowry, Mitchell, Thomas, and Powery, the hermeneutical economy that drives their homiletics is the same. Scripture's value is weighed against the epistemological realities of their respective communities.

53. Powery, *Dem Dry Bones*, 112. Emphasis added.
54. Frank A. Thomas, *Introduction to the Practice of African American Preaching* (Nashville: Abingdon, 2016), 25.
55. Thomas, *They Like to Never Quit Praisin' God*, 85.
56. Mitchell, *Black Preaching*, 67.
57. Ibid., 70.

The Bible, they contend, ought to be employed to alleviate the pain of alienation, estrangement, marginalization, and oppression, which congregants experience in their lives. "Good" or "effective" preaching within this economy is measured by impact: catharsis.[58]

Existential Economies of Scripture

Existential economies of scripture are those that read the Bible with an eye toward *authenticity*, which is communal as well as individual. I stress community here for two reasons. First, as David Buttrick observes, existential concerns have tended in North America to dissipate into a vapid individualism content to focus on "the existential self in psychological self-awareness." To this, Buttrick counters, "Of course, the problem is that the Bible is not addressed to selves in their isolated self-awareness. The Bible does not resonate with pool-gazing Narcissus, as much as it addresses a being-saved community in the world. The true hermeneutic of scripture is ultimately *social*."[59]

Second, even Søren Kierkegaard, the "Father of Existentialism," stressed community as the site of existence:

> In community the individual *is*; dialectically, the individual is crucial as the prior condition for forming community, and within the community the individual is qualitatively essential and can at any moment rise above 'community,' that is, as soon as 'the others' give up the idea. What holds community together is that each is an individual, and then the idea. . . . In community the single individual is the microcosm who qualitatively repeats the macrocosm; here it is a case of *unum noris omnes* in the good sense.[60]

Accordingly, as communities of faith differ, they offer different lenses to their users. There are three communities that operate out of such an economy that I shall treat here: African-American communities, Latino/a communities, and Anglo-American communities.

In his book *The Heart of Black Preaching*, Cleophus LaRue commends an

58. Or, as Powery puts it, "The imagined ends of preaching shape the means [of biblical interpretation]." *Dem Dry Bones*, 112.
59. David Buttrick, *A Captive Voice: The Liberation of Preaching* (Louisville: Westminster John Knox, 1994), 13–14. So too, Fred Craddock, *Preaching* (Nashville: Abingdon, 1985), 27: "the Scriptures, by keeping sentinel watch over the life and faith of the church, blow the whistle on lengthy exercises in self-analysis and self-saving, move the chairs out of the small circle, and scatter moods of self-pity or self-congratulation. Sermons that are self-serving are called into question by the very texts which had been selected to authenticate the message."
60. Søren Kierkegaard, "The Difference Between 'Crowd,' 'Public' — And 'Community,'" in *Papers and Journals: A Selection*, trans. Alastair Hannay (London: Penguin Books, 1996), 465.

existential economy of scripture. He argues that it is neither the creative use of language, nor the emotive capacities of Black preaching that give it its distinctiveness. For LaRue, what is central is the "vital interpretive encounter," wherein one finds in the Bible stories about a God who reveals Godself to be "a God of infinite power who could be trusted to act mightily on their behalf."[61] Scripture bears witness to a God who acts in history to emancipate those on the margins of society. Thus, he argues that African Americans possess a "common master lens" by which to see "a sovereign God acting mightily on behalf of the oppressed."[62] This master lens does not reduce God to one mode of engagement with God's people. LaRue names five "domains" of Black experience and commends an "integral dynamic" capable of seeing God's intervention beyond either pastoral myopia or hermeneutical reductionism.

LaRue writes, "A black homiletic . . . must seek to bring greater clarity to one's understanding of how God and scripture have historically been perceived in the community of the marginalized and powerless, for it is this community that gives formation and shape to the black preacher's identity and proclamation."[63] More forcefully, Teresa Fry Brown advances a homiletic that employs scripture to challenge the ecclesial and societal marginalization of African-American women. She writes, "Use of the Bible solidifies theological grounds for the struggle against injustice. . . . The preacher takes the words of Holy Scripture and makes new theological formulations that provide hope for those who have not attained justice."[64] Her work seeks to extricate such women from "sorrow's kitchen," finding in scripture the ideological and practical means—not of catharsis, per se—but of existential freedom and liberation.

Pablo Jiménez argues that the "true key" to biblical appropriation for preaching is in the "correlation between the social location of the Bible and the social location of the Latino people."[65] Accordingly,

61. Cleophus J. LaRue, *The Heart of Black Preaching* (Louisville: Westminster John Knox, 1999), 2. For LaRue, the "encounter" transcends chatharsis. See his *Rethinking Celebration: From Rhetoric to Praise in African American Preaching* (Louisville: Westminster John Knox, 2016): "A sermon that always ends in celebration (emotional rejoicing) can become a mere whistling past the graveyard or, even worse, the celebration of our captivity to a homiletic gone astray" (26).
62. LaRue, *The Heart of Black Preaching*, 20.
63. Ibid., 122.
64. Teresa L. Fry Brown, "An African American Woman's Perspective: Renovating Sorrow's Kitchen," in *Preaching Justice: Ethnic and Cultural Perspectives*, ed. Christine M. Smith (Eugene, OR: Wipf & Stock, 2008), 47, 48-9. See also Brown, *Can A Sistah Get A Little Help?: Encouragement for Black Women in Ministry* (Cleveland: Pilgrim, 2008) and *Weary Throats and New Songs: Black Women Proclaiming God's Word* (Nashville: Abingdon, 2003).

Jiménez argues for two paradigmatic interventions for Latino/a biblical exchange: marginalization as the site of intervention and *mestizaje* as the condition of being. The former signifies the social location of the Latino/a interpreter; the latter points to the miscegenation between the Spanish conquistadores and the Native peoples, whose offspring were called *mestizos*. Here, however, it is clear that individual/communal existence governs the preacher's approach to scripture and utilization thereof.

From an Anglo context, existential economies of scripture aim to "lure" listeners into new ways of thinking, to "effect a new hearing of the word among those who have been repeatedly exposed to it."[66] Here Fred Craddock is in a league of his own. In his field-shifting *As One Without Authority*, he unabashedly grounds biblical interpretation for preaching in existential theology. He rejects the bifurcation of the "Word of God" into an objective, textual component and a subjective, listener component. He writes, "Of course, Christ is significant *extra nos*, but that significance is in his disclosure of himself to us."[67]

Existential economies of scripture equally value individual-congregational authenticity and God's revealed concern for the same. Accordingly, those who share this theological orientation advance a homiletical approach that aims to set scripture and lived experience along the same vector. Such is not a matter of forcing the text to the velocity and trajectory of lived experience, nor does it ignore those aspects of daily living that are out of sync with biblical precepts. Rather, this economy circulates by articulating a "point of contact" between them.[68]

---

65. Pablo A. Jiménez, "The Bible as *Púlpito*," in *Púlpito: An Introduction to Hispanic Preaching*, eds. Justo L. González and Pablo A. Jiménez (Nashville: Abingdon, 2005), 46. Likewise, in his *Santa Biblia: The Bible Through Hispanic Eyes* (Nashville: Abingdon, 1995), Justo L. González writes that "rather than trying to offer a single perspective or a single clue to a 'reading with Hispanic eyes,' I have decided to organize what follows around five paradigms or perspectives that Latinos employ when reading both the Bible and their own situation" (32). These are marginality, poverty, *mestizaje/mulatez*, exile, and solidarity.

66. Fred B. Craddock, "Inductive Preaching Renewed," in *The Renewed Homiletic*, ed. O. Wesley Allen Jr. (Minneapolis: Fortress Press, 2010), 46; Craddock, *Overhearing the Gospel*, rev. and exp. ed. (St. Louis: Chalice, 2002), 11.

67. Fred B. Craddock, *As One Without Authority*, rev. ed. (St. Louis: Chalice, 2001), 58. He continues, "If the biblical text or the Word of God is objective and the human hearer is subjective, obviously the human is secondary, for the Word is the Word even if spoken into an empty room or into the wind. But that is a contradiction of what a word is. Whether one views word as call (Buber), event (Heidegger), or engagement (Sartre), at least two persons are essential to the transaction, and neither is secondary."

68. "Sermons that move inductively, sustaining interest and engaging the listener do not have points any more than a narrative, a story, a parable, or even a joke has points. But there is a point, and the discipline of this one idea is creative in preparation, in delivery, and in reception of the message." Ibid., 81.

Mimetic Economies of Scripture

Mimetic economies of scripture arise out of the cultural-linguistic philosophical assumptions forwarded by postliberal theology. The arguments this "school" of homiletics advances ramify under the presupposition that scripture establishes not only *what* we should preach but also *how* we should preach. Preachers are to imitate (*mimesthei*) Jesus, these scholars argue, and that means attending closely to the personage of Jesus rendered in scripture.

Such is displayed most cogently in the work of Charles Campbell, Richard Lischer, William Willimon, and Michael Pasquarello III.[69] For these scholars, scripture establishes a particular—even "peculiar" or "odd"—orientation between preaching and the world. They are less concerned with launching propositional excavations of scripture or exploring existential biblical insights that might map onto congregational concerns. Mimetic economies of scripture value the "ascriptive logic" of scripture; that is, they seek to understand an identity (of God) *rendered* by the biblical narratives.[70]

Charles Campbell, who is the most passionate and persuasive proponent of postliberal homiletics, defends his proposal on the assumption that scripture reveals its ultimate value in *rendering* a particular character, namely, Jesus Christ.[71] There is a "foolishness" embraced by

69. Consider Michael Pasquarello III, *Christian Preaching: A Trinitarian Theology of Proclamation* (Grand Rapids, MI: Baker Academic, 2006): "Because words draw their meaning from the company they keep, it is necessary that we recover the primacy of preaching as a theological practice that participates in the scripturally and ecclesially mediated character of truth communicated in Christ, the One of whom we speak" (42) and "As canon, Scripture norms Christian witness as scriptural or evangelical, enabling us to judge whether or not human speech participates in God's self-communicative Word enacted definitely in Jesus Christ" (140).
70. Following the work of Hans Frei, Campbell urges us to follow the "ascriptive logic" of the scriptures. He writes, "According to Frei, the logic of the [Gospel] stories is 'ascriptive,' rather than descriptive. That is, the focus of the stories is the person of Jesus, to whose unique, unsubstitutable person the various titles, characteristics and actions are ascribed. The ascriptive subject, Jesus of Nazareth, is primary, rather than the particular predicates used to describe him." Charles L. Campbell, *Preaching Jesus: New Directions for Homiletics in Hans Frei's Postliberal Theology* (Grand Rapids, MI: Eerdmans, 1997), 39.
71. Ibid., 200. This emphasis on *rendering identity* is central to Campbell's homiletic. It is difficult to tell to what degree, if any, Campbell's thinking has shifted in his later work. In Campbell's *Preaching Fools: The Gospel as a Rhetoric of Folly* (Waco, TX: Baylor University Press, 2012), which he co-wrote with Johan H. Cilliers, we read that "God has already invaded and changed the world through the cross and resurrection. Foolish preaching simply seeks to create the space where new perception becomes possible" (38). Cf. "When the liminality creates its own form of iron philosophy, it develops a theology that gladly speaks about God's omnipotence—often understood as God-with-us—but that ironically struggles to understand this God-with-us in terms of compassion and weakness. An iron theology resists the movement from form to re-form, because it is set in stone; it fails to fathom the reality of fragmentation, because it professes totality and finality; it circles the wagons, because others might endanger this theology's grasp on truth" (65).

this homiletic inasmuch as it runs counter to the "ways of the world."
Campbell explains,

> Like Jesus, who embodied the reign of God and challenged the powers of
> the world, but refused to use violence or coercion in that effort, so the
> preacher, always at a distance, is engaged in this same nonviolent resis-
> tance to the powers in his or her preaching. Not only is the preacher's *mes-
> sage* shaped by the story of Jesus . . . but the very *act* of preaching itself is a
> performance of Scripture, an embodiment of God's reign after the pattern
> of Jesus. The preacher witnesses bodily, announcing the coming of God's
> reign in Jesus Christ and challenging the powers of the world that oppose
> God's way.[72]

We see here not only a valuation of scripture (viz., in rendering a personage, Jesus), but we also witness a mode of circulation (viz., non-
violent resistance). The great strength to this homiletic resides in its
internal consistency: the *how much* (valuation) of scripture informs the
how (circulation) of scripture in and through preaching. These are not
separate elements.

Campbell argues that biblical interpretation for preaching is less
about gleaning meaning from the text or translating the text into contemporary contexts. "The significant thing for the preacher," he contends, "is not Jesus as a model preacher, but rather the identity of Jesus
rendered in the gospels, which provides the pattern for the life of dis-
cipleship."[73] The story of Jesus *shapes* sermonic content and form, but
it also *directs* preachers to see the ecclesial realities of which preaching
is a part.[74] Or, as Willimon puts it, "Our main task is not to be entertaining, or interesting, or thoughtful in our preaching. . . . the *telos*, the end
result of our preaching, that which Jesus intends to do for the world, is
church." This "intrusive word," this "incursion" that challenges thinking and being in the world, structures sermonic production.[75] It gives

72. Campbell, *Preaching Jesus*, 216. Cf. David L. Bartlett, *Between the Church and the Bible: New Methods for
Biblical Preaching* (Nashville: Abingdon, 1999), 164: "What the text says is not as important as whom
the text presents, or re-resents, or entices us to love, or invites us to question, or hides from us
until another day."
73. Campbell, *Preaching Jesus*, 212. So also Michael Pasquarello III, *Sacred Rhetoric: Preaching as a Theological and Pastoral Practice of the Church* (Grand Rapids, MI: Eerdmans, 2005), 135: "Modern strategies that substitute convictions and forms of speech less truthful than the language and claims of
the Gospel have inevitably resulted in a muteness of the church, leaving us with nothing distinctive to say, since there is no way to say it."
74. Ibid., 220. Emphasis added.
75. William H. Willimon, *The Intrusive Word: Preaching to the Unbaptized* (Grand Rapids: Eerdmans,
1994), 129, 97. On the motif of incursion, see also the excellent book by Brian K. Blount, *Invasion of
the Dead: Preaching Resurrection* (Louisville: Westminster John Knox, 2014), 84.

preaching a vocabulary and a grammar, it structures its own (ecclesial) "language game."

In his incisive book *Christian Preaching: A Trinitarian Theology of Proclamation*, Michael Pasquarello III challenges homiletical trends that operate as "popular, pragmatic preaching," that is, those that assess their "primary market value" according to their individualistic and communal utility. In its place, Pasquarello values a "Trinitarian vision of practice by which our thoughts, words, and lives may be more carefully weighed and made true to the One of whom we speak and more fitting for the people God calls to reflect his [*sic*] glory in the form of Christ crucified and risen—'the Word made flesh.'"[76] This economy is mimetic in as much as it provides a standard for *weighing* our words and it presses us to *reflect* a cruciform homiletical style. Accordingly, Richard Lischer contends that if preaching fails to receive its "proper grounding" in the words and ways of God reveled in scripture, sermons can function merely as "a projection of the speaker's personality or as the fabricator of religious consciousness."[77] Preaching, along with church, ought to imitate God's self-revealed way of being in Jesus Christ. The value of scripture is that, without it, we would have nothing after which to model our lives.

Poietic Economies of Scripture

Poietic economies of scripture do not abide by imitation alone but are just as concerned with the performative aspects of the Bible. Such value scripture according to its *disjunctive* capacities, that is, its ability to unsettle the business-as-usual, laissez-faire mentality exhibited by far too many churchgoers. Accordingly, the task of preaching is "to enable the church to discern the world anew according to the script of the Bible," and thus preachers are at their best when they accept the "decentering Word" of the biblical text.[78] Or, as Walter Brueggemann puts it elsewhere,

> The task and possibility of preaching is to open out the good news of the gospel with alternative modes of speech—speech that is dramatic, artis-

76. Pasquarello III, *Christian Preaching*, 9–10.
77. Richard Lischer, *A Theology of Preaching: The Dynamics of the Gospel*, rev. ed. (Eugene, OR: Wipf & Stock, 2001), x. Cf. Walter J. Burghardt, SJ, "Preaching, Role of," in *The New Dictionary of Catholic Social Thought*, ed. Judith A. Dwyer (Collegeville, MN: Liturgical Press, 1994), 779: "the pulpit . . . is the place to *raise* the issues, to raise awareness, to raise consciousness."
78. Walter Brueggemann, *The Word Militant: Preaching a Decentering Word* (Minneapolis: Fortress Press, 2007), 74–75.

tic, capable of inviting persons to join in another conversation, free of the reason of technique, unencumbered by ontologies that grow abstract, unembarrassed about concreteness. Such speech, when heard in freedom, assaults imagination and pushes out the presumed world in which most of us are trapped. Reduced speech leads to reduced lives.[79]

In short, preaching ought to value biblical language highly because the latter's alternative mode of speech *already* affects the change that preaching wishes to make manifest.

On account of our all-too-human tendency to supplant the "Word" of God with a word of avarice in a world of violence, Brueggemann argues that preaching is a kind of "sub-version."[80] He explains, "In my judgment, interpretation that can authorize and evoke transformation must always be quite text-specific, even if a thematization hovers in the background. Such specificity is required because that from which transformation is sought is also, in my judgment, characteristically rooted in quite specific 'text-scripts.'"[81] God has elected scripture, which is anything but laissez-faire, to challenge the status quo.

Significant overlap manifests between poietic and mimetic economies of scripture—in fact, Campbell dedicates an entire section of *Preaching Jesus* to Brueggemann's work. Where the two economies differ is in their focus on language for preaching. Within a poietic economy, scripture's capacity *to do* (*poiéō*) things, *to act* upon and against congregational epistemologies, is valued most highly. Texts circulate within this homiletical economy inasmuch as the preacher unleashes the Bible's *innate* prophetic and po(i)etic capacities. Preaching "evokes" and "discloses" the texts's alternative ways of thinking and being.[82]

For poietic biblical economies, circulation and value arise at the intersection of lived-experience and biblical signification. This inter-

79. Walter Brueggemann, *Finally Comes the Poet: Daring Speech for Proclamation* (Minneapolis: Augsburg Fortress Press, 1989), 3.
80. Brueggemann, *The Word Militant*, 151–52. See Charles L. Campbell, *The Word Before the Powers: An Ethic of Preaching* (Louisville: Westminster John Knox, 2002). Mary Donovan Turner also employs the language of disruption, but grounds it in lived experience. See Mary Donovan Turner, "Disrupting a Ruptured World," 131–40, esp. pp. 135–36. See also Karoline M. Lewis, *John*, Fortress Biblical Preaching Commentaries (Minneapolis: Fortress Press, 2014), xiii: "too much of our preaching is beholden to denominational commitments and obliged to theological constraints that preference dogma and getting the right answer over an event of the Word."
81. Walter Brueggemann, *Texts Under Negotiation: The Bible and Postmodern Imagination* (Minneapolis: Fortress Press, 1993), ix. Nancy Lammers Gross, *If You Cannot Preach Like Paul...* (Grand Rapids, MI: Eerdmans, 2002), 91: "Biblical preaching, therefore, always involves an encounter with a biblical text."
82. Brueggemann, *Finally Comes the Poet*, 9.

section is a point of *disjunction* rather than capitulation or accommo-dation. Roman Catholic homiletician Robert Waznak SS laments that the history of preaching is marred by instances that have "robbed the homily of its prophetic quality," and he urgues us "to detect and resist such similar forces in our time that threaten the prophetic character of the homily." Later he doubles down on this prophetic emphasis, writ-ing in defense of a "strong poetic and prophetic voice that helps to unravel our thoughts and penetrate our hearts so that the gospel can be heard again."[83] Similarly, Brueggemann argues that disjunction is at once "the engine that drives Israel's testimony . . . and the source of the deep vexation that marks Israel's life."[84] Preaching in this vein carries forward this vexation.

Preaching, within a poietic economy of scripture is "an act whereby we are invited and incorporated into an alternative dream about how the world will finally be." Accordingly, the preacher's central task in such an economy is to "establish a fresh universe of discourse in which faithful conversation is possible."[85] In short, preachers ought to *do* (*poieō*) the text in the sermon.

Dialogical Economies of Scripture

Dialogical economies of scripture arise out of insights advanced by revisionary theologians like Paul Tillich, Karl Rahner, and Edward Schillebeeckx. These value scripture as a crucial conversation partner for contemporary persons (alongside historical creeds, doctrines, and practices) in dialogue with worldly perspectives. Accordingly, Ronald Allen wants preaching to begin with the listener in mind and holds that scripture enters the kerygmatic economy when it is a partner in a "mutually critical conversation" oriented to the good news of God's love and justice.[86]

---

83. Robert P. Waznak, SS, *An Introduction to the Homily* (Collegeville, MN: Liturgical, 1998), 26, 67.

84. Walter Brueggemann, *Theology Of The Old Testament: Testimony, Dispute, Advocacy* (Minneapolis: Augsburg Fortress Press, 1997), 268. In his recently published anthology of Brueggemann's writ-ings, Davis Hankins aptly notes that "Brueggemann delights in showing how the utterance of a condition that is unsayable or inconceivable within the dominant social rationality can generate a truth that can be affirmed only by breaking with existing social languages." Davis Hankins, intro-duction to *Ice Axes for Frozen Seas: A Biblical Theology of Provocation*, by Walter Brueggemann, ed. Davis Hankins (Waco, TX: Baylor University Press, 2014), 9.

85. Brueggemann, *Finally Comes the Poet*, 85.

86. See John McClure et al, *Listening to Listeners: Homiletical Case Studies* (St. Louis: Chalice, 2004); Ronald J. Allen, *Hearing the Sermon: Relationship, Content, Feeling* (St. Louis: Chalice, 2004); Mary Alice Mul-ligan and Ronald J. Allen, *Make the Word Come Alive: Lessons from Laity* (St. Louis: Chalice, 2005). As Allen puts it elsewhere, "In my view, the *revisionary* theological movement with its *preaching by means of mutual critical correlation* is the most satisfactory approach because it seeks to make a wit-

For Allen, scripture is important to the degree that it *signifies* the gospel. He maintains that not everything in scripture bears witness to God's love and justice; accordingly, the preaching "conversation" must construe itself as good news for its hearers, be intelligible to the congregation, and be morally plausible.[87] In his introductory preaching textbook, Allen explains, "The correlation is mutual and critical. It is mutual because it presumes that both Christian tradition and contemporaneity can inform and critique one another. It is critical because the Christian tradition criticizes the contemporary setting, even while aspects of today's community criticize the claims, behaviors, and world view of the tradition."[88]

Roman Catholic homiletician Mary Catherine Hilkert advances an alternative form of the dialogical economy. In her book *Naming Grace*, Hilkert juxtaposes the dominant Protestant theology of revelation and proclamation as articulated by the "dialectical imaginations" of Karl Barth and Rudolph Bultmann with the "sacramental imaginations" emerging from the theologies of Karl Rahner and Edward Schillebeeckx. The "dialectical imagination," she argues, stresses the distance of God from humanity, the hiddenness of God, the depth of the postlapsarian condition, the paradox of the cross, the need for grace as redemption and reconciliation and the future-oriented reign of God. By contrast, Hilkert presents a dialogical homiletic based on a sacramental understanding, that emphasizes the mystery of the incarnation, grace as divinizing as well as forgiving, the presence of God as self-communicating love, the creation of humans in the image of God, the mediating role of the Church for salvation, and a present-oriented reign of justice, peace, and love.

For Hilkert, scripture bolsters the dialogical homiletical economy by drawing the listeners into deeper conversation with the world: the site of divine revelation of which scripture is a part. The goal of her

ness that is recognizably Christian and that is intellectually and morally credible in the contemporary world." Ronald J. Allen, *Interpreting the Gospel: An Introduction to Preaching* (St. Louis: Chalice, 1998), 73–74, and Allen, *Preaching is Believing: The Sermon as Theological Reflection* (Louisville: Westminster John Knox, 2002), 130. See also James R. Nieman and Thomas G. Rogers, *Preaching to Every Pew* (Minneapolis: Fortress Press, 2001); and James H. Harris, *The Word Made Plain: The Power and Promise of Preaching* (Minneapolis: Augsburg Fortress, 2004).

87. Ronald J. Allen, "Preaching as Mutual Critical Correlation through Conversation," in *The Purposes of Preaching*, 1–22. See also Allen, *Sermon Treks: Trailways to Creative Preaching* (Nashville: Abingdon, 2013), 5: "a fundamental purpose of preaching is to help the congregation interpret and respond to the presence and purposes of the living God. A preacher needs to approach the sermon from a starting point that gives the preacher a good chance of generating a conversation with the congregation that will help the community move toward a theologically adequate interpretation of the situation in which the sermon comes to life."

88. Allen, *Interpreting the Gospel*, 74.

homiletical theology is to help preachers *listen* for whispers of God's grace and then to *name* the grace that is evident in the world. She writes,

> The role of the preacher is to bring the depth dimension of the mystery of human existence as God's self-offer of love to explicit expression through interpreting that existence in the light of the scriptures, the liturgy, and the whole of the Christian tradition. Thus preaching draws the hearers of the word into a deeper relationship with God that is at the same time a deeper experience of their everyday human life and relationships as graced.[89]

Pope Francis says something similar: "A preaching which would be purely moralistic or doctrinaire, or one which turns into a lecture on biblical exegesis, detracts from this heart-to-heart communication which takes place in the homily and possesses a quasi-sacramental character."[90] Thus, the value of scripture is its role in deepening communicative engagement.

Another manifestation of this economy stresses dialogue to an even greater degree. Here, the Bible is interpreted—and interrupted—by a community whose diversity opens the text more fully to the lived-experiences of its hearers. Lucy Atkinson Rose and John McClure have led this charge. Rose operates out of a "postmodern" understanding of preaching "that seeks to take seriously [her] and other's alternative experiences of [them]selves in the pulpit and the pew."[91] McClure's "roundtable" homiletic is at once *post-semiotic* and *dialogical*, hence the mode of biblical engagement he advances is "collaborative," attending to diverse receptions of the biblical text among its listeners. He writes that "preaching must be embedded within a living dialogical and rit-ual-performative process in which memory-in-community is created, shaped, and put on display."[92]

More recently, in *Youthful Preaching*, Richard Voelz pushes a dialog-ical economy of scripture even farther in the direction of communica-tive engagement. He rightly argues that few homiletical approaches actually collaborate with youth in a way that takes their lived experi-

89. Mary Catherine Hilkert, *Naming Grace: Preaching and the Sacramental Imagination* (New York: Continuum, 1997), 34.
90. Francis, *Joy of the Bishops*, 75.
91. Lucy Atkinson Rose, "Conversational Preaching: A Proposal," *Journal for Preachers* 19, no. 1 (Advent 1995): 26.
92. John S. McClure, "Collaborative Preaching and the Bible: Toward a Practical Theology of Memory," in *Preaching and the Personal*, 63.

ences seriously. Thus, he presses us to reimagine homiletics as a liberative "public sphere" where meaningful interaction may transpire. Drawing on Jürgen Habermas's philosophy of communicative action, Voelz makes space for mutual critique and dialogue between adults and youth around preaching with an eye toward liberation.[93]

Dialogical economies of scripture value the Bible as a "relatively adequate witness" to the gospel. Accordingly, they maintain that the task of preaching is to bear witness to the good news originating in God in a world suffused with systemic injustice and sinfulness. This is preaching's "ultimate word that the preacher is called to speak."[94] Biblical texts enter preaching because their "discursive and intuitive dimensions [are] analogous" to contemporary contexts.[95]

The Law of the House: Giving Scripture a Break

Economic systems in the sociopolitical realm operate out of a logic of scarcity. Within a given country there are limited resources available for production, sale, and consumption. Few, if any, homileticians mentioned above would affirm a logic of scarcity for preaching. We confess that God gives Godself lavishly, even prodigally, and that preaching is a site of reception for God's self-giving. I believe this. However, when we constrain the value and circulation of scripture in and through preaching *qua* homiletics, I fear that we unwittingly commit ourselves to a logic of scarcity and exchange. A sermon is a gift, if there is any, but only if it is given with a recklessness beyond and unaffected by economic calculation. As Derrida rightly observes in *Given Time*, the "transcendental illusion" of the gift presents an implicit demand that the genuine gift reside outside of the oppositional demands of giving and taking, and beyond any mere self-interest or calculative reasoning.[96] How might homiletics aid preaching to share in God's mode and manner of giving, a mode and manner beyond the laws of valuation and exchange?[97]

93. Richard W. Voelz, *Youthful Preaching: Strengthening the Relationship between Youth, Adults, and Preaching*, Lloyd John Ogilvie Institute of Preaching Series (Eugene, OR: Cascade Books, 2016). See also Voelz, "Silence and Deficiency: Contemporary Pictures of Youth and Preaching," *Encounter* 76, no. 1 (2016): 21–49.

94. Allen, *Interpreting the Gospel*, 81.

95. Ronald J. Allen, "Shaping Sermons by the Language of the Text," in *Preaching Biblically*, 35.

96. Derrida, *Given Time*, 30. So also, "A gift is not signed; it does not calculate even with a time that would do it justice" (171).

97. Stephen Webb's insight is instructive here: Conceding the economic character of gifts in general, he observes that every once in a while we surprise ourselves and others with "excessive giving, [which] understood theologically, has the potential to interrupt and disorient the training all of

Scripture is in trouble for preaching because of how it is valuated and regulated by homiletical theologies. Think about it. Even our insistence on the use of pericopes as the basis for sermons suggests a rationing of scripture.[98] We decide, in advance, out of context, how much scripture our congregants can or should handle. If we follow the lectionary, this decision is already decided.[99] But that does not let us off the hook. If we are serious about opening ourselves, and, through us, the church, to "what dreams may come," we must search for a way to break with these economies and economics as such. We must die to (or let die) systems of exchange that regard scripture as a bank from which to withdraw homiletical currency—no matter how these gospel bucks are invested by different homiletical traditions.

The word *economy* comes from two Greek words: *oikos* and *nomos*, *house* and *law*. Homiletics forces preaching to abide by the *laws* of our respective homiletical *houses*. You may be wondering why we do this. I think that we fall back on our economies of scripture because we are afraid to follow the text beyond our comfort zones. We are afraid to lose—our power, our knowledge, our selfhood. We construct these rules to ensure that our hermeneutical investments yield a kerygmatic return. This is a prototypically "masculine" way to think. One feminist thinker puts it this way:

> In the development of desire, of exchange, he [the prototypical man] is the en-grossing party: loss and expense are stuck in the commercial deal that always turns the gift into a gift-that-takes. The gift brings in a return. Loss, at the end of a curved line, is turned into its opposite and comes back to him as profit.[100]

In other words, recuperation lurks within our gift-giving; we are structurally conditioned to take even as we give. My chief concern here is how this affects our relationships. If I'm always taking something from you in the act of giving you a gift (gratitude, self-satisfaction, a sense of magnanimity, etc.), have I not violated you in some way? Even as you

us receive in economizing our resources that ensures that what we give is equal to what we take." Stephen H. Webb, *The Gifting God: A Trinitarian Ethics of Excess* (New York: Oxford University Press, 1996), 8.

98. See Edward Farley, *Practicing Gospel: Unconventional Thoughts on The Church's Ministry* (Louisville: Westminster John Knox, 2003), 83–92.

99. Cf. Long, *The Witness of Preaching*, 83, whose second step in the text-to-sermon process urges preachers to reconsider where the text begins and ends. Long writes, "We should look, then, with a slightly suspicious eye at the way we—or the commentaries or the lectionaries—have cut our text."

100. Cixous, *The Newly Born Woman*, 87.

appear to be the focus of my giving, is it not really I who have asserted myself over you as the gift-giver? I fear that we preachers can be too much like the boy in Shel Silverstein's classic, *The Giving Tree*. We take and we take, when all that God desires is to be in relationship with us. Of course, we get this on a theological level. But as soon as we approach the biblical text homiletically, we get out our saws and axes and, if we are not careful, only a stump remains. This is why scripture is in trouble.

Section Two: Scripture *as* Trouble

> The very language in which Holy Scripture is woven is accessible to all, though, very, very few penetrate it.
>
> — St. Augustine of Hippo[101]

Homiletical theologies must pursue a path beyond scriptural appropriation and consumption. We must orient ourselves otherwise to the Bible in and through our preaching if we are to move toward the Other at work within and beyond its pages. But how to do this? I cannot offer you a new set of rules. Such would merely replace one economy for another. And, paradoxically, rules are the very things that generate circulation and the very things that restrict movement.

Might we conceive a mode of relationality built upon *giving* rather than *taking*? Not really. We could *pretend* that any approach, any reading (which is always already interpreting) was not at once a kind of taking. But an aporia emerges by this approach.[102] But should that stop us from approaching? By no means! The impossible approach is precisely what drives us to approach in the first place. What I want to ask is how we might go to the Bible in such a way that its otherness remains *other*? Moreover, how might such an approach beyond appropriation lead us to *give* sermons without incurring and invoking debt—the gift's own most impossibility? Can the relationship between giver and receiver escape a mode of exchange that makes debt inevitable, an economy that does not bifurcate subject and object, same and other? Is an *an-eco-nomic* structure possible?

---

101. St. Augustine, "Ep. 137: To Volusian," in *Fathers of the Church*, vol. 3, *Saint Augustine Letters* 131–164, trans. Sister Wilfrid Parsons SND (Washington, DC: Catholic University of America Press, 1953), 20.
102. As Derrida observes, ". . . the very form of your proposition, the 'is' ['*est*'] affiliated with *trying-to-say*, essentializes the text, substantializes it, immobilizes it. . . . Writing does not simply weave several threads into a single term in such a way that one might end up unraveling all the 'contents' just by pulling a few strings." Jacques Derrida, *Dissemination*, trans. Barbara Johnson (Chicago: University of Chicago Press, 1981), 350.

No. There is no an-economic homiletical theology. Every giving, to some extent, is a taking. Every approach encroaches. Every valuation devalues. So what are we to do? Leave our Bibles at the altar of the Lord and join the rest of our culture at Starbucks? That won't work for me, and if you're still reading this book, I'm guessing that it won't work for you, either. Once we come face to face with the impossibility of *giving* a sermon—impossible, that is, without also *taking* from scripture—we are left with several options. The first is to give up, which we've already agreed would be insufficient for us. Let's leave that one to the side—for now, at least.

The second option is the most common, and Karl Barth said it best: "Our difficulty lies in the content of our task. . . . As ministers we ought to speak of God. We are human, however, and so cannot speak of God. We ought therefore to recognize both our obligation and our inability and by that very recognition give God the glory."[103] This realization would eventually lead Barth to double down on a kind of planned economy of scripture, naming his radical dependence on *God's* self-revelation witnessed in the Bible and actualized through preaching *as God's Word.*[104] By this approach, God remains the Subject and the Object of God's "Word" in spite of the fact that humans are doing the preaching. This theo-linguistic problem informs Barth's ban on all points of contact between lived-experience and God's self-revelation.[105]

Another option is to double-down on lived experience, making it the sun around which the elements of preaching revolve. But we already observed in chapter 2 that the identity of the preacher is unstable, and that an anthropocentric homiletic falters before both the theolog-

103. Karl Barth, "The Word of God and the Task of the Ministry," in *The Word of God and the Word of Man,* trans. Douglas Horton (Gloucester, MA: Peter Smith, 1978), 186. Concluding this essay, Barth writes, "The word of God is at once the necessary and the impossible task of the minister. This is my ultimate conclusion. Further than this I have nothing to say" (213).
104. Karl Barth, *The Church Dogmatics,* I/1, ed. G. W. Bromiley and T. F. Torrance, trans. G. W. Bromiley (Edinburgh: T & T Clark, 1975), § 4, p. 93: "From all these angles the actualization of proclamation might still be understood as an external and accidental characterization, as a kind of clothing or enlightening of an event which as such is ultimately still the event of the willing and doing of proclaiming man. . . . It is the miracle of revelation and faith when the misunderstanding does not constantly recur, when proclamation is for us not just human willing and doing characterized in some way but also and primarily and decisively God's own act, when human talk about God is for us not just that, but also and primarily and decisively God's own speech. It is this miracle that in the fourth and innermost circle of our deliberations we have not so much to explain as rather to evaluate as this specific miracle."
105. See Karl Barth, *Homiletics,* trans. Geoffrey W. Bromiley and Donald E. Daniels (Louisville: Westminster John Knox, 1991), 124–25. Angela Dienhart Hancock notes that in the student notes to Barth's *Predigtvorbereitung* we find in the parentheses, "the basic question of whether a person can actually speak to another at all . . . cannot interrupt our presentation of this." Hancock, *Karl Barth's Emergency Homiletic: 1932-1933: A Summons to Prophetic Witness at the Dawn of the Third Reich* (Grand Rapids, MI and Cambridge, UK: Eerdmans, 2013), 287n143.

ical argument and the humanistic argument.[106] And so I want to suggest that another way forward is to pursue a kerygmatic economy that resists valuation and circulation, that is, the "masculine" economy that appropriates otherness, forcing it to comply with the metrics of sameness.

Seeking a Path Beyond Kerygmatic Economy

A few homileticians have mounted a resistance to "masculine" economies of scripture, and it is they who have led us farthest down the way that is no-way (*a-poros*, without-passage).[107] I am deeply indebted to their work; in fact, the book you are now reading would not exist apart from the insights and guidance of Anna Carter Florence's *Preaching as Testimony* and John Mcclure's *Other-wise Preaching*.

In *Preaching as Testimony*, Florence seeks a way to affirm the polyvalence of biblical meaning as it arises out of the reading practices of particular communities, especially marginalized communities. And yet, she stresses that this does not mean that we can make the text say whatever we want it to. Florence laments the tendency to force a confession out of the text, and so she points us toward a mode of biblical engagement beyond domination. This is what preaching *as testimony* gives us: a way of naming what we see in the text from our unique social locations and confessing what we believe about it. Such a noncoercive approach presses against centuries of kerygmatic hermeneutics. In an important essay she makes this case even clearer. She tells us to "put down our swords," our exegetical and hermeneutical machetes that maim and kill the otherness of the text. She writes that

> somewhere along the way, [my students] have picked up the idea that preaching is not about textual exploration and refraction, but about *solving the problem that is the text*. They cannot see it, hear it, feel it, or even wonder about it; they are too worried about solving it. And this stifles them. It keeps them anxious, fretful, and unable to engage in any creative

---

106. Consider Michel Foucault, *The Order of Things: An Archeology of the Human Sciences*, trans. Alan Sheridan (London: Routledge, 1989), xxv: "Strangely enough, man—the study of whom is supposed by the naïve to be the oldest investigation since Socrates—is probably no more than a kind of rift in the order of things, or, in any case, a configuration whose outlines are determined by the new position he has so recently taken up in the field of knowledge."

107. A fine example of this is Phil Snider's Caputo-inspired "homiletic of the event" that challenges David Lose's attempt at a non-foundational homiletic in the latter's *Confessing Jesus Christ: Preaching in a Postmodern World* (Grand Rapids, MI: Eerdmans, 2003). Snider, *Preaching After God: Derrida, Caputo, and the Language of Postmodern Homiletics* (Eugene, OR: Cascade Books, 2012).

conversation with the Word of God that does not immediately yield results.[108]

Florence urges us to take a different tact, one in which we immerse ourselves—or better, allow ourselves to become immersed—in the "deep logic and grace of God." Thus, her approach is less about presence and knowledge than it is about absence and unknowing. "I believe," she confesses, "that such absence sets in motion a hunger that the Spirit moves in to fill."[109] I think she's right.

In *Preaching as Testimony*, her emphasis on subjectivity and social location also resists an anything-goes hermeneutic feared by some. She approaches the limits of economy as she draws upon the work of Mary McClintock Fulkerson, and particularly Fulkerson's metaphor of "graf(ph)ting."

Engraf(ph)ting, as Fulkerson employs it from the world of horticulture, signifies the way in which all readings are *grafted* onto institutional practices (e.g., hermeneutics) that at once precede and nourish further practices (viz., readings).[110] At the same time, the reader writes herself and her particularity *into* texts and practices. Such subjective grafting functions like a *graphton* (which is Greek for *stylus*). In other words, the preacher writes herself into the text; the grapht is also a graft. The semantic polysemy of this neologism graf(ph)t, which was coined by Derrida, tethers the reading/writing binary to that of inserting/extracting. As Fulkerson explains, "A graft is other than the plant, even as it redirects the flow of sap, and depends for its life on the host; it creates a new plant. Similarly a reading is an engraf(ph)ting on a text; it is not a mirror of a text, a repetition or imitation. A reading writes a text anew, stimulates its flow of meaning in new directions."[111] This

---

108. Anna Carter Florence, "Put Away Your Sword! Taking the Torture Out of the Sermon," in *What's the Matter With Preaching Today?*, 96.

109. Ibid., 105.

110. Fulkerson writes, "Just as a plant graft is sustained by the sap-flow of a stronger sapling onto which it is grafted, we academics are engraf(ph)ted onto and therefore sustained by the nourishment of institutional practices. . . . The practice is not innocent of its larger stem, nor can it be simply plucked and moved without alteration—and alteration there must be before the kind of changes that could allow respect for difference, affinity with the 'other' woman, can occur." Mary McClintock Fulkerson, *Changing the Subject: Women's Discourses and Feminist Theology* (Eugene, OR: Wipf & Stock, 2001), 17–18.

111. Ibid., 152. This is not quite right. Derrida would contend that every reading is *precisely* a repetition. Indeed, it is the paradox between necessary repetition in/as language and possible event in/beyond language that structures the impossible as such: "To give up neither the event nor the machine, to subordinate neither one to the other, neither to reduce one to the other: this is perhaps a concern of thinking that has kept a certain number of 'us' working for the last few decades." Jacques Derrida, "Typewriter Ribbon: Limited Ink (2)," in *Without Alibi*, ed. and trans. Peggy Kamuf (Stanford: Stanford University Press, 2002), 74.

sounds great, but it is not quite right. It still leaves the preacher with a bloody scalpel/pen in her hand, having "cut" into the text to forge newness. A certain violence forever marks her writing/cutting.

Florence follows Fulkerson's error in failing to note that the graf(ph)t is not a way around the aporia of scripture reading/sermon writing; rather, it names the aporia as such. It is not the case, as Florence suggests, that a graf(ph)t is a "signal that *something* is *wrong*" with a community's interpretation of a text, that it is "functioning as a roadblock." The graf(ph)t points instead to the fact that *penetration* has always already taken place. As Derrida puts it, "[The text's] active translation has been clandestinely inseminated; it has for a long time been (under)mining the organism and the history of your domestic text."[112] Thus, in spite of her advances, Florence cannot quite leave economics behind. Even as she urges us *to take* liberties with the text in order *to make* liberty with the text, we are still taking, still tethered to the logic of circulation and valuation: the *law* of the *house, eco-nomics.*

John McClure takes us farther. In his groundbreaking text *Other-Wise Preaching,* he argues that "the Bible as scripture does not hold on to itself. It deconstructs even its own revelation, exits its own house . . . in such a way as to place the exegete into a certain proximity to the texts of others."[113] Undecidability and uncertainty are not obstacles to be overcome by clever hermeneutical methods for McClure; instead, they constitute the Bible *as scripture.* Furthermore, the greater the exegete/preacher's proximity to the text *as other,* the greater his/her/their dissolution as exegete/preacher.

The leading conversation partner for McClure in *Other-wise Preaching* is the Jewish philosopher Emmanuel Levinas. With Levinas as his guide, McClure espouses a radical passivity on the part of the preacher in relation to the Bible *as Other.* The preacher becomes one "under erasure," that is, one whose signifying position (as subject, as "I") loses or abdicates his/her/their position of recognizing or understanding the Bible as scripture.[114] The only approach that does not arrest the play of

---

112. Anna Carter Florence, *Preaching as Testimony* (Louisville: Westminster John Knox, 2007), 85; Derrida, *Dissemination,* 357.
113. John S. McClure, *Other-wise Preaching: A Postmodern Ethic for Homiletics* (St. Louis: Chalice, 2001), 20.
114. Ibid., 21. He continues, "This deep centripetal quality of scripture does much to nudge the reader-preacher into a similar erasure-posture *within culture at large and within the church.* This posture is precisely one of position-losing, position-shifting, and ultimately position-erasing/writing/speaking. It is not merely the oddness of the language that makes preachers into readers/writers/speakers who operate under erasure. . . . rather the fact that the Bible as scripture disseminates its now (non-)positions of authorship and reading by differing them, however elliptically, to that which is profoundly otherwise than Being, language and preaching."

the "writerly" text, the only approach that does not radically reduce and thus nullify the Bible's "Saying" in a "Said," is an "other-wise" approach, which would be an-economic.

With McClure, I would suggest that such an erasure, such a death, is the *terminus ad quem* of biblical engagement and the *terminus a quo* of preaching. The problem with McClure's homiletic, however other-wise and other-oriented it may be, is that it turns impossibility into possibility through the metrics of impossibility itself. Let me explain.

For Levinas, the "approach of the other" is *endured* by the subject, who is rendered radically passive.[115] Everything about the preacher may come under erasure save this: her impulse to approach scripture *in order to* take or receive something from scripture for her sermon. McClure speaks of this approach in terms of a "task." He initiates a kind of phenomenological reduction that holds the subject's subjectivity in reserve in order to approach the other that/who is invited to overcome the preacher's subjectivity.[116] The problem here is that this initial *decision*, this *task*, this *beginning*—even if this beginning harbors an "other-wise *commitment*"[117]—cannot submit this constituting gesture to erasure. I sustain my I-ness as the one straining to bracket my I-ness.

There can be no pure, no originary, movement or approach toward the Bible that does not harbor—and retain in its harboring—a secret

<hr/>

115. As Levinas's translator, Alphonso Lingis, explains, "The approach of the other is an initiative I *undergo*. I am *passive* with regard to it—and *even passive in a more pure sense than the sense in which a material substrate receives*, with an equal and opposite reaction, the action impressed on it, and in the sense that the sensibility is passive as a receptivity that synoptically, or syndotically, receives the medley of sensation given to it. Here no form, no capacity preexisted in me to espouse the imperative and make it my own. . . . Not being able to arise by my own forces here is just in what the sense of an appeal made to me, an invocation or a provocation, consists. Not being able to take up the order put to me and appropriate it, and make it into my own principle, is just in what the sense of being contested consists. . . . *One is passive with regard to the approach of alterity, one sustains its impact without being able to assimilate it, one is open to it, exposed in its direction, to its sense, susceptible to being affected, being exalted and being pained.*" Emmanuel Levinas, *Otherwise Than Being, or, Beyond Essence*, trans. Alphonso Lingis (Pittsburgh: Duquesne University Press, 1981), 4–5. Emphasis added.

116. This phenomenological "bracketing" is identified by Husserl as a "putting into action." It is *not* passive. Eugen Fink explains that under Husserl's *epoché or reduction proper*, "The transcendental tendency *awakening in man* [sic] is nothing other than the transcendental onlooker's 'internal *phenomenologizing that is already at work in the projection of motivation.* In that in his action (the universal epoche) the onlooker brings himself out into the open, he is also the *first* transcendental I (and transcendental life) that comes to itself as such. But the coming-to-himself of the phenomenological onlooker only makes possible a *more fundamental* coming-to-oneself: in the cognitive life of the phenomenologizing I transcendental subjectivity comes to itself *as constituting*. In other words, the onlooker is only the *functional exponent* of transcendentally constituting life, an exponent that of course does not itself in turn perform a constituting action but precisely though its *transcendental differentness* makes self-consciousness (becoming-for-oneself) possible for constituting subjectivity." *Sixth Cartesian Meditation: The Idea of a Transcendental Theory of Method*, trans. Ronald Bruzina (Bloomington: Indiana University Press, 1995), 40.

117. McClure, *Other-wise Preaching*, 133.

desire to say something to someone about something. It is still a hermeneutical phenomenology. Accordingly, any "saying," any alterity, is always already reduced by the primal gesture to approach the Bible *as* scripture. McClure asserts that "[t]he subversive function of the Bible as scripture . . . is not fundamentally a dialectical, centrifugal subversion in service to identity." Rather, he regards such as a "centripetal self-erasure in service to an absolute witness to glory," which he argues will disintegrate identity in the process of "making signs" toward and on behalf of the other.[118] The problem with this is that McClure asserts and inserts an ethic prior to ethics. Such retains valuation and circulation in spite of its efforts. Such remains economics—even in its resistance thereto.

Following the lead of homileticians like McClure and Florence, we must reconfigure our understanding of scripture vis-à-vis preaching. Preaching is not about *understanding* or *applying* God's Word as/in scripture. Preaching is a way to dream. It is a way of opening us to the impossible event we cannot know or coerce into being. Preaching is a desire for the impossible. Thus, it is a "desire beyond desire" and an impossible beyond impossibility.[119]

Toward a "Feminine Economy" of Scripture

Recognizing that there is no path that is otherwise than economics, feminist philosophers like Julia Kristeva, Luce Irigaray, and Hélène Cixous offer us another way to think about how our homiletical theologies might engage scripture kerygmatically. Together their work ramifies under the banner of what has come to be known as *Women's Writing* (*L'Écriture Feminine*). Such submits so-called "standard" (read: masculine) modes of discourse to deconstructive erasure by challenging the (unconscious) sexualized biases always already at work within Western

---

118. Ibid., 26.
119. It is thus a kind of "transcendental illusion" in the order of the gift. See Derrida, *Given Time*, 30: "But the effort to think the groundless ground of this quasi-'transcendental illusion' should not be . . . a sort of adoring and faithful abdication, a simple movement of faith in the face of that which exceeds the limits of experience, knowledge, science, economy—and even philosophy. On the contrary, it is a matter—desire beyond desire—of responding faithfully but also as rigorously as possible both to the injunction or the order of the *gift* ('give' ['*donne*']) as well as the injunction or the order of meaning (presence, science, knowledge): *Know* still what giving *wants to say, know how to give,* know what you want and want to say when you give, know what you intend to give, know how the gift annuls itself, commit yourself [*engage-toi*] even if commitment is the destruction of the gift by the gift, give economy its chance."

philosophy and discourse in general.[120] We saw this in action in chapter 1.

"Masculine" economies are all about appropriation, calculation, and outcomes. They are economic *as such*. They are *closed* systems, hard-wired to capitalize on investments and returns. This way of thinking and relating to otherness undergirds Western thought. I speak or write with an *intention to say* (*vouloir dire* in French, wherein "saying" and "meaning" are synonymous) something, to get my meaning implanted in your mind so that together we can share in understanding. Along the way, certain approaches are valued over others.

"Get to the point."

"Don't equivocate."

"Say what you mean."

These are "masculine" in their approach because these psychological-semantic preoccupations map onto gendered and sexual assumptions that are generalizably *andro*centric, man-centered. This is the discursive genus of which homiletics is a species.[121]

Sexually (and psychologically) speaking, man's drive to climax makes him task-oriented. I'm sad to admit it, but such is also the governing mode of homiletics. What are focus, theme, or topic statements if not means to get our homiletical point across, to achieve theological climax and ethical insemination, so to speak? There is little room for excess, for (fore)play. Moreover, the "masculine" economy militates against the possibility of multiple climaxes of meaning.

The "feminine" alternative economy does not mark one's anatomical makeup; rather, it points to one's "relationship to pleasure." It is less about consumption than it is about tasting: "knowledge could begin with the mouth, the discovery of the taste of something"; it arises when the body enters the system of exchange, disrupting the masculine ("phallic") economy of superimposed linearity and hegemony.[122] The "feminine" is the "overflow" of "luminous torrents" that

---

120. NB: Men are not excluded from such a feminine economy; in fact, at numerous points in her writings Cixous lifts up the writing of men like Jean Genet and James Joyce as emblematic of "feminine writing."

121. Lamentably, this is the case even for the most gynocentric homileticians. For instance, in spite of her many advances for homiletics, the work of Christine Smith remains within the masculine economy that establishes the currency values (subject matter) and governs the exchange rates (method) of preaching. Her "feminist hermeneutics of proclamation," which is always a hermeneutics of suspicion, operates within the system of meaning mining and distribution. The target of her challenge is on who benefits from this system (hint: it's the dudes). She writes that the "ultimate authority" is not the Bible in and of itself; "rather, it is the degree to which the text is liberating and redemptive." Smith, *Weaving the Sermon*, 98.

122. Hélène Cixous, "The Author in Truth," in *"Coming to Writing" and Other Essays*, ed. Deborah Jenson,

spill over the pre-ordained margins through an "excess" of eroticism and free-play not directly attributable to the fixed hierarchies of masculinity.[123] In response to patriarchal systems of homiletical control, which are totalizing in the way that an economy is totalizing, feminist philosophy merely laughs.

This laugh is articulated most poignantly by Hélène Cixous. In one of her most illuminating essays, "The Laugh of the Medusa," she offers a critique of conventional (read: male-dominated) modes of meaning-making that maps perfectly onto the kerygmatic economies of scripture we've been investigating. Taking the time to walk through the flow of this essay offers much. And since I find her thinking so instructive for preaching, I'll be sounding echoes of her thought directly into the homiletical arena, and, following her lead, I'll attempt to embody through my writing the alternative mode of discourse I'm suggesting for preaching.[124]

With an overwhelming effusion of poetic expression, Cixous hearkens "woman" from the dark—the secret, marginal places where her body as well as her preaching are, like Medusa, feared by men. Woman must preach, not according to the law of the house, but in accord with *her* way of knowing and becoming that is beyond masculine forms of Knowledge and Being. The only way this can happen, the only way woman may preach herself, is to preach according to a feminine—embodied—mode of discourse, a mode that does not accord with phallogocentrism, that does not genuflect before the phallus.[125]

trans. Sarah Cornell (Cambridge: Cambridge University Press, 1992), 150-51. The association between the penis, a man's "manhood" (*andreia*), and logic is articulated in the second-century CE text, *Oneirokritika* (Dream Analysis) of Artemidoros of Daldis: ". . . some people call [the penis] their 'manhood'. It resembles reason and education since, like reason [*logos*], it is the most generative thing of all. . . ." Cited in Stephen D. Moore, "Que(e)rying Paul: Preliminary Questions," in *Auguries: The Jubilee Volume of the Sheffield Department of Biblical Studies*, ed. David J.A. Clines and Stephen D. Moore (Sheffield, UK: Sheffield Academic Press, 1998), 271.

123. Hélène Cixous, "The Laugh of the Medusa," trans. Keith Cohen and Paula Cohen, *Signs I* (1976): 876.

124. Here I take my lead from Cixous herself, who takes her leave from normative scholarly practices of citation. In an exchange with Catherine Clément, she eschews direct quotation and even citation because she rejects the notion that one is ever in possession of an idea. Cixous, "A Woman Mistress: An Exchange with Catherine Clément," in *Newly Born Woman*, 136. Therefore, I will engage with her thoughts obliquely.

125. The phallus does not map perfectly onto the male member, the penis; but neither is it completely apart from it. In the work of Jacques Lacan, which is always an engagement with Freud, the phallus serves a psychosocial function. It drives signification. In his essay "The Significance of the Phallus," in *Écrits: A Selection*, trans. Bruce Fink (New York: Norton, 1977), 575-83, Lacan articulates the difference between "being" and "having" a phallus. Men are positioned as men insofar as they are seen to have the phallus. Women, not having the phallus, are seen to "be" the phallus. The symbolic phallus is the concept of being the ultimate man, and having this is compared to having the divine gift of a god. See Judith Butler's critique in *Gender Trouble* (London: Routledge, 1990), 144: "The law requires conformity to its own notion of 'nature.' It gains its legitimacy through the

It is not enough to challenge the hegemony of the phallus, to enter into a dueling match with the boys who play according to *their* rules and employs *their* tools. No. Woman must preach herself! She must bask in the glory of her heterogeneity, her erotogeneity, and let that encounter with herself burst forth, gushing onto and beyond the pages of scripture. Cixous blows the whistle. The game is over. The boys can take their ball(s) and go home. This is not seminal. This is a new game, a game played by a different set of rules. These rules are not repressive but liberating. The only rule is this: there are no rules.

Only a new game will free women from the bonds that enslave them. But not only women: men and others, too; not only women-identifying women, but women-identifying men and men-identifying women —even, perhaps, with a little help, men-identifying men. Woman can neither sing nor laugh, gagged as she is with the pollinous residue of that libidinal and cultural economy that silences her, her mouth *covered* and *concealed* according to the *pro-tecting* logic and politics of the pollinators.

Masculine preaching fills every nook and cranny, leaving no space for woman to express herself; man has spilled his ink everywhere, on the pages of history, law, and theology—often at woman's cost even as she is the blank space where his ink is spent. Man takes (from) her (to be) *the very possibility of change*, the space that can serve as a springboard for subversive thought, the precursory movement of a transformation of social and cultural structures. So woman preaches as she laughs.

She refuses to participate in an exchange of theological reason, which is always already philosophical. She refuses to be ruled by a phallocentric dictator: the dic(k)tating phallus. She has been silenced and so she refuses to speak in a fashion considered appropriate by the colonizing hoard. She speaks as she writes: according to her own "logic." Thus, she breaks the codes that negate her by preaching from and with her body. She returns to her body just as she laughs with her whole body. And with her body she forges for herself a *path* that disrupts every charge of *path-ology*.[126]

---

binary and asymmetrical naturalization of bodies in which the phallus, though clearly not identical to the penis, deploys the penis as its naturalized instrument and sign."

126. I.e., the charge of hysteria (from French *hystérie*, from Ancient Greek *hustéra*, meaning "womb/uterus"), which pathologizes woman for being woman. Cixous avers, "It is by writing, from and toward women, and by taking up the challenge of speech which has been governed by the phallus, that women will confirm women in a place other than that which is reserved in and by the symbolic, that I, in a place other than silence. Women should break out of the snare of silence. They

Man uses only the tiniest part of himself/his body when he preaches. He urges woman to do the same and then confirms his own suspicion when her temerity gets the better of her, when she loses her wind (Hebrew: *ruah*, spirit), when she cannot find her breath (Greek: *pneuma*, spirit). He shrugs when she cannot speak from the lack he has marked her with, stemming from his own grotesque fears. Woman, by contrast, preaches from her own body, a body prior to the mark of man.[127] She doesn't preach, she p/reaches, throwing her trembling body forward, letting go of herself. She flies. All of her passes into her voice, and it's with her body that she vitally supports the pathologic of her preaching. Woman's speech and woman's writing resonate, echo, within woman's preaching.

The key needed to open the rusty lock of patriarchy and thereby liberate woman from her forced enslavement is ana-logos to economy: a logos *alongside* and *up to* something other than logos.[128] To be woman, to preach as woman, is to split open, spread out, push forward, and fill every struggle according to the prodigious extravagance of the feminine economy rather than the restrictive economy of male thrift. It is in the confluence of a particular woman's history and that of all women that is embodied in her preaching.[129]

So what exactly is this "feminine practice" of preaching? Such a question is a man's question. To offer a single definition would always already obviate the possibility of a definition.[130] We must wait. We must listen. But we will know it when we hear it. Woman's preaching is accomplished to the degree that it shatters the scepter of philosophical-theoretical-theological-hermeneutical domination; it is found as a trace of the preaching subject, liberated from subjectivity at the point where Bible becomes scripture, when it opens, unfolds, and unfurls itself before the other, the preacher whom it receives. Scripture plays host to the p/reacher.[131]

shouldn't be conned into accepting a domain which is the margin or the harem." Cixous, "Laugh of the Medusa," 881.
127. "Women must write through their bodies, they must invent the impregnable language that will wreck partitions, classes, and rhetorics, regulations and codes, they must submerge, cut through, get beyond the ultimate reserve-discourse, including the one that laughs at the very idea of pronouncing the word 'silence,' the one that, aiming for the impossible, stops short before the word 'impossible' and writes it as 'the end.'" Ibid., 886.
128. "Woman un-thinks (*dé-pense*)," writes Cixous, "the unifying, regulating history that homogenizes and channels forces, herding contradictions into a single battlefield." Ibid., 882.
129. It is precisely this mode of (feminine) discourse that sublates (*aufheben*) other struggles (class, race, etc.) according to the "fundamental struggle." Ibid.
130. Cixous asserts, "It is impossible to *define* a feminine practice of writing, and this is an impossibility that will remain, for this practice can never be theorized, enclosed, coded—which doesn't mean that it doesn't exist." Ibid., 883.

There is no getting around the fact that to be a woman is to be a body. Preaching woman is to p/reach the (female) body. Such an economy is *more than subversive*. It "gives" with reckless abandon because, for Cixous, woman is a giver.[132] She does not participate in the androcentric economy of exchange by her very generosity, her willingness to give in accord with the gift of scripture.

Woman p/reaches *from* a plentitude, not a void. In fact, she p/reaches *into* a void as she discovers through the process of preaching the new worlds just waiting to be discovered, worlds where no man has gone before.[133] This is her *destination* as much as her *distinerring*. Woman's p/reaching claims no beginning, submitting to no origin (*arche*) or rule (*archon*). Woman p/reaches from herself in order to discover herself in and against scripture and experience:

> *P/reach! And your self-seeking text will know itself better than flesh and blood, rising, insurrectionary dough kneading itself, with sonorous, perfumed ingredients, a lively combination of flying colors, leaves, and rivers plunging into the sea we feed.* The unknown is the originary—commencing without beginning—of woman's p/reaching, even as it does not end and it cannot know to where it goes.[134] This is (feminine) preaching, a mode of p/reaching that—like Medusa—is not deadly, but beautiful.

From Homiletical Economics to Echognomics

Cixous is a trailblazer, leading us farther toward an alternative to "masculine" ways of thinking than any I've yet to encounter. Her work both models and signifies, signifying in her modeling, an alternative mode of discourse that can destabilize the homiletical economy: homiletics *as* economics. This is crucial because if homiletics continues to press its

---

131. Here I draw upon the full measure and etymological insight that structures Derrida's thinking of impossibility/undecidability vis-à-vis the host/hospitality. See Jacques Derrida and Anne Dufourmantelle, *Of Hospitality*, trans. Rachel Bowlby (Stanford: Stanford University Press, 2000).

132. See Cixous, "Laugh of the Medusa," 888–89. This is a point of contention among feminist philosophers. See *Women and the Gift: Beyond the Given and All-Giving*, ed. Morna Joy (Bloomington: Indiana University Press, 2013).

133. "I am spacious, singing flesh, on which is grafted no one knows which I, more or less human, but alive because of transformation." Ibid., 889.

134. Cixous concludes her essay with a warning: "Beware, my friend, of the signifier that would take you back to the authority of the signified!" (Ibid., 892). She fears that woman, when "threatened by the big dick" of masculine writing, will lose heart. Instead, she calls for woman to follow her example. She loves her body. She loves her writing. "When I write," ends Cixous, "it's everything that we don't know we can be that is written out of me, without exclusions, stipulations, and everything we will be calls us to the unflagging, intoxicating, unappeasable search for love. In one another we will never be lacking" (893).

rules upon us, we will remain locked in modes of biblical engagement that are, in effect if not by intent, idolatrous.[135]

Unfortunately, Cixous only gets us part of the way. Her work falls short of providing a new horizon for preaching for three reasons. First, she and all who come after her are forced to perform all kinds of philosophical gymnastics in order to parse the difference between the feminine (*féminin*) and femininity (*féminité*).[136] At its best, her philosophy minimizes the complexities inherent in gender identity; at its worst, it occludes them.[137]

Second, in stressing the feminine as an alternative to a masculine economy, she falls under the trenchant critique of third- and fourth-wave feminists who challenge second- and first-wave feminists for essentializing "woman" and ignoring supra-biological factors such as race, class, religion, and technology.[138] Moreover, it is this aspect of her work that stymies engagement by scholars who happen to be men. Men have no epistemological access to women's bodies (apart from women's testimonies and our own lived-experiences with them), and thus we have minimal basis for assuming the connections Cixous makes between women's ways of knowing and women's embodiment—they *seem* right to me, but my experience is quite limited.

---

135. See Stephen D. Moore and Yvonne Sherwood's attack on "methodolatry" in *The Invention of the Biblical Scholar: A Critical Manifesto* (Minneapolis: Fortress Press, 2011), esp. section 1: "Theory has fueled the biblical-scholarly susceptibility to methodolatry and methodone addiction. Method is our madness" (31).

136. Cixous, "Author," 155: "It is not anatomical sex or essence that determines us in anything; it is, on the contrary, the fable from which we never escape, individual and collective history, the cultural schema, and the way the individual negotiates with these structures, with these data, adapts to them and reproduces them, or else gets around them, overcomes them, goes beyond them, gets through them. . . ." See also Chris Foss, "'There is No God Who Can Keep Us From Tasting': Good Cannibalism in Hélène Cixous's *The Book of Promethea*," in *Scenes of the Apple: Food and the Female Body in Nineteenth-and Twentieth-Century Women's Writing*, ed. Tamar Heller and Patricia Moran (Albany: SUNY Press, 2003), 163n1.

137. See Judith Still, "A Feminine Economy: Some Preliminary Thoughts," in *The Body and the Text: Hélène Cixous, Reading and Teaching*, ed. Helen Wilcox et al. (New York: St. Martin's, 1990), 51: "Can we usefully talk about 'women,' or more controversially 'woman'? Is a biological definition a sufficient bond such that the term 'women' can function in non-tautological statements without greater precision of, say, time and place being necessary in terms of accuracy? . . . slippage into essentialism or biologism is a constant—and necessary—danger." In her book-length treatment of this topic, Still writes, "The feminine, between Cixous and Derrida, slips from a bond with women to an evocation of something which is before or beyond sexual opposition." *Feminine Economies: Thinking Against the Market in the Enlightenment and the Late Twentieth Century* (Manchester: Manchester University Press, 1997), 168.

138. See Kira Cochrane, *All The Rebel Women: The Rise of the Fourth Wave of Feminism* (London: Guardian Books, 2003). Judith Still, "A Feminine Economy," 57, writes, "A feminine economy is about mutual knowing and knowing again . . . *Ecriture féminine* therefore should be a writing shot through (like shot silk) with otherness. Does this require it to be 'difficult' (since we are trained in conservative forms), modernist, expressionist, James-Joyce writing? If so, much contemporary women's writing (especially black women's writing) fails."

Furthermore, such thinking has led some philosophizing men to valorize, if not deify, women's bodies.[139] Such is problematic because neither misogyny nor deification corroborates the majority of women's self-attestation or understanding of themselves. This thinking reinforces a classical bifurcation concerning women as either agents of lasciviousness and temptation *or* quasi-divine in their capacity for childbirth and breastfeeding. Of course, these latter aspects of womanhood are neither experienced nor desired by all women.

Third, Cixous's feminine economy is still an economy—albeit a subversive, transgressive economy. This goes beyond the slippage manifested between the English *economy* and the French *économie*.[140] For Cixous, following Derrida, the alternative to economy is gift—or at least the *idea*, the *possibility* of the gift, which is given, in theory, beyond any thought of remuneration or recuperation of loss.[141]

Cixous pushes us to find ways of relating that are altogether different from "masculine" economic structures. She pursues "a kind of desire that wouldn't be in collusion with the old story of death." Such a desire would open onto a new horizon: that of love. This alternative relation would risk re-cognition, of alterity, of difference. Such a desire would resist the temptation to feel inadequate or threatened by the strangeness of the other, but would instead work to "discover, to respect, to favor, to cherish."[142] Following Cixous's profluence, I desire a new way of relating scripture with preaching, a new homiletical "scene," so to speak. And I affirm that the starting point arising out of said desire would be to "invent Love," which I have attempted to do in some of my other published works.[143]

139. See Rosalyn Diprose's critique of Levinas here in *Corporeal Generosity: On Giving with Nietzsche, Merleau Ponty, and Levinas* (Albany: SUNY Press, 2002), 141–42.
140. French poststructuralists frequently invoke *l'économie* without any reference to its mercantile connotations. The French word is more abstract than its English equivalent. See, for instance, the careful parsing conducted by Christopher Johnson, *System and Writing in the Philosophy of Jacques Derrida* (Cambridge: Cambridge University Press, 1993), 57–64.
141. Cixous puts it this way: "How does one give? It starts in a very simple way: in order for a gift to be, *I* must not be the one to give. A gift has to be like grace, it has to fall from the sky. If there are traces of origin of the *I* give, there is no gift—there is an I-give. Which also signifies: say 'thank you,' even if the other does not ask you to say it. As soon as we say thank you, we give back part or the whole gift. We have been brought up in the space of the debt, and so we say thank you. Is it possible to imagine that there can be a gift?" Verena Andermatt Conley, "Interview with Hélène Cixous," in *Hélène Cixous: Writing the Feminine*, exp. ed. (Lincoln, NE: University of Nebraska Press, 1991), 158–59.
142. Cixous, "Sorties," 78.
143. See Jacob D. Myers, "Before the Gaze Ineffable: Intersubjective *Poesis* and the Song of Songs," *Theology and Sexuality* 17, no. 2 (May 2011): 139–60; Myers, "The Erotic Approach: Homiletical Insights form the Work of Georges Bataille," *Theology and Sexuality* 19, no. 1 (2013): 26–37; Myers, "Toward an Erotic Liturgical Theology: Schmemann in Conversation with Contemporary Philosophy," *Worship* 87, no. 5 (September 2013): 387–413; and Myers, *Making Love with Scripture*.

The best of contemporary homiletics also wants to lead us here. McClure, following Levinas, writes, "The subject of saying does not give signs, it becomes a sign, turns into an allegiance."[144] From this, McClure infers that "[o]nce the knower releases his or her thematizing control in the event of knowing, uncovering oneself, and becoming exposed to the other, to infinite strangeness and otherness, the knower's ability to solidify or rigidify into a stable identity or position (as fixed sign) is considerably undermined."[145] Florence nudges us in the same direction. Drawing upon the work of Rebecca Chopp, she wants to affirm the alterity and sanctity of "the Word as perfectly open sign." Florence writes, "It is Word that opens up many voices, any of which can push and challenge and transform the present order. This Word is always open to new meaning; it is a perfectly open sign; it is God. It is also a bet against all odds that good news can still be proclaimed, even from the margins. It is a wager that women can speak of freedom."[146] Bringing McClure and Florence together, we might say that other-wise homiletics is testimonial homiletics under erasure.[147]

I, too, want to lead us toward an approach to scripture that does not take (*prendre*) from scripture in order to learn (*apprendre*) or understand (*comprendre*) scripture. In French this connection is more overt than it is in English. I desire a way with scripture that would not have its way with scripture, *taking* in order to *give* a sermon. I am interested in what Cixous identifies as "the paradoxical logic of an economy without reserve."[148]

So, how do we get there? What would such p/reaching look like? What would it sound like? Preaching at the limits of economics, perhaps beyond the limits of a priori valuation and regulation, arises out of an oblique way of knowing. I want to call such a homiletic *echognomic*. This neologism is more than paronomastic; I'm not just playing with words to display my cleverness or cheekiness. An *echognomic homiletic* begins by working to undo beginning. Like an echo, its sound is not original to itself. The source of an echo is elsewhere and other-

144. Levinas, *Otherwise than Being*, 49, cited in McClure, *Other-wise Preaching*, 121.
145. McClure, *Other-wise Preaching*, 121.
146. Florence, *Preaching as Testimony*, 95.
147. McClure, *Other-wise Preaching*, 131, writes, "The movement toward the other must be more than a simple reframing exercise—the grafting on of a new perspective or a therapeutic disorientation-reorientation that is somehow managed by a still autonomous subject. Testimony, as it emerges from witness, is not simply counter-testimony. It is *erasure*-testimony, through which one term of the binary must go under erasure, as one would erase any error. . . . Something (perhaps everything) in the homiletic theme or narrative is erased, not merely countered or reframed, by approaching its other."
148. Cixous, *Newly Born Woman*, 86.

wise—not, I hasten to add, because it comes from nowhere, a universal sound that sounds the same in every time and place. The source of an echo is *particular*. It is fixed spatially and temporally; but that does not mean we can pin it down or isolate it. It is aural, but its aurality may not collapse into orality.[149] We begin with a response to an originary call. It is this call that we can *think* and *host* but never *know*.[150]

Moreover, the echo requires a certain kind of spatial configuration in order to rebound. It demands particular acoustics—in us, in our communities. Physics stipulates that delay be proportional to the distance of the reflecting surface from the source and the listener. Echoes emerge from many places: the bottom of wells, concrete buildings, the walls of an enclosed and empty room. In other words, an echo will not appear just anywhere. Echognomically inclined homiletics will attend to the physicality of the preacher's environment. Where does the preacher "stand" in relation to the text? What detritus lies in between the "Word as perfectly open sign" that might consume its soundings before it can echo in her consciousness?

Lastly, the echo tethers us to time in unique ways. Unlike most mainstream hermeneutical and homiletical schemas, this temporal delay would not be viewed as a problem to be overcome. It is a "masculine" preoccupation to fill every gap, to close every space. Such an approach would render the echo impossible. Without a temporal gap—a necessary absence—between original sound and resound, there can be no echo. Echognomics requires time. The echo is always and necessarily diachronic; it moves through time. Temporal foreclosure silences all; synchrony is otherwise than sound. Therefore, the echognomic preacher will concern themselves less with the world behind, in, or in front of the text (as if such a world *exists*). They will instead attend to the movement of forces and regimes of power *though* time.[151]

149. N.B. Here I am being metaphorical with regard to sound. The echo's o/aurality holds no privileged place or special means to access God. Writing, too, shares in the logic I am espousing (see chapter 4).
150. See Derrida, *Given Time*, 80 on "thinking the gift."
151. Foucault's approach is thus to enter into the inside, to reinscribe a certain return at the origin of regimes of discourse, to enter into "regimes of power" at the source of their power and thereby rupture "truth" from within. He writes, "The essential political problem for the intellectual is not to criticize the ideological contents [of a discourse] . . . but that of ascertaining the possibility of constituting a new politics of truth. The problem is not changing people's consciousness—or what's in their heads—but the political, economic, institutional regime of the production of truth. It's not a matter of emancipating truth from every system of power (which would be a chimera, for truth is already power), but of detaching the power of truth from the forms of hegemony, social, economic, and cultural, within which it operates at the present time." Michel Foucault, "Truth and Power," in *The Foucault Reader*, ed. Paul Rabinow, trans. Christian Hubert (New York: Pantheon Books, 1984), 74–75.

Turning to the second aspect of this compound word, I maintain that preaching in the trajectories established by Florence, McClure, and Cixous will aim to be *gnomic* rather than *nomic:* it is *epistemological* more than it is *methodological*. The Greek word *gnómé* is often translated as "mind-set," "judgment," or "decision." Unlike its near synonym, *gnôsis*, *gnómé* is less about externalized, abstract knowledge than that which sets one in motion. *Gnómé* is knowledge coupled with resolve. Both nouns share in the noetic capacity of a person, but *gnómé* denotes a firm purpose that is based on prior knowledge and experience. It signifies the volitional and agential dimension of knowing, a kind of fusion of intellect and will.[152]

Gnómé does something else for homiletics: it moves us from the metrics of economy, rationality, and logic toward gift, hospitality, democracy, justice, and friendship. Even as these later "concepts" "are"— strictly speaking—impossible, they serve to move preaching beyond an immanent frame. Indeed, it is their very impossibility, their elusiveness, their subversion of Being that drives preaching (mad).[153] Cixous points to much the same thing when she writes of giving. "Giving isn't sacrificing," she argues. "The person who gives has to be able to function on the level of knowledge without knowing." Such a "state of weakness" particular to the gift/giving that presses (beyond?) the limits of economy and exchange may be weak, but it is not passive: One would have to "have the guts to occupy the position one has no right to occupy and that one show precisely how and why one occupies it. I set my sights high: I demand that love struggle within the master against the will to power."[154]

When homiletics strives to extricate itself from economics, even if this extrication may be impossible, it requires an alternative imagination for helping preachers approach scripture *in a certain way* for p/reaching. Such does not provide a new law (*nomos*); it does not con-

---

152. This intentional and agential dimension of knowing denoted by *gnómé* is evident in Ignatius's *Letter to the Ephesians*, 3:2—4:1a: "But since love does not allow me to be silent concerning you, I decided to encourage you, that you may run together in harmony with the mind [*gnómé*] of God. For also Jesus Christ, who cannot be distinguished from our life, is the Father's mind [*gnómé*], just as also the bishops who have been appointed throughout the world share the mind [*gnómé*] of Jesus Christ. For this reason it is fitting for you to run together in harmony with the mind [*gnómé*] of the bishop, which is exactly what you are doing." *The Apostolic Fathers: I Clement, II Clement, Ignatius, Polykarp, Didache*, Loeb Classical Library, vol. 24, ed. and trans. Bart D. Ehrman (Cambridge, MA: Harvard University Press, 2003), 222–23.

153. Derrida identifies these concepts/ideals/invocations of gift, hospitality, etc. as nondeconstructible inasmuch as they force us continually to reconsider concrete constructions or instantiations of gift, justice, etc. according to an internal disquiet that cannot be stilled or silenced.

154. Cixous, "A Woman Mistress," 140.

fine preaching to a new house (*oikos*). Rather, the echognomic orientation offers itself as a re-frame, a summons even, to receive the text *in a certain way* and to share one's thoughts, voice, and body with others by preaching *in a certain way*. I maintain no delusions that this reorientation and its accompanying labors will be easy. But if you signed up for this p/reaching life because you wanted easy, then, my friend, you are in the wrong business.

Conclusion: Disrupting the Homiletical Economy

> We need the books that affect us like a disaster, that grieve us deeply, like the death of someone we loved more than ourselves, like being banished into forests far from everyone, like a suicide. A book must be the axe for the frozen sea inside us.
>
> — Franz Kafka[155]

We opened this chapter in conversation with *Moana*. I suggested that preachers are not that different from the demigod, Maui: we just want to give that which is life-giving to the people we love and serve. Unfortunately, like Maui, we have overstepped our bounds in taking that which only God may give. Furthermore, as Cixous has taught us, the propensity to seize what is not ours and to abscond with the gift has devastating effects on the "feminine economy." The history of preaching has been one of stealing the heart and voices of women and others who do not abide by the rules of the homiletical game, its economics. To move forward, we will have to completely rethink the laws of our homiletical houses, approaching the im-possibility of giving a sermon by setting fire to these houses.

Economics will not go away from preaching any more than it will from our sociopolitical contexts. We need economics to live in community. But might we resist a certain economic orientation to preaching that is promulgated by homiletical systems? That is the question that drives me (mad) because I do not want to reduce scripture to a commodity. As soon as scripture enters as "source" as "given," we are caught in an economy. The *house* of homiletics sets the *law* of preaching, and laws and houses always serve the powerful and exclude the powerless. Theologian Marion Grau puts it this way: "Economy comes to stand for the masculine, hom(m)osexual process of exchange

155. Franz Kafka, "Letter to Oskar Pollak, January 27, 1904," in *Letters to Friends, Family, and Editors*, ed. Max Brod, trans. Richard Winston and Clara Winston (New York: Schocken Books, 1977), 15–16.

between men, while the gift stands for the rebellious feminine departure from this phallic economy that has excluded women and attempts to inscribe the different relationality of women."[156] I think that she is right.

What if we didn't try to take anything *from* scripture? How might we give *to* scripture? How would that shift our kerygmatic econometrics? What if we gave without any thought of receiving something in return? What if preaching were about saturation, saturation added to saturation? What if we didn't try to *extract* or *exegete* scripture? What if we were to *inhabit* it? To *invest* in it? As Anna Carter Florence so poignantly puts it, "Maybe the problem with preaching ha[s] less to do with form than with relationships—*our* relationships. Our need to preach sermons that [are] right, rather than true. Our need to illuminate a text instead of living it."[157] How ought our relationship with scripture change in order to *live* in and with the text?

Making *Kontax* with Scripture

Feminist philosopher Judith Still reminds us that "While it may well be the case that no pure feminine economy could ever be available to us, the evocation of such a utopic term may enable a displacement in thinking."[158] In other words, even to *inquire* against the kerygmatic economy marks a coefficient of doubt over our homiletical metrics. Such questioning forces us to think more deeply about how and why we use the Bible for our preaching. How we respond to this question says much about how we understand God working in and among us; such questioning is as theological as we can get.

To get here, our language has to change. Can homiletics begin to think echognomically against economics? I believe we can. But this theoretical questioning is all well and good until homileticians have to teach this stuff to their students. Economic thinking makes homiletical pedagogy easy—perhaps too easy. Go to the ATM/Bible, withdraw some funds/verses, invest them in your sermon and voila, you have preaching. I do not want to leave you with a big fat question mark. I want to give you something, an image that you may use to reconfigure your relationship to the Bible in your preaching. I want *to give* something to you, and thus I want the *impossible* for you.

---

156. Marion Grau, "Erasing Economy: Derrida and the Construction of Divine Economies" *CrossCurrents* 52, no. 3 (Fall 2002): 363.
157. Florence, "Put Away Your Sword!" 106.
158. Still, *Feminine Economies*, 20.

I find much to celebrate in the work of poet and philosopher Jean-Louis Chrétien. He offers homiletical theologies an image sufficient to reframe our conception of scripture: "To read the Bible today is not to decipher all by oneself a score written by the very hand of the composer; it is to allow to come toward me that immense sonorous ocean made of a thousand voices and a thousand instruments and *to have the joy of becoming in it a wavelet.*"[159] This last part is key. Rather than thinking in terms of extraction and exchange, how much better is it to become a part of scripture in some way, to harmonize with it? Moving in this direction with Chrétien, I suggest the image of the *kontax,* a pole around which a scroll is wound. The word signifies a certain movement in accord with the way in which words on a scroll unfurl as they are read, and it maps nicely onto Cixous's "feminine" economy and the homiletical echognomy I'm offering.

This image has already done some work in the Christian tradition. In the Byzantine church, *kontákia* are hymns or poems recited as a dialogue between chanter and choir. I love this because it points to a space in between speaker and listener, caller and responder, that is open. It is hallowed and hollowed space wherein we play host to the God who might always (not) show up. It is as close to a pure gift as we may achieve because it is so utterly saturated with undecidability and hope.

Philosopher Richard Kearney argues that "we have to read sacred Scriptures as carefully as we greet strangers who come to us out of the night."[160] He's right. Let us no longer go to scripture with our homiletical pickaxes sharpened to mine meaning, truths, dogmas, or practical wisdom. Let us put violence aside. Instead, let's go to scripture as one falls asleep, viz., obliquely. We must not force it, or it will never come. Let us allow the words of scripture to unfurl around us, calling us, haunting us. Let us give ourselves to the Bible's echo, even as the Bible is the Bible's echo, bearing witness to an originary testimony and "counter-testimony" that wills to remain silent even as it is the only sound we seek to hear.[161]

159. Chrétien, *Under the Gaze of the Bible*, 3. Emphasis added.
160. Richard Kearney, *Anatheism: Returning to God After God* (New York: Columbia University Press, 2011), 170.
161. Walter Brueggemann describes this biblical echo resounding within itself through the work of "cross-examination," whereby Israel challenges Israel's own theological "core testimony" through a "counter-testimony" informed by lived experience. Brueggemann explains, "Cross-examination does not proceed frontally or in large, sweeping generalization. It is conducted, rather, by the slow, attentive process of teasing out detail, of noticing hints of incongruity that fly in the face of the main claims; as such hints accumulate, a rereading and reuttering of the primary narrative is required. This cross-examination of Israel's testimony concerning Yahweh, in

This is *biblical* preaching. We host the text *in a certain way*, a way that honors our professed belief in the (divine) alterity at work within the words of scripture and in the life of our communities of faith. Such an approach, an approach that subverts every kind of encroachment, simultaneously constitutes a *rapprochement*. At day's end, we do not speak so that others will hear what we have to say about scripture; we speak so that an originary silence might whisper in a way that overwhelms our speaking and our hearing. This is the way of death, a way to dream, perchance.

the end, will require a considerably revised narrative about Yahweh." *Theology of the Old Testament: Testimony, Dispute, Advocacy* (Minneapolis: Fortress Press, 2005), 324.

4

Giving Up the Ghost: Troubling God

Theology is idolatry if it means what we say about God instead of letting ourselves be addressed by what God has to say to us.

— John D. Caputo[1]

The film *Inception* centers on a man named Cobb, a thief-for-hire who infiltrates the unconscious minds of corporate magnates to extract valuable information. Following a botched assignment, Cobb is forced to accept a seemingly impossible mission: *inception*. Inception is the implantation of an idea into a target's unconscious, thereby altering the target's psyche. If he is able to achieve inception, Cobb's criminal record will be expunged, and he will regain his freedom.

Complications ensue when Cobb's deceased wife, Mal, appears. She begins to haunt his efforts, threatening to unravel his work from within (himself). The nearly impossible task of inception becomes more than impossible because the very component needed for inception (viz., Cobb's mind) has turned against itself. *Inception* illumines the (troubled) relationship between God and homiletics in several ways, but I shall focus on one element in particular: the ghost.

Cobb is haunted by his wife's memory. Having spent decades together in the dream world exploring the furthest recesses of the

---

1. John D. Caputo, *What Would Jesus Deconstruct? The Good News of Postmodernism for the Church* (Grand Rapids, MI: Baker Academic, 2007), 131.

143

unconscious, Mal lost touch with reality. Her dream world supplanted the real world, and so she saw no need to "wake up" to reality. In an effort to save her, Cobb turned his psychological skills against his wife. He planted the idea in her mind that her world wasn't real, hoping that she would come to see the truth and return to reality with him.

The shadow side of inception is that once an idea is planted in another's mind, it can consume her. In an effort to draw her out of her dream world, Cobb convinces Mal that the only way to return to reality is for them to kill themselves. (This is a central element in the film's narrative universe, by the way; if you die in the dream world, you wake up.) Even after Mal "awakes," she continues to believe that her world is not real. In an effort to snap herself out of this delusion, to return to her *real* husband and children, she actually takes her own life.

Homiletics pursues a kind of *theological* inception. On us. It has planted in our minds an idea that pervades our most primal homiletical understanding: that preaching *is* the Word of God. This ontological declaration shapes preaching as such. Homiletics has planted this proposition so deeply in preaching's unconscious that it leads us to say things like, "The word of God is at once the necessary and the impossible task of the minster."[2] Such an aporia drives preaching (mad).

Thankfully, that about which we speak when we speak theologically—namely, God—haunts preaching, disturbing and destabilizing it. The more homiletics represses the uneventful event, the "unworkable work" (*désœuvrement*) harbored in the name/ing (of) God, the greater its power over preaching. Here I want us to consider the "hauntological" capacities of preaching, capacities that, like Mal, trouble the metaphysical underpinnings of homiletical inception.[3]

I realize that this is counterintuitive. If preaching *is* the Word of God,

---

2. Karl Barth, "The Word of God and the Task of the Ministry," in *The Word of God and the Word of Man*, trans. Douglas Horton (Gloucester, MA: Peter Smith, 1978), 213. Also: "Our difficulty lies in the content of our task. . . . As ministers we ought to speak of God. We are human, however, and so cannot speak of God. We ought therefore to recognize both our obligation and our inability and by that very recognition give God the glory" (186).

3. Hauntology (a portmanteau of *haunting* and *ontology*) signifies a state of (ontological) disjunction in which presence is haunted by the "ghost" of its own (unrealized) possibilities. On the "unworkable work" and the "ghost" of Surrealism see Maurice Blanchot, "Reflections on Surrealism," in *The Work of Fire*, trans. Charlotte Mandell (Stanford: Stanford University Press, 1995), 85–97. On the "haunting" of Marxism, see Jacques Derrida, *Specters of Marx: The State of the Debt, the Work of Mourning and The New International*, trans. Peggy Kamuf (New York: Routledge, 1994), where he speaks of an opening that preserves its heterogeneity "as the only chance of an affirmed or rather reaffirmed future. . . . In the experience of the end, in its insistent, instant, always imminently eschatological coming, at the extremity of the extreme today, there would thus be announced the future of what comes. . . . The question is indeed 'wither?' Not only whence comes the ghost but first of all is it going to come back? Is it not already beginning to arrive and where is it going? What of the future? The future can only be for ghosts. And the past" (45).

then isn't preaching guided *by* God? Well, yes and no. As we'll see in the forthcoming investigation, the only way for preaching to sur-vive, to live (*vivre*) beyond (*sur*) its living, is for preaching to give up, or perhaps give in to, the (Holy) Ghost. Preaching must die to ontology to live, per-chance, in God.

Section One: God *in* Trouble

If only we lacked sight and knowledge so as to see, so as to know, unseeing and unknowing, that which lies beyond all vision and knowledge. For this would be really to see and to know.

— Pseudo-Dionysius[4]

Is preaching the Word of God? Homileticians unite in their affirmation of this ontological conjunction between *verbum Dei* and *verbum homini*; but this was not always the Church's position.[5] It was not until the Second Helvetic Confession (1562 CE) that preaching's ontological sta-tus received an upgrade. Having asserted that the Bible is the Word of God, Heinrich Bullinger (the confession's principal author) turns to preaching. "The Preaching of the Word of God Is the Word of God," he declares.[6] Thus he assigns preaching a mode of being, an ontology, that

4. Pseudo-Dionysius, *The Mystical Theology*, in *Pseudo-Dionysius: The Complete Works*, trans. Colm Luib-heid (New York: Paulist, 1987), 138.
5. A major problem with most homiletical thought is that this conviction is merely asserted with little to no argument. Consider William H. Willimon: "Preaching is not merely what we say. . . . Preaching is what God says." *Proclamation and Theology* (Nashville: Abingdon, 2005), 8. Craddock declares, "Preaching is both words and the Word. To deny any relationship between one's own words and the Word of God, whether due to one's notion of proper humility or to an abdication of the authority and responsibility of ministry, is to rob preaching of its place and purpose." Fred B. Craddock, *Preaching*, 25th ann. ed. (Nashville: Abingdon, 2010), 18–19.
   Ronald Allen offers a necessary word of caution here, writing that "there is no guarantee that every word of every sermon is altogether God's word." Ronald J. Allen, *Interpreting the Gospel: An Introduction to Preaching* (St. Louis: Chalice, 1998), 13. Accordingly, Allen commends theologi-cal humility when he writes that "a preacher cannot casually claim that everything relating to a sermon is of God. Ministers sometimes speak simplistically of the sermon as 'God's word.' This nomenclature emphasizes that God can work through preaching. However, I have reservations about the causal use of that phrase to describe the sermon. In sermons, pastors can pawn their own idiosyncrasies and idols as God. Pastors can even use the sermon to abuse."
6. Bullinger adds several addendums that homileticians seldom mention: *if* the preacher is "lawfully called," and *if* the Word is "received by the faithful," and *if* no "other Word of God is to be invented nor is to be expected from heaven," *then* preaching is the Word of God. "The Second Helvetic Con-fession," in *The Book of Confessions* (Louisville: Office of the General Assembly Presbyterian Church USA, 1999), 53–54. Cf. "The Scots Confession of 1560": "Although the Word of God truly preached, the sacraments rightly ministered, and the discipline executed *according to the Word of God*, are *cer-tain and infallible signs* of the true Kirk, we do not mean that every individual person in that com-pany is a chosen member of Jesus Christ" (Ibid., 24–25, emphasis added).
   In a recent study, Daniël Timmerman maps a shift in Bullinger's thinking in response to con-flicts with more radical reformers. Timmerman writes that "the early Bullinger adheared to the right of the congregation to judge the prophecy of their preacher—as an application of 1 Cor

guarantees preaching's authority (and unassailability). Such serves to insulate preaching from critique, to protect it against every specter of uncertainty.[7]

St. Augustine radically differentiates the Word through whom all things were made, namely Jesus Christ, from human words—be they homiletical or not. It's no wonder, he observes, that we can find no words about which to speak adequately concerning the one Word of God, "who spoke us into being and about whom we seek to say something." He goes on to note that even though our minds may ponder over this non-created Word, we must acknowledge that our minds were themselves formed *by* the Word. Furthermore, St. Augustine asserts that we are incapable of making words in the same way that we humans are made by the Word because

> the Father did not beget His one and only Word in the same way He made all things through the Word. For God begot God, but the Begetter and the Begotten are together one God. God certainly made the world; the world, however, passes away while God endures. And so these things that were made did not make themselves, but by no one was God made, the One by whom all things were made. It is no wonder, then, that a human being [like me], a creature in the midst of it all, cannot explain the Word through Whom all things were made.[8]

Human words, which are *created*, can never attain the status of Word, who was *begotten* of God.

As with Bullinger, whenever homileticians stress the ontological status of preaching it is in response to some perceived threat. For instance, in responding to a so-called language crisis, Richard Eslinger stresses that preaching is the Word of God because he believes that

14:29-32. Yet, like other mainstream reformers, due to conflicts with the radical reformation over the authority of the ordained ministry, Bullinger soon abandoned this idea. An overview of the works from the period 1532-1537 confirms that this development continued after Bullinger's accession to office of Zurich's first pastor. Moreover, a survey of the reformer's previous publications reveals a growing concern with the authority of the ministry. Especially in the New Testament commentaries from these years, the Zurich antistes frequently highlights the authority (*authoritas, potestas*) of preachers." *Heinrich Bullinger on Prophecy and the Prophetic Office (1523-1538)* (Göttingen: Vandenhoeck & Ruprecht, 2015), 230.
7. Historically, Christian thinkers reserved the moniker "Word of God" for Jesus. See, for instance, St. Irenaeus, *On the Apostolic Preaching*, trans. John Behr (Crestwood, NY: St. Vladimir's Seminary Press, 1997), 44: "for those who bear the Spirit of God are led to the Word, that is to the Son, while the Son presents [them] to the Father, and the Father furnishes incorruptibility." See also St. Augustine, *On the Holy Trinity*, in *Nicene and Post-Nicene Fathers*, vol. 3, ed. Philip Schaff, trans. Stephen McKenna (New York: Cosimo, 2007), ch. 6, §9, p. 21: "For it is plain that we are to take the Word of God to be the only Son of God . . ."
8. St. Augustine, "Sermon 188," in *Augustine in His Own Words*, ed. William Harmless (Washington, DC: Catholic University of America Press, 2010), 128.

only the Word is able to restore preaching to its pristine ontological state, to its "oral/aural immediacy."[9] Here he reinscribes the hallmark of Western logocentrism: the privileging of speech over writing.

Contemporary homiletics is only able to bolster preaching theologically (as Word) because the spoken word has already been bolstered philosophically (as presence). This I label a *homiletic of presence*.[10] In elevating speech over writing, homiletics rehearses the metaphysical assumptions underwriting Western philosophy since (at least) Plato. Such assumptions allow Fred Craddock to link "words in their original form, their purest form" to those "that pass orally from person to person, words in their native setting in the world of sound."[11] It undergirds Richard Lischer's assertion that preaching, as an "event-from-above," is mediated by "pure sound" and that proclamatory faith "is an acoustical affair."[12] And it is what allows Wilson to get away with declaring, "Sermons are spoken: This is essential to their nature, not incidental."[13]

I want to challenge the tripartite elision of word/Word, Word/speech, and speech/presence. Not only does such elision ignore—nay, repress—the trace of absence that makes discourse possible (see chapter 1), it also commits preaching to idolatry, as John Caputo so rightly observes above. In our fear of God's absence, that God always might not show up in our preaching, we have suppressed a certain troubling that, ironically, puts our understanding of God in trouble.

Breathing One's Last: Aural Homiletical Theology

In his book, *Blue Note Preaching in a Post-Soul World*, Otis Moss III writes, "No other medium can carry the supernatural message with such

9. "There is a crisis in language, a diminution in the ability of words to express potency . . . And since preaching is by its very nature born out of an oral tradition and becomes an event by returning the Word to its oral/aural immediacy, the performative power of its language is now being reaffirmed." Richard L. Eslinger, *The Web of Preaching: New Options in Homiletic Method* (Nashville: Abingdon, 2002), 18. See also, Eslinger, *A New Hearing: Living Options in Homiletic Method* (Nashville: Abingdon, 1987), 14. His proposed remedy takes several things for granted: 1) the nature of God's Word; 2) the slippage between Word and words; and 3) what is involved in hearing said Word. These matters are thus theological (God-oriented), semiological (sign-oriented), and epistemological (knowledge-oriented).
10. The work of George Steiner has provided much philosophical credence to the belief that the spoken word is only able to convey meaning because it is underwritten by the presence of the Divine. See George Steiner, *Real Presences: Is There Anything in What We Say?* (London: Faber & Faber, 1989).
11. Fred B. Craddock, *As One Without Authority*, rev. ed. (St. Louis: Chalice, 2001), 23. Elsewhere he writes, "After all, in a very real sense, the word of God is located not on a page nor on the lips, but at the ear." Fred B. Craddock, "The Sermon and the Uses of Scripture," *Theology Today* 42, no. 1 (April 1985): 14.
12. Richard Lischer, "Preaching as the Church's Language," in *Listening to the Word: Essays in Honor of Fred Craddock*, ed. Thomas G. Long and Gail R. O'Day (Nashville: Abingdon, 1993), 121.
13. Paul Scott Wilson, *The Practice of Preaching*, 2nd ed. (Nashville: Abingdon, 2007), 47.

power as sound." Moss goes on to add that sound "delivers something external but cannot be controlled. The written word can be copyrighted, and someone can say, 'I own it.' But once a word goes out, no one can own it or grab it."[14] There are several problems with this claim. First, as we saw in chapter 1, language—spoken, written, gestural—cannot lead us beyond language. Its every effort to lead us to an *outside* only ever roots us more firmly on the *inside* of language as such.[15] Second, Moss is off on his understanding of the materiality of the spoken word, which *can* be copyrighted. Furthermore, written words are just as intangible as spoken words—you can take hold of a piece of paper, but that's not the same as taking hold of the word inscribed on that paper. Written words rely on sight to the same degree that oral/aural words rely on sound—neither of which is retainable apart from memory.

Moss is not alone in the way he affirms the oral/aural milieu over the visual. Nor is he unique in privileging sound as the medium par excellence of the divine. As we will see, the elevation of speech as the supreme vehicle for the Word unites homiletics most supremely.

Homiletics United in Contradiction: Preaching is Writing Spoken Over Writing

Homiletics achieves a rare point of confluence amid its diversity in its unswerving confidence that preaching is an *oral/aural event*. And yet, the orality/aurality of the preaching "event" is tempered by an event of writing, which disqualifies it as *event*.[16] To illustrate, in his short but influential book *Homiletics*, Karl Barth writes, "To be sure, a sermon is a speech. It has to be this. But in this speech we should not leave it up to the Holy Spirit (or some other spirit!) to inspire the words. . . . Instead,

---

14. Otis Moss III, *Blue Note Preaching in a Post-Soul World: Finding Hope in an Age of Despair* (Louisville: Westminster John Knox, 2015), 38.
15. Derrida avers, "The death of speech is therefore the horizon and origin of language. But an origin and a horizon which do not hold themselves at its exterior borders. As always, death, which is neither a present to come nor a present past, shapes the interior of speech, as its trace, its reserve, its interior and exterior *differance*: as its supplement." Jacques Derrida, *Of Grammatology*, trans. Gayatri Chakravorty Spivak, corr. ed. (Baltimore: Johns Hopkins University Press, 1997), 315.
16. Philosophers are adamant on this point. See Jean-Luc Marion, *Being Given: Toward a Phenomenology of Givenness*, trans. Jeffrey L. Kosky (Stanford: Stanford University Press, 2002), 167: "Now, it happens that the event—precisely because it arises in an unpredictable landing—overcomes measure and the understanding, and therefore is excepted from all adequate cause." Richard Kearney puts it this way: "If what happens is only that which is possible in the sense of what is anticipated and expected, then it is not an event in the true sense. For an event is only possible in so far as it comes from the impossible." Kearney, "Deconstruction, God, and the Possible," in *Derrida and Religion: Other Testaments*, ed. Yvonne Sherwood and Kevin Hart (New York: Routledge, 2005), 298.

a sermon *is* a speech which we have prepared word for word and written down. This alone accords with its dignity."[17] Barth does not tell us
how these graphic and oral/aural elements relate to one another, but
it does trouble preaching's ontological status as *God's* Word if its very
structure precludes the work of the Holy Spirit!

In his book *God's Human Speech*, Charles Bartow offers a robust
defense of speech's prominence over writing in and for preaching. In
his impassioned defense of speech, Bartow doubles down on a classical
distinction between *living speech* and *dead letter*. The former he deems
"full," "present," and that which "reveals interiority" (i.e., conscious
intention); the latter he views as an "arrested performance," a "dead-
letter," or that which "is about to be lived." Bartow argues that through
speech and concomitant "physical gestural virtuosity," the preacher
conditions herself to "experience and understand presence and the
Presence." Embodied speech, for Bartow, is the human performance
that ignites the flow of presence from its inert state in "the dead-letter
of the text"; it transforms—to invert a phrase from T. S. Elliot—"ink
into blood."[18]

Bartow's assertion raises many questions. How is such presence/
Presence mediated through the preacher's voice and gestures? How
might we account for the fact that so much of what the preacher says
is absented from the congregation via the sermon manuscript? How do
we account for such absence at work on the *inside* and at the *origin* of

17. Karl Barth, *Homiletics*, trans. Geoffrey W. Bromiley and Donald E. Daniels (Louisville: Westminster John Knox, 1991), 119. Emphasis added. We must quickly note that this in no way suggests that the sermon was constituted by whatever the *preacher* wanted to say. See Barth, "The Word of God and the Task of Ministry," in *The Word of God and the Word of Man*, trans. Douglas Horton (Glouces-ter, MA: Peter Smith, 1978), 183–217: "one can *not* speak of God simply by speaking of man in a loud voice." See also Angela Dienhart Hancock, *Karl Barth's Emergency Homiletic, 1932–1933: A Sum-mons to Prophetic Witness at the Dawn of the Third Reich* (Grand Rapids, MI: Eerdmans, 2013), 325: "The *Predigtvorbereitung* [viz., Barth's "Exercises in Sermon Preparation"] artifacts demonstrate that Barth steadily, repeatedly, relentlessly worked to decenter these young preachers, urging them to lay down their weapons and their agendas, to listen with empty hands and open hearts to the unsettling Word from the Lord at the dawn of the Third Reich."
18. Charles L. Bartow, *God's Human Speech: A Practical Theology of Proclamation* (Grand Rapids, MI: Eerd-mans, 1997), 64, 66, 121. Bartow writes, "Revelation thus evokes within us awareness of God's dis-tance from us and nearness to us, God's accessibility to us and hiddenness from us, God's coming and God's going, God's speech and God's silence. The history of revelation, therefore, is marked by episodes of continuity and discontinuity. There is sufficient continuity to enable us to speak to each other about God and to have some idea of what we are talking about when we do. But there is sufficient discontinuity to keep us aware of the fact that we can never sum it all up" (21). Here Bartow recognizes the paradoxical nature of revelation, which is beyond totalization. Why then is Bartow so insistent on re-inscribing the classic Western tendency to associate speech with presence and writing with absence? When we invite our congregants to hear the Word of God might this not be a call to recognize God's presence in God's absence and, mutatis mutandis God's absence in God's presence? In what way, then, is the text an "arrested performance" if both text and proclamation *are* the Word of God?

sermonic P/presence? Lastly, if speech itself is the means of semantic resurrection from its textual tomb, do we really need God to be present in preaching?

Thomas Troeger asserts, "We value speech because its aural properties suggest the ineffable character of personhood and the source of being from whom that personhood springs." Note the paradox: for Troeger, the ineffable, that which cannot be uttered, is made available through speech, the actualization of effability. "Preaching will never die," he continues, "because a witness to the precise personal center of reality—God—is most effective when we receive it through a medium that expresses the fullness and wonder of what personality is, and that is accomplished more completely by speech than by the written word."[19] Paul Scott Wilson goes so far as to assert, "The passive words we use for God may in fact stand as barriers to God's coming to us. . . . Both the Bible and oral cultures suggest practical guidelines for using concrete language and action statements about God."[20] For Wilson, it seems, if we pick the wrong words, God will not enter into preaching. Yikes! All the more incentive to polish that manuscript, the written word, before Sunday morning.

It is not all that surprising to hear mainline homileticians and preachers defend the importance of the sermon manuscript. What is surprising, in light of the ecclesial propensity to the dynamism of call-and-response, is how many African American homileticians encourage the use of sermon manuscripts. William Turner Jr. writes that the "instrument of the preacher is the script."[21] In much the same vein, Cleophus LaRue writes,

> What you hear from black pulpits is a carefully crafted selection of words in which the preachers *give the impression of spontaneity*, pleasing the expectations of a listening congregation that prizes spontaneity as a sign of the movement of the Spirit. But *in actuality*, much thought and careful

19. Thomas H. Troeger, *Imagining a Sermon* (Nashville: Abingdon, 1990), 69. Troeger is right: "Vocal inflections represent dimensions of reality that exceed rational analysis, meanings that go beyond the denotations of a dictionary definition" (74). Where he is less helpful is in the assumption that the "musicality" of speech in the realm of sound is not itself a mode of signification. It is. Moreover, the musicality of a culture is situated in, if not determined by, that culture.
20. Paul Scott Wilson, *The Practice of Preaching* (Nashville: Abingdon, 1995), 37.
21. William Clair Turner Jr., *Preaching That Makes the Word Plain: Doing Theology in the Crucible of Life* (Eugene, OR: Wipf & Stock, 2008), 22. Turner differentiates between "the script" and "the scribble." He explains that "[t]here is a sense in which scribble offers a moment for the searching and trying of the heart in the presence of God who knows the wickedness of the preacher. It is like prayer in sighs that are too deep for words, but that are suited to one's temperament and mood. Scribble is the extension of meditation in a moment when one can be real with God before standing in the congregation" (23).

consideration have gone into the selection of each word, thought pattern, and argument that the black preacher speaks (or intends to speak).[22]

Is oral/aural spontaneity a ruse, then? Is this "sign" of the Spirit's movement in and through the preacher's words mere subterfuge? In his seminal text *The Heart of Black Preaching*, LaRue argues that literary devices such as antiphonality, repetition, alliteration, syncopation, oral formulas, thematic imagery, voice merging, and sacred time "continues to be a compelling concern of the African American preacher. Such rhetorical tools in the hands of a skillful black preacher can evoke a sense of God's awe and mystery in the listening congregation."[23] Taking these words at face value, it seems that LaRue has a hearty confidence in our human capacity to elicit an experience of divine presence. Is this merely a function of rhetorical flair, or is something less anthropocentric going on in and through the preacher's words?

Though informed by LaRue's perspective, Kenyatta Gilbert urges his preaching students to follow the Spirit away from their manuscripts in the preaching moment. This risky endeavor, Gilbert writes, "should be about letting God revise our manuscripts to speak a truer and more faithful expression of the good news." Thus, Christian proclamation "involves the unleashing of the gospel in the context of human community."[24] How, then, is the manuscript (writing) understood to function in relation to what Gilbert deems a "truer" and "more faithful expression" of the gospel manifested through speech?

We find the same arguments in Roman Catholic homiletics. Stephen DeLeers states, "In a very real way, of course, the phrase 'written homily' is an oxymoron. A written text is an object, produced in private, fixed in space. A homily is an oral event, the product not of a sin-

---

22. Cleophus J. LaRue, *I Believe I'll Testify: The Art of African American Preaching* (Louisville: Westminster John Knox, 2011), 83. Emphasis added.

23. Cleophus J. LaRue, *The Heart of Black Preaching* (Louisville: Westminster John Knox, 1999), 10. Likewise, Teresa Fry Brown addresses the same orientation in terms of *musicality*. She explains, "The preacher's use of musicality is the linguistic intonation, ebb and flow, call and response, inflection and physicality inherent in many forms of black and charismatic preaching. It often evokes and expresses the emotional content of the sermon." Teresa L. Fry Brown, *Delivering the Sermon: Voice, Body, and Animation in Proclamation* (Minneapolis: Fortress Press, 2008), 36.

24. Kenyatta R. Gilbert, *The Journey and Promise of African American Preaching* (Minneapolis: Fortress Press, 2011), 88. See also the recent study of Gardner Taylor's improvisational manuscript preaching in Jared E. Alcántara, *Crossover Preaching: Intercultural-Improvisational Homiletics in Conversation with Gardner C. Taylor* (Downers Grove, IL: InterVarsity, 2015). Alcántara notes, "Taylor was not an ad-hoc preacher. He was highly prepared. Spontaneity arose out of intense preparation and memorization. His Manuscript was more like a *manutemplate* from which improvised sermonic discourse could emerge" (71–72).

gle agent, but of the interplay of preacher, hearer, and the Holy Spirit. A homily is not a text."[25] What is it about orality/aurality that is fundamentally different from textuality? Might not the interplay of sermon scriptor, reader, and the Holy Spirit be equally efficacious? If not, why not?

I'm not picking on these fine scholars, nor am I singling out a minority report within the guild. If time and space allowed, we could amble together through the annals of homiletical theology to find much the same privileging of speech over writing—in fact, I can find no case in which a homiletician has questioned the hierarchical relationship of speech over writing, or one who has even questioned the relationship between written and oral/aural sermonic discourse.

Voice Over: How Speech "Works"

Before we wade too deeply into the marshes of philosophy, let's get something straight: speech "works" as a form of communication. I say something. You hear something. In this act, *something* is communicated between us, and this something is communicated differently than through other mediums (e.g., writing, texting, Facebook). That which appears in your mind may not be a perfect copy of what I have in my mind; nevertheless, spoken discourse functions as a sufficient mode of communication. So why the scare quotes? Well, I want preachers and homileticians to think through some of the philosophical and theological assumptions that facilitate the *work* of speech. There are three aspects of speech I'd like us to consider together.

The first thing to note is that the "I" who speaks is not stable (see chapter 2). As the nineteenth-century poet Arthur Rimbaud famously wrote, "I is an other" (*Je est un autre*).[26] I "am" someone else. To myself. To you. To God. In other words, the "I" that others perceive is other than the "I" that I understand myself to be. We would hope that this is especially apropos to the "I" who preaches, who is changed—transformed, even—in the uneventful event of preaching. The Pope himself

25. Stephen Vincent DeLeers, *Written Word Biomes Living Word: The Vision and Practice of Sunday Preaching* (Collegeville, MN: Liturgical Press, 2004), 157–58.
26. Arthur Rimbaud, "À Georges Izambard (Charleville, 13 mai 1871)," in *Rimbaud: Complete Works, Selected Letters, A Bilingual Edition*, ed. Seth Whidden, trans. Wallace Fowlie, rev. ed. (Chicago: University of Chicago Press, 2005), 370. Leading up to this, Rimbaud writes, "I want to be a poet, and I am working to make myself a *Seer*: you will not understand this, and I don't know how to explain it to you. It is a question of reaching the unknown by the derangement of *all the senses*. The sufferings are enormous, but one has to be strong, one has to be born a poet, and I know I am a poet. This is not at all my fault. It is wrong to say: I think: One ought to say: people think me.—Pardon the pun [*penser*, 'to think'; *panser*, 'to groom']" (371).

argues that "before preparing what we will actually say when preaching, we need to let ourselves be penetrated by that word which will also penetrate others, for it is a living and active word." And he continues, writing that if the preacher "does not take time to hear God's word with an open heart, if he does not allow it to touch his life, to challenge him, to impel him, and if he does not devote time to prayer with that word, then he will indeed be a false prophet, a fraud, a shallow impostor."[27] Linguistically, the "I" who speaks is but an evanescent instantiation of conscious and unconscious energies. Much as sound is expressed in its departure, so too is the "I" who speaks manifested in her speaking.

The tenuousness of the preacher as subject makes the spoken word just as shaky as the written word. All who preach know this to be true in a very practical way. Have you ever listened to a recorded sermon from earlier in your preaching ministry or returned to a sermon preached in the last lectionary cycle? Do you agree with everything you said? Would you say it the same way today? No. So you see, the plentitude of your presence can no more be secured by spatial and temporal proximity (speech) than it can through graphic signification (writing). The "I" who communicates is an "I" in flux, regardless of the medium of communication.

Second, we need to think more critically about how speech is related to life. Breath is a stable marker of existence; the prolonged absence of breath indicates death (for mammals, at least). Furthermore, a *certain* symmetry obtains between the self that speaks and the self that hears oneself speak. This transcends the mere linguistic synchronicity of my first point. I feel my lungs expand, sense my diaphragm supporting my breath, perceive the vibration of my vocal chords as my body transforms breath into sound. It all seems kind of magical.[28] But here's the rub: the concord I perceive between my consciousness and my embodied speech is not real.

The power of the voice is experienced by the speaker differently than the hearer. When I hear myself speak, I do not seem to need to transcend myself, to move outside myself in order to be affected by my own expressive activity. My words appear to be *alive* in a way that others' words do not. I carry my voice through my breath, which I

27. Francis, *The Joy of the Bishops: Evangelii Gaudium* (Dublin: Veritas, 2013), 80.
28. See Ruthanna B. Hooke," The Spirit-Breathed Body: Divine Presence and Eschatological Promise in Preaching" (paper, Annual Meeting for the Academy of Homiletics, San Antonio, Texas, November 2016).

alone can experience as exhalation. Thus, in my speaking, my embodied voice claims ownership of the words I intend; I require nothing outside myself to experience the fullness of my own voice.[29]

My experience I have with myself differs when I write. Writing makes me feel alienated. I am forced to transcend my body. Furthermore, the marks I inscribe on a page do not dissipate, as does my voice. They remain. They linger. I lose control over them once they have left my mind through the movements of my hand. Moreover, writing *seems* to constrain expression in a way that speaking does not. My hand must conform to the rule of the letter, with my gaze enforcing the letter's hegemony.[30] But when I speak, my body and mind *seem* more fully united. All of it—diaphragm, lungs, larynx, mouth, tongue—seems to achieve a miraculous harmony in my voice.

In spite of this appearance, a necessary gap persists between my speaking and my hearing. It is a brief gap, faster than the blink of an eye, but a gap supervenes nevertheless. "My words are 'alive' because they seem not to leave me: not to fall outside me, outside my breath, at a visible distance; not to cease, to belong to me, to be at my disposition 'without further props.'"[31] This is how we convince ourselves of *truth* and how we teach ourselves to value truth over mere *appearance*. This myth bolsters much of Western thought. In order for speech to "work" as communication it requires that which is *other* than life. In that briefest of moments between speaking and hearing, my *living speech* is sustained by a certain *dead space*—within me, between us. This space is *necessary*; have you ever placed your lips on another's ear and spoken? No meaning is made. All they get is a tickle, which communicates something else entirely. So, a certain *absence*, a kind of death—spacing, hiatus, gap—is required for speech to live.[32] Presence through speech is a compelling fiction. I'll say more about this in a moment.

29. See Jacques Derrida, *Speech and Phenomena; And Other Essays on Husserl's Theory of Signs*, trans. David B. Allison (Evanston, IL: Northwestern University Press, 1973), esp. chs. 5 and 6.

30. See Luce Irigaray, "The Rape of the Letter," in *To Speak is Never Neutral*, trans. Gail Schwab (New York: Routledge, 2002), 123, who writes of "the enslavement of the hand" and the "dictatorship of the eye."

31. Derrida, *Speech and Phenomena*, 76. "This self-presence of the animating act in the transparent spirituality of what it animates, this inwardness of life with itself, which has always made us say that speech [*parole*] is alive, supposes, then, that the speaking subject hears himself [*s'entendre*] in the present. Such is the essence or norm of speech. It is implied in the very structure of speech that the speaker *hears himself*: both that he perceives the sensible form of the phonemes and that he understands his own expressive intention" (78).

32. See Jacob D. Myers, "Dying to be Creative: Playing in/with the Homiletical Hiatus," *Homiletic* 38, no. 2 (2013): 17–29.

Third, and this point draws upon points one and two, we need to think more carefully about the relationship between speech and presence. Jared Alcántara writes, "In sacramental human speech in the public recitation of Scripture, God manifests God's presence."[33] This view is commonplace. Richard Ward describes the recitation of scripture as an "intentional act of turning something as fixed and abstract as a text into concrete, embodied human speech." We might challenge Ward as to just how "fixed" the Bible is (see chapter 3), but even more central here is what Ward says next: "Any *coherent* understanding of what language is and does, of how language performs, of the capacity of human speech to communicate meaning and feeling is, in the final analysis, underwritten by an assumption of God's presence."[34] How so? Why must we assume God's presence in order for human speech to function? Are all atheists mute, then?

Contemporary homileticians desire to save presence by protecting speech. Thomas Long, for instance, hopes for preaching to participate in "the eventfulness of God" by "recovering voice." This, he argues, "will involve recovering a confidence in the capacity of language to be the carrier wave for divine encounter, or, perhaps better to say, trust that God in freedom will in freedom choose to be present in our little words."[35] Such a presence can neither tolerate nor abide alongside absence. So too, LaRue writes that in the Black church tradition, congregants expect and appreciate "rhetorical flair and highly poetic language in the preaching of the gospel." Such a style is commended "to free the poet in the preacher and allow the presence of God through the power of language to lift the sermon to higher heights." The questions I wish to pose to Long, LaRue and others are these: Is it right to tether God's presence to the power of oral rhetoric? Is the human voice a sufficient "carrier wave" for divine encounter? Furthermore, what does this commit us to theologically? If I master a way with words, have I mastered the divine presence in some sense? Might not this feeling of God's presence in the "storm" of pulpit proclamation be merely a function of language? When "[t]he listening ear becomes the privileged sensual organ as the preacher attempts through careful and precise rhetoric to embody the Word," are we not claiming an a priori "point of contact" between God and humanity?[36]

---

33. Alcántara, *Crossover Preaching*, 92–93.
34. Richard F. Ward, *Speaking of the Holy: The Art of Communication in Preaching* (St. Louis: Chalice, 2001), 64.
35. Thomas G. Long, *Preaching from Memory to Hope* (Louisville: Westminster John Knox, 2009), 41.

What all this points to is that the voice, which is seemingly at one with itself in the thought world of the proclaimer and the empirical world of the listener, is always already structured by a certain dissimulation for which homiletics has failed to account. Homiletics is not alone it this; indeed, it is the central presupposition of Western thought: truth or meaning as a presence without difference from itself. This leads me to a second proposition: living speech is contaminated by death.

Living Speech is Contaminated by Death

When I open my mouth to speak—whether from the pulpit or not—I willingly participate in death. When my words leave my lips they are severed from the very thing believed to give them life: breath. Moreover, a structural necessity for speech is the "dead space" between speaker and listener. Even if my words are alive in my mouth in some necessary sense, their articulation as such forces them into the realm of death as absence. This is paradoxical to be sure.

You'll recall from chapter 1 that no act of discourse (spoken, writing, gestural, etc.) can be a *singular event*. It must employ some form of signification that is recognizable to an interlocutor. Its very *repeatability* prevents its singularity.[37] Furthermore, every time I speak I am doing something *new*. Nobody in the history of the world has ever stood where I now stand to say what I now say *at this particular point in time.*[38] But in spite of how speaking/hearing might make us feel, speech participates in the vicissitudes of language in general. To put this another way, in spite of the apparent unity of signification in speech caught up in the realm of sound, speech requires language, difference. When I preach, I employ my voice. The sound leaves me, transcends me, in order to arrive at the intended target of my speech (the congregation); but it does this without ever *seeming* to leave me.[39] Such transcendence

36. LaRue, *The Heart of Black Preaching*, 10. Cf. John W. Hart, *Karl Barth vs. Emil Brunner: The Formation and Dissolution of a Theological Alliance, 1916-1936* (New York: Peter Lang, 2001).

37. Derrida, *Speech and Phenomena*, 50: "A signifier (in general) must be formally recognizable in spite of, and through, the diversity of empirical characteristics which may modify it. It must remain the *same*, and be able to be repeated [iterable] as such, despite and across deformations which the empirical event necessarily makes it undergo."

38. Ibid. "A phoneme or grapheme is always to some extent different each time that it is presented in an operation or a perception. But, it can function as a sign, and in general as language, only if a formal identity enables it to be issued again and to be recognized."

39. Some thinkers, like the ancient sophist Gorgias (c. 375 BCE), have questioned whether or not language is capable of capturing thought at all: "speech can never exactly represent perceptibles, since it is different from them, and perceptibles are apprehended each by the one kind of organ, speech by another. Hence, since the objects of sight cannot be presented to any other organ

is both real and apparent: it is real in that I really am communicating something to *someone else*; it is apparent because every act of speech tethers me all the more to language.

This point bears repeating. The meaning (signified) of my speech (signifier) appears immediately present to the speaker in the act of expression. This *appearance* of self-presence in the act of speaking also causes us—in the Western tradition, at least—to link the sound of our own voice to meaning, breath, presence, and truth. Because the meaning-intention of my speaking/preaching is in absolute proximity to me, it seems to make no detour through language or the world. Space and signification are erased in what philosophers will label "pure auto-affection."[40] This is that feeling I've been describing wherein my spoken words affect me differently than they affect others. The assumption of speech as pure auto-affection is a mark of most, if not all, homiletical theologies.

Allow me to illustrate. Lischer writes, "Our cultural perception has so long been dominated by the visual—script, print, electronic image—that from time to time voices are needed to remind us that the visual words we see are *representations* of a more fundamental and primal reality, namely, the word as sound. Words are for hearing." Lischer continues along these lines, arguing that sound is the "key to interiority."[41] This assertion overlooks the general operation of language that we discussed above. Spoken words (phonemes) are just as susceptible to the vicissitudes of signification as written words (graphemes); they share equally in the *arbitrary* and *differential* web that is signification.

Bartow displays the philosophical problematic of speech and writing, and how such a bias against writing trips up his theological claims, in the following passage: "The Word of God is face to face, oral-aural, situated, and suasory discourse. It is not a dead letter. It is not reason alone. It is an event of *actio divina* (God's self-performance, if you will). It is in fact God's human speech."[42] But we now know better than to follow Bartow's simplistic distinction between *dead letter* and *living speech*.

but sight, and the different sense-organs cannot give their information to one another, similarly speech cannot give any information about perceptibles. Therefore, if anything exists and is comprehended, it is incommunicable." Gorgias, *Philosophic Classics*, vol. 1: *Thales to Ockham*, ed. Walter Kaufmann, trans. Kathleen Freeman (New Jersey: Prentice Hall, 1968), 56.

40. Derrida, *Of Grammatology*, 98. See also Irigaray, "The Setting in Psychoanalysis," in *To Speak is Never Neutral*, 199.
41. Richard Lischer, *A Theology of Preaching: The Dynamics of the Gospel*, rev. ed. (Eugene, OR: Wipf and Stock, 2001), 48, 50. See Walter J. Ong, *The Presence of the Word* (New Haven, CT: Yale University Press, 1967) and Ong's later work *Orality and Literacy* (London: Routledge, 1982).
42. Bartow, *God's Human Speech*, 3.

Inherent in the structure of human communication is a certain vacillation between life and death, presence and absence, and this situation is necessary for both speech and writing.[43] Life and death are not as dualistic as we have been led to believe. Life is contaminated by death. Language is always already infected.

There is "a power of death in the heart of living speech," writes Derrida, "a power all the more redoubtable because it opens as much as it threatens the possibility of the spoken word."[44] In spite of Derrida's philosophical insights, which are now a half-century old, there persists in homiletics an implicit confidence in speech as capable of delivering (God's) full presence. Michael Brothers writes, "Through distance and participation, the preacher invites the hearer to *participate freely* in life over death."[45] Here the choice he names proves my point. Brothers urges his readers to exploit the gap, the hiatus, the dead zone, between speaker and hearer to inaugurate a life-giving sermonic event that is set in opposition to the death-dealing droning of direct sermonic discourse. The possibility of the former relies on the rejection of the latter.

In its preoccupation with sameness, presence, and life—along with its fear of contamination by otherness, absence, and death—homiletics has followed lockstep with Western philosophy and theology. This causes homiletical theology to fear philosophical fears that subvert theology as such. In rushing to avoid contamination, impurity, and death, homiletics ignores the spacing necessary for signification in general (sign of sign). There's a gap, a difference, an absence, a death always already at work in sameness, presence, and life. What is there to fear if our hope in God is truly more than hope in the power of human discourse?

43. See Derrida, *Speech and Phenomena*, 40: "All these 'goings-forth' effectively exile this life of self-presence in indications. We know now that indication, which thus far includes practically the whole surface of language, is the process of death at work in signs. As soon as the other appears, indicative language—another name for the relation with death—can no longer be effaced." Even in a book titled *Preaching without Notes*, Webb insists that "the sermon preached without script or notes is a well-developed, meticulously crafted sermon, open to the guidance of the Holy Spirit, but prepared under the same constrains of procedure and time, and energy that guide every preacher week in and week out." Joseph M. Webb, *Preaching Without Notes* (Nashville: Abingdon, 2001), 23.
44. Derrida, *Of Grammatology*, 141.
45. Michael Brothers, *Distance in Preaching: Room to Speak, Space to Listen* (Grand Rapids, MI: Eerdmans, 2014), 79.

Preaching the Death of God

Preaching is not the Word of God. To the degree that preaching *is* anything, preaching is the death of God. Let's discuss this proposition linguistically and then theologically.

First, the linguistic argument. For a word to be anything it must first sacrifice the very thing it signifies—that is, to be a word, it must *not* be the word's referent. This is true for all words. The word *dog*, arbitrary and differential as it is (see chapter 1), *is* not an animal that lives and breathes. It is a *sound* that gives rise to a *thought*; it is an *inscription* on a page made of ink or lead or wax, which has no heartbeat and draws no breath. This word cannot fetch your slippers.

The word *God* is no different. It has no special access to being, to life. Blanchot instructs us here. He asks, "How can the Sacred, which is 'unexpressed,' 'unknown,' which is what opens provided only that it is not discovered, which reveals because unrevealed—how can it fall into speech, let itself be alienated into becoming, itself pure interiority, the exteriority of song?" This is a question that homiletics has failed to ask. Blanchot the atheist reminds us that all worldly language concerning God has as its origin an "event that cannot take place."[46] Or, as the novelist and critic Jean-Richard Bloch argues in his 1931 collection of essays *Destin du siècle* (*Fate of the Century*), our every attempt at discourse is stymied because "there are large corpses lying across our path. These are dead words." For Bloch, words only serve to draw us into their deadness.[47] Kind of like zombies. In a similar way, Henri Bergson writes of the impossibility of achieving existence itself through mere representation when the latter necessarily suppresses the former.[48] Preaching is only possible as the *impossible* and the preacher is the very incarnation of this impossibility.

Language produces a kind of death. The literary critic Jean Paulhan

---

46. Blanchot, "The Sacred Speech of Holderlin," in *The Work of Fire*, 126.
47. Jean-Richard Bloch, *Destin du siècle* (Paris: Presses Universitaires de France, 1996), 147–52.
48. "To transform [the living thing's] existence into representation, it would be enough to suppress what follows it, what precedes it, and also all that fills it, and to retain only its external crust, its superficial skin. That which distinguishes it as a *present* image, as an objective reality, from a *represented* image is necessarily what obliges it to act through every one of its points of all other images, to transmit the whole of what it receives, to oppose to every action an equal and contrary reaction, to be, in short, merely a road by which pass, in every direction, the modifications propagated throughout the immensity of the universe. . . . Representation is there, but always virtual—being neutralized, at the very moment when it might become actual, by the obligation to continue itself and to lose itself in something else." Henri Bergson, "Images and Bodies," in *Key Writings*, ed. John Mullarkey and Keith Ansell Pearson (London: Bloomsbury Academic, 2014), 117–18.

articulates this as clearly as you'll find anywhere. Language, he notes, is made up of signs on the one hand and ideas on the other. Language tethers the latter to the former by way of evocation; that is, the sign *evokes* an idea, calls it into presence. Language is thus partly material (signs) and partly spiritual (ideas). Paulhan concludes, "The power of words would thus be precisely, in the microcosm of its expression, the material oppressing the spiritual . . . a thought that is subjugated to words, however hard it tries to keep up appearances, is already dead and reduced to nothing: just one thing among others that falls over when you push it, and that stays down once it has fallen over."[49] You cannot take the word *dog* for a walk; you cannot climb the word *tree*.

And so I ask, *How might preaching, as a form of language, overcome the death that is always already at work in sermonic speech, as well as sermonic writing?* It cannot and it ought not—not if it truly believes in a God who can overcome death! Preaching has no privileged access to the *presence* of God. By tethering itself ontologically to the "Word" of God, preaching displays the very faithlessness it eschews. The word *God* only ever evokes an *idea* of God, which renders only the *concept* of God present. Homiletical theologies can do better than this.

Theologically speaking, as if theo*logy* were not already a form of speaking, preaching unwittingly proclaims the death of God. Preaching necessarily places conditions upon God, as my survey of aural homiletical theology reveals. To follow the arguments of those homiletical defenders of speech all the way would mean that God is dead in the realm of written language. Because writing is inextricable from absence, God's absence is inextricable from writing. For these thinkers, speech rushes onto the scene to resurrect God from God's death, to resuscitate God through the preacher's breath. This, I have argued, is an illusion. It only *seems* like speech conjures presence. We are alive when we speak, but it does not follow that our breathing-presence may overcome writing's silence-absence through speech.

Here is where the work of John Caputo is especially helpful. He has written much about the dangers of linking the idea harbored in the name/ing (of) God with existence, Being. God does not *exist*, argues Caputo; God *insists*. The "insistence of God" seeks to interrupt a metaphysics of presence, troubling theology's logocentrism, its every condition of possibility. It gestures toward the provocation of an event. And as such, the insistence of God, which "is" not a *thing*, *agent*, or *subject*,

---

49. Jean Paulhan, *The Flowers of Tarbes*, trans. Michael Syrotinski (Urbana: University of Illinois Press, 2006), 33.

gives rise to a *radical* homiletics that is more theological than any confessional theology could ever be on account of the latter's blindness to its own philosophical commitments. Following Caputo's charge, I want us to pursue a *radical homiletics* that participates in the "hope beyond hope" that God will show up in our preaching, *might* even call upon us through preaching: that God *may be* experienced kerygmatically as a solicitation.[50]

What is more, Caputo teaches us that the *event* of God's presence—in preaching as well as theology—never takes place, cannot take place, for (at least) two reasons: 1) Any event worthy of the name cannot be conditioned by theology, and 2) Theo-logy, as a mode of *logos*, can only posit ideas; it cannot address events as such.

The *event* of God, if such an event is ever possible, takes (its) place without condition. Caputo explains, "The unconditional is a homeless, uncanny sort of thing or nothing that does not inhabit the house of being." Here Caputo is challenging a certain Heideggerian assumption, which has done much for the New Homiletic.[51] Caputo continues, "It is not God's life on earth as the Absolute Spirit (Hegel) but rather something more spectral that gives us no peace. It is not Divine Providence transcribed into space and time but a more radical roll of the dice, a promise/threat, where the risk runs all the way down, where the folly is to follow the risk all the way without turning back."[52] Homiletics, with all of its sophisticated theological and rhetorical strategies, cannot teach preaching to conjure God's presence.

To speak of God vis-à-vis theology is already to misspeak. Caputo argues that a theology "turning on the insistence of God," one that arises out of a "resolutely un-sovereign and anti-imperial and un-

50. John D. Caputo, *The Insistence of God: A Theology of Perhaps* (Bloomington: Indiana University Press, 2013), 53. In his own words: "As with justice so with God, which the insistence of God, which is an interruption, a solicitation, a promise, occurring in a disjunction or dislocation. Disjoining is the work of the event, which does not mean what the event 'does,' but the way the event opens the space in which things get themselves done. The 'axiom' of any hauntology of the event, were such a thing possible, is that when it comes to events, to be is to provoke. . . . The event is not what happens but what is going on in what happens, what is provocative about what happens. The provocation means that we can never see God coming. God can happen anywhere. Even God cannot see God coming."
51. See, for instance, Robert Stephen Reid, "Commentary," in *The Renewal of Preaching in the Twenty-First Century*, 2nd ed. with commentary by Robert Stephen Reid (Eugene, OR: Wipf & Stock, 2008), 130, and Craddock, *As One Without Authority*, 31–36.
52. John D. Caputo, *The Folly of God: A Theology of the Unconditional* (Salem, OR: Polebridge, 2016), 78–79. Citing Derrida, Caputo continues, "The unconditional in Derrida is not infinite being, not being itself, not the being of beings, not a hyper-being, but something otherwise and elsewhere, an infinitival in-finite, a to-come, a messianic promise (without a Messiah), a figure of hope against hope—how foolish is that?—in the coming of something that we cannot see coming, which may turn out to be a disaster" (79).

monarchical theology, a theology that insists without quite existing," ought to take the form of a *theopoetics*.[53] Such a shift from theology to theopoetics could move homiletics from its mythological and ideological harbor into a sea of discursive possibilities that nurtures a space for the *possibility* of encountering God, perhaps.

Preaching, like life itself, is conditioned by death. Death is only possible for that which lives. Therefore, the majority report of contemporary homiletics, presuming that preaching as speech can somehow skirt the death-dealing effects of speech, ignores preaching's own most possibility. Homiletics must move beyond its (Western) preoccupation with presence if it is not to proclaim God's death though the conditions it places upon preaching. But there is another way. Even as God is in trouble on account of our homiletical techniques and theological presuppositions, when we shift our perspective to view God as the trouble that simultaneously animates and jeopardizes preaching, we discover that preaching the death of God isn't such a bad or scary prospect after all.[54]

I propose, therefore, a moratorium on the Word of God in reference to preaching. Preaching "is" not the Word of God. To the extent that it "is" anything, preaching is the secret of God. This secret of God is not the same thing as Luther's "hidden" God or Barth's "veiled" or "unknowable" God.[55] Rather, beyond Being and beyond appearing as such, the secret (of) God spooks preaching. The secret (of) God, which always already animates/torments the "Word" of God manifested in our words about God, can reorient homiletics to embrace the ghost of preaching's own impossibility—a thoroughly troubling homiletical theology.

Section Two: God *as* Trouble

The whole idea is to haunt confessional theology, to expose it to what it contains but cannot succeed in containing, to expose it to an event it can-

---

53. Caputo, *The Insistence of God*, 63.

54. This does not mean that homiletics should become atheistic in some simple sense. "The death of God is not simple atheism but a radical atheism that converges with radical faith. Conventional understandings of atheism are not radical enough." Clayton Crockett, "The Death of God, Death, and Resurrection," in *Resurrecting the Death of God: The Origins, Influence, and Return of Radical Theology*, ed. Daniel J. Peterson, G. Michael Zbaraschuk (Albany, NY: SUNY Press, 2014), 152.

55. Joshua Miller, *Hanging by a Promise: The Hidden God in the Theology of Oswald Bayer* (Eugene, OR: Pickwick, 2015), 89, puts the difference between Luther and Barth in this regard more succinctly than you'll find anywhere: "Any hiddenness of God in this picture is a hiddenness of God within revelation."

not prevent, after which it will continue to be, perhaps, but it will never be the same.

— John D. Caputo[56]

God troubles preaching. A radical homiletics, inasmuch as it embraces the divine trouble driving preaching, ought to drive preaching (mad). Like a ghost, the spectrality harbored in the name/ing (of) God structures the impossibility of bifurcating presence and absence. As Caputo puts it, "the ghost is a kind of 'pres/absence,' there but then again not there, the source of a general disturbance in the present."[57] How might we embrace such a disturbance? How might we embrace God when so much of homiletical thought braces us structurally against the event harbored in the name/ing (of) God? When the *raison d'être* of homiletics is to make preaching possible, to teach preachers how to wrangle the impossible, how might we lean into an alternative way of being that troubles the necessary supposition of Being?

If we as homileticians and preachers are not to go mad, we must find a way to participate in the madness (of) God. This, precisely, is what radical homiletics offers to homiletical theology: madness, a troubled soul. Such a madness, such a troubling, such a haunting, disturbs every kind of preaching. It is an equal opportunity offender. Rather than establishing its own kingdom, its own kind-dom, radical homiletics would lurk in the shadows of every kind of preaching, spooking it by pointing to/out preaching's own ghoulishness.

Homiletics needs to articulate a better theological understanding of itself and its purpose. We do not preach because preaching offers us any guarantees, any assurances that the event harbored in the name (of) God will take place: that God will arrive. *God always might (not) show up.* This necessary possibility (not) is my claim. This is why I regard the ontological correlation between preaching and the Word of God to be insidious if not idolatrous. That is why enfolding presence in speech ignores the structural impossibility it creates. It is time we call bullshit on every kerygmatic ontology and thereby expose it to a homiletical "hauntology."[58]

56. Caputo, *The Insistence of God*, 104.
57. John D. Caputo, "Teaching the Event: Deconstruction, Hauntology, and the Scene of Pedagogy," *Philosophy of Education* (2012): 25.
58. This need not collapse into what David Schnasa Jacobsen labels a "purely deconstructive homiletic"—as if any deconstruction could ever be pure (enough)!—and confusedly identifies such with the work of John Caputo, namely, one "that places both divine grace and justice in a kind of hall of mirrors constructed out of parentheses, brackets, and ellipses." Jacobsen, "Promise as an Event of the Gospel in Context: Toward an Unfinished Homiletical Theology of Grace and Justice"

But this in no way means that we ought to abandon confessional theo-logy, only that we not ignore the ways God haunts theology's *logos*. Such is not completely alien to confessional theology as such. We catch glimpses of this trouble. Barth, for instance, gets it right when he declares that, "the Center cannot be apprehended or beheld" and thus the preacher

> will not if he can help it allow himself to be drawn into giving direct information about it, knowing that *all* such information, whether it be positive or negative, is *not* really information, but always *either* dogma *or* self-criticism. On this narrow ridge of rock one can only walk: if he attempts to stand still, he will fall either to the right or to the left, but fall he must. There remains only to keep walking—an appalling performance for those who are not free from dizziness—*looking from one side to the other*, from positive to negative and from negative to positive.[59]

Such difficulties, Barth seems to realize, cannot be overcome by theology, except, perhaps, by a radical theology that is troubled, dizzying, mad(dening)—"out of joint," as Hamlet declares.

Even as God "is" in trouble in/as Being, God spells trouble for preaching as p/Presence. But how, we may ask, are we to receive this theological troubling in and for preaching when homiletical theology wants to silence, to erase, to occlude the trouble that we name "God" in English? Harbored in the name/ing (of) God there stirs the radical secret of God that troubles our homiletical ontologies. Every "God is . . ." shifts the homiletical register toward Being, reducing God to our level. Most homiletical theologies arrest the play of otherness and absence always already at work within preaching. Here is where a homiletical hauntology saves preaching, saves it by spooking it (to death).

(paper, Annual Meeting for the Academy of Homiletics, San Antonio, Texas, November 2016), 76. I say confusedly because elsewhere Jacobsen praises Caputo's work and commends it to homiletics. See Jacobsen, "Promise and Cross: Homiletical Theology, the Vocative Word *Extra Nos*, and the Task of a Revisionist Eschatology," in *Homiletical Theology in Action: The Unfinished Theological Task of Preaching*, ed. David Schnasa Jacobsen (Eugene, OR: Cascade Books, 2015), 115, along with Jacobsen's endorsement of Caputo's recent books in his reviews of *The Insistence of God: A Theology of Perhaps* in *Homiletic* 39, no. 2 (2014): 57 and of *Hoping Against Hope: Confessions of a Postmodern Pilgrim* in *Homiletic* 41, no. 1 (2016): 91–92.

59. Barth, "The Word of God and the Task of Ministry," 206–207. Dialectical speech in no way *guarantees* that the preacher will not encroach upon hallowed ground. Barth writes, "There is no reason why the dialectic theology should be *specially* capable of leading one up *to* a gate which can be opened only from within. If one should fancy that it possesses a special preeminence, at least in preparing the way for the action of God, let him remember that it and its paradoxes can do no more *to this end* than can a simple direct word of faith and humility. . . . a stool may be high enough and the longest ladder too short to take the kingdom of heaven by force" (212).

Derrida writes, "The last one to whom a specter can appear, address itself or pay attention is a spectator as such. . . . As theoreticians or witnesses, spectators, observers and intellectuals, scholars believe that looking is sufficient. Therefore, they are not always in the most competent position to do what is necessary: speak to the specter."[60] A certain radical theology of *perhaps*, a certain theology turned (theo)poetics of the *unconditional* can help homiletics critique its own inheritance from theology. When we bracket our looking (*spectāre*), we homileticians and preachers are able to see the trouble of God in preaching that theology tries to shield from view.

Haunting Homiletics

William Turner Jr. hits the mark when we writes, "Being prepared to preach requires touching the mystery that is not accessible on the preacher's terms. The mystery of God is given in self-disclosure in moments that are inherent to that mystery." This is why Turner commends the preacher to allot much time to spiritual and homiletical contemplation and communion. He continues, "When the mystery has not been touched there is no vitality, no power. Preaching that does not live cannot give life; preaching that has no power cannot give power."[61] Turner urges preachers to open themselves to the Holy Spirit in hopes of achieving a spiritual state of "saturation." Out of this overflow, the Spirit speaks, perhaps.

But in preaching, in responding to the call harbored in the name/ing (of) God, in playing host even as we are played as host, we *say* "come" to that which we could never see coming. Our summons is a séance. We have no control over the Spirit, which is why we call the Spirit *Holy*. Because our speaking and writing (of) God are always already ghostly, the life and the "living" of which Turner speaks—and most of all the receiving and giving of power—always already participates in a kind of death. The mystery remains mysterious or it's not really a mystery but a quandary. There can be no *touching*, no *handling*—indeed, no *preaching*—apart from death.

Preaching must be exposed to a certain haunting, an exposure of the radically o/Other irreducible to sameness. Such will be the task of radical homiletics. We teachers of preaching do our students no favors when we show them how preaching is possible. Better to drive them

---

60. Derrida, *Specters of Marx*, 11.
61. Turner, *Preaching That Makes the Word Plain*, 22.

(mad) to grasp for the ungraspable truth of preaching as a "possibility of the impossible," which is the most theological—because it is the least theological—"truth" homiletics may approximate.

I want to suggest that homiletics accept a more humble status: that of host. The God who we seek and of whom we speak is *strange*. This is how God responds to the impertinence of Moses and Job (e.g., Exod 3:14; Job 38:4-7). And that is why preaching is so risky. Caputo offers a glimpse of what is at stake in such a posturing in naming hospitality for what it is: dangerous. Risking a visitation by the stranger (*hostis*) who might always be/come *hostile* affirms the arrival—perhaps—of the radically other, to wel-come whatever or whomever may *come*, with no guarantees or foreknowledge that such a coming will work out *well* for us. Caputo observes that this is why Derrida invented the portmanteau "hosti-pitality," and why Jesus declared love of friends to be far less dicey than loving our enemies.[62]

Imagine the homiletics classroom that welcomed and played host to the specters of language, identity, scripture, and theology that haunt preaching. Homiletics professors would need to attend less to what students were saying, or trying to say, about God and more to the attempts to speak forth and body forth a call, a summons. In very practical terms, embracing the specters of God in/as a radical homiletics, a homiletics that haunts every homiletic, will strive toward three tasks: 1) G/hosting the strange(r) before us; 2) G/hosting the strange(r) within us; and 3) G/hosting the strange(r) among us.

G/hosting the Strange(r) Before Us

Our route toward a radical homiletics that haunts homiletics as such must begin without beginning. This is impossible, and this impossibility tells us we are starting on the right foot, so to speak. The way forward is the aporetic way, a way that is no-way. Such is not an apophatic way, which always has a way of turning negation into affirmation.[63]

To begin without beginning is necessary in light of the ghoulishness of preaching. To speak (of) God is to proceed by way of death. As Blanchot reminds us, "Whoever sees God dies. In speech what dies is what gives life to speech; speech is the life of that death, it is 'the life that endures death and maintains itself in it.' What wonderful

---

62. Caputo, *The Insistence of God*, 40.
63. See Jacques Derrida, "How to Avoid Speaking: Denials," in *Languages of the Unsayable: The Play of Negativity in Literature and Literary Theory*, ed. Sanford Budick and Wolfgang Iser, trans. Ken Frieden (Stanford: Stanford University Press, 1987), 82.

power."[64] Radical, haunting homiletics must nurture a g/hostly perspective, playing host to the ghost that haunts our preaching.

The first step, which is already a mis-step, a *faux pas*, is a step that takes place before every step. It welcomes the (Holy) ghost before us; it greets the strange(r) before us with a prayer and a breath—our most sacred offering. At the same time, in a time without time, the preacher plays host to the strange(r) before us. This is a radical step because it exposes every inference, every prejudice (*Vorurteil*) that works to delineate and determine who or what this strange(r) might "be" within a horizon (*Horizont*) of possibility.[65] As Caputo puts it, "What exists is always already inscribed in 'perhaps,' caught up in the insistent condition of an ancient archi-spacing, in an ancient non-originary condition that is as old as time, an archi-space from time out of mind."[66] It is this originary givenness, prior to every foundational "there is" (*il y a/es gibt*), that the writer of Genesis signifies as *tohu wa-bohu*, the "formless and void" into which God breathed light.[67] We must find ways to become this *tohu wa-bohu*, which is kenotic without being deprecatory.

For a haunting homiletics—one that is as much haunter of preaching as haunted by p/reaching—moving toward God (perhaps!) demands that it distances itself, in a step (not) beyond (*le pas au-dela*), homiletics as such.[68] Here is where things get really scary. The p/reacher, as reacher for God, for words of God, enters an in-between, a liminal space that is no place, not even a middle or mediating place. What is said in its saying *takes* place in the middle voice, in between every agency and prior to every decision of passivity. This is what it means to play host before, to be-for(e) the strange(r) who may come.

The originary spacing that is at once before us in its archi-temporality is also be-*fore* us spatially. To play host to the (Holy) ghost deconstructs every effort to rule (*árchein*) this o/Other who always might

---

64. Blanchot, "Literature and the Right to Death," in *The Work of Fire*, 327.
65. The concepts of prejudice, or prejudgment, and horizon are Gadamer's. Han-Georg Gadamer, *Philosophical Hermeneutics*, ed. and trans. David E. Linge (Berkeley: University of California Press, 1976), 9: "Prejudices are our biases of our openness to the world. They are simply the conditions whereby we experience something—whereby what we encounter says something to us."
66. Caputo, *The Insistence of God*, 260.
67. See Catherine Keller, *The Face of the Deep: A Theology of Becoming* (London: Routledge, 2003), 1–24, 183–99. Here my thinking sides with Irigaray against Levinas, Derrida, and Caputo concerning the supposed originary taking place of the *il y a/es gibt*. See Luce Irigaray, *The Forgetting of Air in Martin Heidegger*, trans. Mary Beth Mader (Austin: University of Texas Press, 1999), esp.1–21, 79–94.
68. See Maurice Blanchot's book *The Step Not Beyond*, trans. Lynette Nelson (Albany, NY: SUNY Press, 1992), which performs its own fragmentation at the limits of discourse. Here we find a kind of displacement of the self as present to him/her/themself and the conventionality of language employed against language as convention. It has much to teach homiletics and preaching, but that must wait for a forthcoming volume.

(not) come. This "perhaps," as Caputo reminds us, "does not mean we should lose our faith that the world is worth the risk or that we should descend into tragic complaint. On the contrary, it calls for what is coming, strange and unforeseen though it be."[69] There is something at work within this "perhaps," which overruns and consumes theology as such, that is more faithful, faith-ful to God. The "perhaps" will not strengthen preaching except in tightening its sense of a sacred anarchy that rules over preaching by making preaching impossible.

G/hosting the Strange(r) Within Us

A second prospect toward haunting homiletics is to host the strange(r) within us.[70] As we have already devoted much attention to the strangeness of language (chapter 1) and our *estrangement* from ourselves (chapter 2), we need not reiterate those points here. Suffice it to say that the otherness that structures the possibility of our language and the otherness that ghosts our identity in the production or performance of our selfhood haunts our speaking and our being.

In addition, as we embrace the God, perhaps, who troubles homiletics by troubling preaching, we are confronted by a third "kind" of alterity. This third "kind" is not really or not quite a "kind" of anything. It has no kind—and this is where confessional theology/homiletics gets it right in stressing the otherness/righteousness of God. Unfortunately, we have seen throughout this book that too much of God's otherness is enervated by an economy of sameness (chapter 3). Derrida leads the way—leads us away from kind-ness and sameness—when he declares, "Every other (one) is every (bit) other" (*Tout autre est tout autre*).[71] The force of this shibboleth is theological *and* ethical, even as it marks by obscuring the line dividing ethics and theology. Said differently, it names with haunting parsimony one of the central theological claims of Barth and one of the primal ethical claims of Levinas.[72]

---

69. Caputo, *The Insistence of God*, 261.

70. This prospect is second only on account of *our* temporality, *our* inability to undergo multiple operations at once. I want to stress that these are not steps like those one may follow to build an IKEA bookshelf. There is no temporal or ontological priority to any of these tasks.

71. Derrida, *The Gift of Death*, 82. Derrida observes that even though this looks like a tautology, this declaration "instead utters a radical heterology, the very proposition of the most irreducible heterology." And yet, Derrida concedes, "That has never stopped it from 'functioning,' as one says, on the contrary. It operates so much better to the extent that it serves to obscure the abyss or fill in its absence of foundation, stabilizing a chaotic becoming in what are called conventions" (83, 84).

72. See Steven G. Smith, *The Argument to the Other: Reason Beyond Reason in the Thought of Karl Barth and Emmanuel Levinas* (Chico, CA: Scholars Press, 1983).

G/hosting the strange(r) within us compels the p/reacher to respond to the call of (the) otherness at work within us, to surrender to its very impossibility, which inverts the classical hierarchy between Being/theology and ethics/being. Caputo characterizes this call as *folly*. He writes, "The folly of God is that God does not exist; God insists. God does not exist; God calls. . . . The insistence of God means that the name of God is not the name of a Supreme Being, but the name of a call, to which we may or may not respond."[73] Haunting homiletics, a homiletics that haunts preaching even as it is haunted by p/reaching, nurtures a hospitable disposition to this call of the strange(r) that takes (its) place within us.

This call that is at work within p/reaching as its innermost possibility structures the impossibility of preaching. This strange(r) call that comes, perhaps, to the p/reacher solicits God in *our* response, or what Richard Kearney labels, the "poetics of the possible God." The God-Who-May-Be—*or May-Be-Not!*—elects the weakness of the call within p/reaching and is thus dependent upon our response to be and to work within p/reaching.[74] If this is the mode of God's being (perhaps) that

73. Caputo, *The Folly of God*, 83.
74. Kearney explains, "Hermeneutically retrieving Cusanus's idea of God as absolute possibility (*absoluta potentia*), I hold firm to the view that such *potentia* cannot be reduced to a totalizing necessity where every possible is ineluctably actualized from the beginning of time—history being reduced, by extension, to a slow-release 'unfolding' of some pre-established plan. On the contrary, from an eschatological perspective, divinity is reconceived as that *posse* or *possest* which calls and invites us to actualize its proffered possibles by our poetical and ethical actions, contributing to the transfiguration of the world to the extent that we respond to his invitation, but refusing this transfiguring task every time we do evil or injustice or commit ourselves to non-being. In short, while Nicholas of Cusa's initial bold challenge to the traditional priority of actuality over possibility is a welcome contribution to the rethinking of God as *posse*, it does not go far enough." Richard Kearney, *The God Who May Be: A Hermeneutics of Religion* (Bloomington: Indiana University Press, 2001), 105.
    David Jacobsen likes to cite Kearney's illuminating text to invoke an "onto-eschatological" theology of God's presence in/as God's promise for homiletics. See David Schnasa Jacobsen and Robert Allen Kelly, *Kairos Preaching: Speaking Gospel to the Situation* (Minneapolis: Fortress Press, 2009), 172; David Schnasa Jacobsen, "The Promise of Promise: Retrospect and Prospect of a Homiletical Theology," *Homiletic* 38, no. 2 (2013), 12; Jacobsen, "The Unfinished Task of Homiletical Theology," in *Homiletical Theology: Preaching as Doing Theology*, ed. David Schnasa Jacobsen (Eugene, OR: Cascade Books, 2015), 52; Jacobsen, "Promise and Cross," 115; Jacobsen, "Promise as an Event of the Gospel in Context." What Jacobsen misses in Kearney's book—and in Kearney's later work, which he never, to my knowledge, considers—is that the tendency to ground God's promise in actuality over and against possibility is antithetical to Kearney's notion of the "Possible God," the God without conditions, the "eschatological May-be." Furthermore, Jacobsen unwittingly places conditions on God's promise-making and promise-keeping that work against his declared reliance on an Austinian philosophy of perlocutionary acts.
    For Austin, conditions of felicity are met by the speaker (see Conclusion). Kearney, by contrast, argues that the "future of the covenant is wide open—nothing is predetermined. It is up to us to remain as faithful to God as God promises to remain faithful to us." Kearney stresses that the self-revelation of God to Moses in Exodus 3 is "less predicative than appellative." In other words, in disclosing Godself to Moses, God is revealing nothing about God's *Being* as such, if we can even speak in such terms; rather, God's self-naming is beyond substance and syllogism; the name of

God reveals to us in scripture, a mode of being that haunts our all-too-human conceptions of Being, ought we not nurture such folly in/as p/reaching?

Preachers must find a way to host in their bodies and in their words the strangeness at work within preaching. Such strangeness is radical in that its strangeness, its uncanniness, its mysteriousness, can never stop being strange. It never finds expression in a sameness of thought or language, for such sameness nullifies the (command to) secrecy at the heart of preaching. As Derrida makes clear in *The Gift of Death*, the irreducible strange(r)ness at the heart of linguistic expression and rationality transcends irrationality. The strange(r)ness within reason inheres in the very structure of reason, so this is not a paean to non-sensical preaching but a reminder that preaching spooks rationality from within. Or, as Derrida puts it elsewhere, "If I am to share something, to communicate, objectify, thematize, the condition is that there be something non-thematizable, non-objectifiable, non-sharable. And this 'something' is an absolute secret."[75] Preaching is thus spooky/ed on account of the originary summons to secrecy inhering with(in) it.

G/hosting the Strange(r) Among Us

Thirdly, a radical and haunting homiletics g/hosts the strange(r) among us by nurturing space to receive from others in our church communities and beyond. John McClure describes this better than any. He urges us to imagine the preaching ministry as an act of hospitality itself. In his own words: "... the preacher, like the disciples on the road to Emmaus, is a *host* who welcomes strangers into the preaching ministry. As hosts, we welcome all with a word to share into dialogue so that the word and wisdom of God might be discerned for the community."[76] Such an effort on the preacher's part also calls for her to be hosted by the other, to take the role of guest. In attending to whatever may come from the other, the preacher's preconceived understandings of God's agency in the world and in biblical texts become haunted by a

---

God marks a "relation rather than an abstraction" (26). God's self-revelation is more vocative than indicative. It is therefore completely off base for Jacobsen to set Kearney's thinking here against Caputo's reflections on the "insistence" of God. The God whom Kearney and Caputo e/in-voke is not the "God" of metaphysics, not the omnipotent "God," but a God who reveals Godself in the weakness/folly of the call, which always might not come—promise notwithstanding.

75. Jacques Derrida, "I Have a Taste for the Secret," in Jacques Derrida and Maurizio Ferraris, *A Taste for the Secret* (New York: Polity, 2001), 57.
76. John S. McClure, "Preacher as Host and Guest," in *Slow of Speech and Unclean Lips: Contemporary Images of Preaching Identity* (Eugene, OR: Cascade Books, 2010), 123.

possibility that belongs only to the other as such. In claiming the undecidable and nontotalizable role of guest/host, the other who may come and speak exposes confessional theology to the possibility of divine disclosure, to an "emergent word," to borrow McClure's language.

Charles Campbell provides radical homiletics with another angle on this g/hosting the strange(r) among us through what he labels "dislocation." Drawing from the ethical insights of William Stringfellow, Campbell challenges p/reachers to place themselves into intentional proximity to preaching's historical others, particularly the poor and marginalized. Campbell explains that "genuine dislocation involves much more than simply going to an unusual space; it involves preachers having their own *lives* "dislocated" by learning from the "other" and by allowing crucial homiletical practices—for example, biblical interpretation—to be shaped by a new space and different voices."[77] This is as radical as preaching gets, provided that in the p/reacher's dislocation she is ever wary of the propensity to turn the other into a sermon illustration, a mere commodity within the homiletical economy of sameness.

Radical homiletics can also learn much in this regard from the subversive work of Peter Rollins. Rollins, the founder and former leader of Ikon in Belfast, Ireland, developed two programs that inform this g/hosting of the strange(r) among us that participates in a radical homiletics. The first program Rollins designed is called the Omega Course. This multi-week venue plays off and against the Alpha Course, which aims to lead participants to a unified doctrinal understanding of the supposed essentials of Christianity. The Omega Course, by contrast, tries to create a space within Christian communities for those elements of faith and doubt that are repressed or suppressed by Christianity as such. In playing host to theology's other/ness, something like Rollins's Omega Course would receive this other/ness to haunt preaching and homiletics without attenuating the spookiness of the other/ness.

A second program designed by Rollins is called the Evangelism Project. The Evangelism Project works against traditional modes of evangelization, whereby the evangelist seeks to convert the other to his beliefs. Rollins's Evangelism Project aims instead for participants to host spaces wherein the "evangelist" aims to be converted to another's beliefs. Moreover, this Project invites religious others to name what

---

77. Charles L. Campbell, *The Word Before the Powers: An Ethic of Preaching* (Louisville: Westminster John Knox, 2002), 171.

they see in the "evangelist's" beliefs, to help the latter understand the effects of their faith on others.

These approaches to sermon development could become a part of the practices and rhythms taught by radical homiletics.[78] Such sites of hospitality, of receiving the other *as such*, foster a kind of hiatus at the heart of homiletics. In Derrida's terms, "This hiatus opens the rational space of a hypercritical faith, one without dogma and without religion, irreducible to any and all religious or implicitly theocratic institutions."[79] Such a faith beyond faith haunts a faith reduced to reason by exposing faith itself to the possibility of who or what may come. This is our task.

Specters of God: Preaching as Séance

We preachers are charged with the impossible task of enunciating the ineffable.[80] We are supposed to open our mouths and somehow, miraculously, God is supposed to speak. Unfortunately, our sermonic discourse often falls short. How might it be the case, as the Second Helvetic Confession insists, that "The Preaching of the Word of God *is* the Word of God"? Moreover, *how* does this happen? How do we know if/when this has happened? It *looks* like a human preaching. It *sounds* like a human preaching. What might be going on in and through preaching that conjoins it with God's Holy Word?

For preaching to move beyond a homiletics of presence it must allow radical homiletics to trouble its discourse. This begins by divesting ourselves of the privileging of speech. If our task is to "effect a *new hearing* of the Word among those who have been repeatedly exposed to it,"[81] as Craddock declares, then we must begin by placing our confessional (homiletical) theologies under erasure. Again, McClure helps us here, as does Snider.[82]

78. See John S. McClure, *The Roundtable Pulpit: Where Leadership and Preaching Meet* (Nashville: Abingdon, 1995) and Lucy Atkinson Rose, *Sharing the Word: Preaching in the Roundtable Church* (Louisville: Westminster John Knox, 1997).
79. Jacques Derrida, "To Arrive—At the Ends of the State," in *Rogues: Two Essays on Reason*, trans. Pascale-Anne Brault and Michael Naas (Stanford: Stanford University Press, 2005), 153.
80. "The word of God on the lips of a [person] is an impossibility; it does not happen: no one will ever accomplish it or see it accomplished." Karl Barth, "The Need and Promise of Christian Preaching," in *The Word of God and the Word of Man*, 124. And "God is distinguished from everything created, distinct, and finite by his indistinction and his infinity. . . . Thus, the more one tries to speak about the ineffable, the less that one says about it as ineffable. . . ." Meister Eckhart, "Commentary on Exodus," in *Meister Eckhart: Teacher and Preacher*, ed. and trans. Bernard McGuinn (New York: Paulist, 1986), 82.
81. Fred B. Craddock, *Overhearing the Gospel*, rev. ed. (St. Louis: Chalice, 2002), 11. Emphasis added.
82. See John S. McClure, *Other-Wise Preaching: A Postmodern Ethic for Homiletics* (St. Louis: Chalice,

When we open ourselves to this risky endeavor we find that we are not alone. The specters of God have always abided alongside confessional theology. St. Augustine puts it this way: "Have I spoken something, have I uttered something worthy of God? No, I feel that all I have done is to wish to speak; if I did say something, it is not what I wanted to say. How do I know this? Simply because God is unspeakable?"[83] Or consider the words of Meister Eckhart, whose p/reaching pursues a "light that is uncreated and not capable of creation," whose p/reaching ventures into "the quiet desert, into which distinction never gazed," who leads us into "the innermost part, where no one dwells."[84] Homiletics would do well to revisit his preaching.

To the degree that preaching "is" anything, it is a specter of God. By no means are we able to make the Spirit of God present. This is why I have argued that every homiletical ontology must give way to a kind of hauntology. Such is not seduced by a homiletics of presence; rather, it summons us to consider the marks of a philosophical/theological inheritance that simultaneously inhabits and spooks preaching.

I am not proposing a new task for preaching. Here I'm being more descriptive than prescriptive. The church is already haunted. Such a task is always already operative within a *wanting to hear* (God) and a *wanting to say* (God). Preaching expresses itself as a *yearning* for a "Word" that might always never come, and that is why only an erotic epistemology is sufficient to preaching.[85] Preaching is tasked with host-

---

2001) and Phil Snider, *Preaching After God: Derrida, Caputo and the Language of Postmodern Homiletics* (Eugene, OR: Cascade Books, 2012).

83. St. Augustine, *On Christian Teaching*, trans. R. P. H. Green (Oxford: Oxford University Press, 2008), 10. Later, he concedes, "Yet although nothing can be spoken in a way worthy of God, he [*sic*] has sanctioned the homage of the human voice, and chosen that we should derive pleasure from our words in praise of him" (11).

Cf. Karl Barth, *The Church Dogmatics*, II/1, ed. G.W. Bromiley and T. F. Torrance, trans. T. H. L. Parker, W. B. Johnston, Harold Knight, and J. L. M. Haire (Edinburgh: T & T Clark, 1957), 448, will put it like this: "God Himself [*sic*] is simple, so simple that in all His glory He can be near to the simplest perception and also laugh at the most profound or acute thinking—so simple that He reduces everyone to silence, and then allows and requires everyone boldly to make Him the object of their thought and speech. He is so simple that to think and speak correctly of Him . . . does not in fact require any special human complexities or for that matter any special human simplicities, so that occasionally and according to our need He may permit and require both human complexity and human simplicity, and occasionally they may both be forbidden us. For the simplicity of God is His own simplicity. His simplicity is God Himself as comfort, exhortation and judgment for all [people] and over all human endeavor."

84. Meister Eckhart, "Sermon 48," in *Meister Eckhart: The Essential Sermons, Commentaries, Treatises, and Defense*, trans. Edmund Colledge and Bernard McGinn (Mawhaw, NJ: Paulist, 1981), 198. Earlier in the sermon he speaks of "the man who has annihilated himself in himself and in God and in all created things; this man has taken possession of the lowest place, and God must pour the whole of himself into this man, or else he is not God" (197).

85. See Jacob D. Myers, "The Erotic Approach: Homiletical Insights form the Work of Georges Bataille," *Theology and Sexuality* 19, no. 1 (2013): 26–37.

ing the spirit of God, ever aware that preaching is only ever a specter of God.[86] Ironically, here is where preaching *might* be understood as Word, as that which is summoned and harbored in the phenomenality of words.[87] The subjunctive mood is key!

Preaching as séance calls upon God's spirit to haunt our theological certitude, our kerygmatic hubris. It forces the question upon us: Is God going to answer our call? Such a "frightening hypothesis of visitation" deconstructs homiletical ontologies of presence; it confesses that speech is an insufficient medium for presence.[88] Such a homiletic points to our all-too-human tendency to forget that we are haunted. The church is always already a haunted house.[89] Imagine if such an ecclesiology took hold of/as preaching: we enter a haunted house *in order to be spooked*, to drive us out into the world. Even as the church provides us sanctuary and comfort, it also ought to scare the hell out of us.

I myself am haunted by what is harbored and concealed by the insistence that preaching *is* the "Word" of God. That is why I appreciate Herbert McCabe OP's insight that through our words about God we do not access the Word as such, but that we access "a mystery beyond our understanding which we do not create, but which rather creates us and our understanding and our whole world."[90] It is far from irrelevant, I hasten to add, that homiletics has been dominated by mostly white, mostly straight, mostly male voices. The origin of the preacher's authority then, as *Word*, arises alongside that which bell hooks identifies as "imperialist white supremacist, capitalist patriarchy."[91] If

---

86. Here is where our English is less than helpful; the denotative distinction between *spirit* and *specter* is muted. German distinguishes between *der Geist* and *das Gespenst*. Likewise, French differentiates between *l'esprit* and *le spectre*.

87. St. Augustine argues that the Word of God is "neither utterable in sound nor capable of being thought under the likeness of sound such as must needs be with the word of any tongue; but which precedes all the signs by which it is signified." St. Augustine, *On the Trinity*, 411, 505–6.

88. Jacques Derrida, *Specters of Marx*, 124.

89. Karl Barth writes, "Real proclamation, then, means the Word of God preached and the Word of God preached means in this first and outermost circle man's talk about God on the basis of God's own direction, which fundamentally transcends all human causation, which cannot, then, be put on a human basis, but which simply takes place, and has to be acknowledged, as a fact." *Church Dogmatics*, I/1, 90.

90. Herbert McCabe OP, "The Logic of Mysticism," in *God Still Matters* (London: Continuum, 2005), 28.

91. bell hooks, *The Will to Change: Men, Masculinity, and Love* (New York: Atria Books, 2004), 17–18, and hooks, *Feminism is for Everybody: Passionate Politics* (London: Pluto, 2000), 46: "Since unenlightened white feminists were unwilling to acknowledge the spheres of American life where they acted and act in collusion with imperialist white supremacist capitalist patriarchy, sustained protest and resistance on the part of black women/women of color and our radical white sisters was needed to break the wall of denial." See also Delores S. Williams, *Sisters in the Wilderness: The Challenge of Womanist God-Talk* (Maryknoll, NY: Orbis Books, 1993), who highlights the intersectionality of race and gender in theology, advancing a womanist hermeneutic.

p/reaching is going to reach toward anything worthy of the name, it must exorcise these spirits of privilege from its body politic (viz., homiletics); it must enact and embody a kind of *revenir*, a return to the originary acts of suppression and marginalization that animate the ghosts (*revenants*) of oppression. When the God, perhaps, who troubles homiletical theologies is embraced beyond metaphysical suppositions, we release preaching to participate in the "chaosmic" undecidability that deconstructs every homiletic.[92]

Conclusion: Spook(ing/y) Homiletics: The Word of God, Perhaps

All kinds of theoretical and practical difficulties are connected with the fact that the Church's preaching is the Word of God.

— Karl Barth[93]

In some ways, to describe preaching as *Word* is about as perfect a designation as we can find—but in a completely different way than homileticians tend to suggest. To signify preaching as *Word* is to say that preaching performs itself as otherwise than Being. Words are otherwise than the things they signify. They are *destinerring*, that is, they aim at a target they must always miss. They never arrive at their intended destination, which is the thing itself (*die Sache selbst*). Even as preaching words come from God—perhaps!—words never arrive at God (see chapter 1).

Only when God gives Godself do we receive God's Word as such. This cannot be planned by picking the best words in advance of sermon delivery, nor in employing the most evocative rhetorical strategies. We can only ever *experience* this arrival, this event—which, by definition, we could never have seen coming. Even so, even when we seem to experience the event (perhaps) harbored in the name/ing (of) God, what we name by this "event" is not a naming of God, nor is it even the *event* of God, but what is going on in what happens. As Caputo puts it, with the insistence of God all we get is an "interruption, a solicitation, a promise, occurring in a disjunction or dislocation." Disjoining and disjunction are marks of the event, which Caputo conceives as the opening of a space in which "things get themselves done" rather

92. The neologism "chaosmic" is from James Joyce. Caputo explains that this word signifies a state that is neither chaos nor cosmos, neither pure order nor pure disorder. Caputo, "Teaching the Event," 28–29.
93. Barth, *Church Dogmatics*, I/2, 747.

than instances where we do anything event-ful. He concludes, "The 'axiom' of any hauntology of the event, were such a thing possible, is that when it comes to events, to be is to provoke. Events are not present, but what is provocative about what is present."[94] That is why the evocation of prayer goes hand-in-hand with a provocation of the event. We would not say that the event is, but that the event provokes. Drawing heavily from Caputo, Phil Snider moves us in the right direction with his "homiletic of the event," which "doesn't preach about God, but instead preaches *after* God."[95] For Snider, preaching "is" irreducible to the Word of God conceived as (pure) presence.

The spectral impulse of preaching is to leave congregants disturbed, impelled, provoked by the haunting Word/Secret of God. This is what it truly means to declare scripture *in-spired* (cf. 1 Tim 3:16): scripture is at once God-breathed (*in-spirare*) and it inspires a certain yearning above the homiletical branches that simultaneously protect and stifle the event. The haunting, harbored in the name, the "Word," the Secret (of) God, like the coil of a tree trunk (*speira*), continues above the point where branching begins.

Scripture ought not comfort and preaching ought not synthesize or explicate. Preaching must die to such impulses. Face to face with a homiletical hauntology that at once provokes and terrifies it, p/reaching discovers its truest calling: to die. Preaching should scare us to death. It is a summons to die to the fear that imperils our actions, that stymies the gift, that squelches the im-possibility of event. Preaching succeeds when we start seeing ghosts everywhere.

I'm calling for a moratorium on associating preaching with the Word of God. How long this ideological embargo lasts remains to be seen, but I say that we'll be ready once again to associate preaching with God's Word when we learn some theological humility. Preaching is *in* trouble in our postmodern, post-Christian, postcolonial world because preachers have misconstrued its purpose. Preaching is only in trouble because preachers peddle it as a miracle drug capable of curing maladies of the modern soul. This is wrong. To the degree that it *is* anything, preaching *is* trouble. Only when we are willing to embrace its troubling, destabilizing function will we be able once again to speak of preaching as the Word of God, perhaps.

The Word of God, if such a thing *exists*, spooks preaching. It inhabits and haunts preaching, troubling our kerygmatic foundations, calling

94. Caputo, *The Insistence of God*, 53.
95. Snider, *Preaching After God*, 114.

preaching to a kind of death. That should be our aim when we preach: to give up and give in to the (holy) ghost, to allow a homiletical hauntology to do its work against our various homiletical ontologies (e.g., preaching *is* teaching; preaching *is* practical wisdom). To embrace the ghost of preaching is to embrace the im-possibile event, which is quasi- or proto-phenomenological, which "is not what visibly happens but what is going on invisibly in what visibly happens."[96]

The Word of God, if there *is* such a thing, haunts preaching by troubling preaching's spatio-temporal stability. It spooks what we see and hear in preaching—not merely through the necessary re-contextualization of scripture, but through its unexpected and spectral arrival, its coming, which subverts every homiletical economy (see chapter 3). This is how we must understand God, perhaps, and anything worthy of the name "Word of God," at work in and through preaching.

96. Caputo, "Teaching the Event," 26.

Conclusion:
Preaching Meets Its Maker, Perchance

In a sense the sermon does not matter, what matters is what the preacher cannot say because the ineffable remains the ineffable and all that can be done is to make gestures towards it with the finest words that can be used.
— R. E. C. Browne[1]

I like the dead, they are the doorkeepers who while closing one side 'give' way to another. . . . It's true that neither death nor the doorkeepers are enough to open the door. We must have the courage, the desire, to approach, to go to the door.

— Hélène Cixous[2]

Even as homiletics lives not for itself, so too its death is not its own. Homiletics must die because preaching must die. That is its lot, its trouble, its troubling—its "mortal coil," as Hamlet declares. And it is Hamlet who offered the first words of this book. It is he who set us on our course with his famous soliloquy. "To be, or not to be, that is the question." For homiletics. For preaching.

This *coil* of which Hamlet speaks has done some work for us throughout this book. The word enjoys a peculiar etymology, hence its facility for a homiletical theology most concerned with words and their power over and within preaching. On the one hand and in its most familiar sense, the word denotes something that is wound in the shape of a helix or spiral (e.g., a *coil* of electrical wire). The shape of the coil, like that of Being, is circular: a movement outward only ever to return to

1. R. E. C. Browne, *The Ministry of the Word* (London: SCM, 1958), 27.
2. Hélène Cixous, *Three Steps on the Ladder of Writing*, trans. Sarah Cornell and Susan Sellers (New York: Columbia University Press, 1993), 7.

its source: the same. And also like a coil, Western ontology, the *logos* of *ontos*/Being, circulates around a center it can never penetrate or perceive. Western thought revolves around that which is ineffable. And yet it cannot stop speaking about that which it cannot speak—a peculiar inversion of Wittgenstein.[3]

On the other hand, Shakespeare's use of the word *coil* connotes something quite different. This *coil*—plucked from its now obsolete Elizabethan vernacular milieu—means *trouble*. This *tumult*, these *vicissitudes* of Hamlet's life following the murder of his father, is what drives him to contemplate death, to consider the prospect of a *not to be*. It is also in this sense of *coil* that we have oriented ourselves to the conditions of preaching's possibility, which have turned out to be also its conditions of *impossibility*. The trouble innate to preaching, along with homiletical theologies' efforts to ignore or get around this trouble, is what I have attempted to bring to homiletics *as trouble*. This book's troubling of homiletics has been about exposing homiletics to a certain death in order to help preaching dream, *perchance*. Aye, there's the rub!

Our difficulty as well as Hamlet's is that of undecidability. Henceforward, *perchance* should be a watchword for homiletical theologies—for radical homiletics, to be sure. We cannot know with certainty "what dreams may come." The death of preaching offers us no guarantees. It abides in the subjunctive mood. Perhaps. Per/chance. By and through chance. Even as this grates on our modern sensibilities, obsessed as we are with certitude, the realm of chance is the realm of faith, Christianity's native land. Every radical homiletical theology, as hope for preaching beyond hope, forces us into an alternative epistemological frame, a frame that transcends immanence without deciding between immanence and transcendence.[4]

This *preaching to come*, perhaps, perchance, calls for, summons, a certain disposition toward the impossible—a certain p/reaching, I have argued. It aims to nurture a kerygmatic disposition by reaching beyond every possibility. Such a p/reaching to come is fueled by hope. Homiletics doesn't need hope. Sure, homiletics talks about hope but

---

3. Ludwig Wittgenstein, *Tractatus Logico-Philosophicus*, trans. B. F. McGuinness and D. F. Pears (London: Routledge, 1961), 3: "What can be said at all can be said clearly and what we cannot talk about we must pass over in silence."

4. On the concept of an "immanent frame," vis-à-vis a "supernatural" or "transcendent" one, see Charles Taylor, *A Secular Age* (Cambridge, MA: Harvard University Press, 2007), 242–93. Taylor identifies the central marks of this "immanent frame" as a buffered (as opposed to a porous), individualized identity that is incredulous toward the supernatural and the dominance of instrumental rationality. These are the *sine quibus non* of our so-called "secular age."

only as a theological commodity. Genuine hope is superfluous when certitude is grounded in and by promise.

Standing on the Promises

To stand on a promise is to stand nowhere—even, perhaps especially, if God is the one doing the promising. This assertion points to (at least) two elements that are all too often occluded by homiletical theologies. First, assuming that God *will continue* to speak through human speech ignores the always already *human element* intrinsic to God's promise of presence. God's promise of presence is mediated through scripture, through human words. Can we peel back the layers of the hermeneutical onion to arrive at pure promise?[5] Surely not!

Second, if God's promise is guaranteed, then it is not a promise. Promise is haunted by a necessary *perhaps*.[6] By definition, a promise must *always possibly not* come to fulfillment. This is why homiletical theology—indeed, homiletics as theology—is in trouble. As promise it is troubled by an undecidability that is at once structural and theological. A promise might always be broken. Even after such-and-such has come to pass *as promised*, its structural tenuousness remains. Furthermore, if God *must* honor God's promises then God's sovereignty as promise-maker comes into question. For those who want to hold on to a belief in God's sovereignty, God must remain sovereign even over God's own word of promise.

Here we must push back against the otherwise fine work of James Kay and David Schnasa Jacobsen. In spite of their many important contributions to homiletics respectively, both Kay and Jacobsen run away from the trouble of God, the troubling God, at work in and through preaching. They seek solace from uncertainty in the metaphysical

---

5. This seems to be the *terminus ad quem* for mainstream homiletical theologies, especially for advocates of what I might call the "theology first" school of Richard Lischer, James Kay, Paul Scott Wilson, and David Schnasa Jacobsen. To illustrate, Jacobsen writes, "I am now willing to contend that the starting point of homiletical theology is a theology of *the gospel itself*. It seems to me that this particular *locus* really helps to drive the others and provide a center point for our work going forward." "The Unfinished Task of Homiletical Theology," in *Homiletical Theology: Preaching as Doing Theology*, ed. David Schnasa Jacobsen (Eugene, OR: Cascade Books, 2015), 55. Emphasis added. Do we have access to the gospel itself (*die Sache selbst*)? Is not such a "locus" a vanishing point? Is not such a homiletical *mise en place* a theological *mise en abyme*?

6. As Caputo reminds us, the *perhaps* is irreducible to the possible: "'Perhaps' does not mean the onto-possible, the future present, where it is only a matter of time until it rolls around at some later date. . . . It belongs to a different register altogether, not the presential order of ontology but a weaker, more dove like order, what Derrida amusingly (but he is dead serious) calls the order of 'hauntology,' which means the order of the event which haunts ontology." John D. Caputo, *The Insistence of God: A Theology of Perhaps* (Bloomington: Indiana University Press, 2013), 4–5.

"God" of onto-theology, the "God" whose promise becomes a guarantee, which defaces its promissory quality. A quick word on each of these thinkers will help to close us out.

The most productive aspect in Kay's *Preaching and Theology* is his chapter on preaching as "promissory narration," wherein he gleans from the work of Christopher Morse and Jürgen Moltmann. Building on the "theology of hope" articulated by Moltmann, Kay argues that God's presence is tied up with God's self-revelation as promise-maker and promise-keeper. Kay writes, ". . . Christian preaching and the life of faith are occurring in the interval created by the promise of God to reconcile the world to Godself. . . . In this interval, can more be said for preaching, not only as an act of proclaiming God's promised salvation, but as the linguistic medium for God's own promise making?"[7] Even as Kay offers an exciting and compelling vision for preaching as promissory narration, that vision has failed to notice several lingering problems, especially in Kay's association with the philosophy of "speech acts."

There is a slippage between Kay's deployment of Moltmann's theology of promise and Kay's subsequent homiletical proposal. Citing Moltmann, Kay writes, "A promise is a declaration which announces the coming of a reality that does not exist."[8] This promise "binds man [sic] to the future" even as it "stands in contradiction to the reality open to experience now and heretofore." These are Moltmann's words.[9] The "contradiction" is lost, however, when Kay makes his constructive move, in which a promise does not merely announce a coming reality as that reality stands in contrast to the present, but serves "to constitute a new state of affairs in the present."[10] By my reading, the power of a promise is produced by the tension between a current state of affairs and the *hope* that the promise entails concerning the (im)possibility of *another* state of affairs. Kay has lost or ignored the *necessary possibly*

7. James F. Kay, *Preaching and Theology* (St. Louis: Chalice, 2007), 122. Cf. Jürgen Moltmann, *A Theology of Hope: On the Ground and Implications of a Christian Eschatology* (New York: Harper & Row, 1965), 103–4, which Kay cites (121).

8. Kay, *Preaching and Theology*, 121, citing Moltmann, *A Theology of Hope*, 103.

9. Kay leaves out of his discussion Moltmann's distinction between history and existence "in general," and the "peculiar history" oriented toward hope that God will make good on God's promise: "The promise takes man [sic] up into its own history of hope and obedience, and in so doing stamps his existence with a historic character *of a specific kind.*" Moltmann, *A Theology of Hope*, 103. Emphasis added.

10. Kay, *Preaching and Theology*, 122. Cf. Karl Barth, "The Need and Promise of Christian Preaching," in *The Word of God and the Word of Man*, trans. Douglas Horton (Gloucester, MA: Peter Smith, 1978), 124: "*Speaking the word of God* is the *promise* of Christian preaching. Promise is not fulfillment. . . . Promise does not do away with the necessity of believing but establishes it. Promise is man's [sic] part, fulfillment is God's."

not—the fact that every perlocutionary act contains within its essential makeup the conditions by which it might *not* perform the speaker's intention.

J. L. Austin, who figures prominently in Kay's book, identifies conditions by which a speech act might fail. Austin calls these "impure" or "infelicitous," and his philosophy of performative utterances necessitates an originary exclusion of such instances.[11] To lose the future-oriented aspect of God's promises in scripture, as well as the elision of God's promise into the human preacher's "promissory narration," constitutes a double fault. The third strike arises from Kay's uncritical appropriation of Austin's, and Searle's, philosophy of "speech acts."[12]

David Schnasa Jacobsen commits a similar fault. Pushing against the theology of Oswald Bayer, Jacobsen writes, "Yet I am convinced that the performative nature of promise does more than promote faith in the *vita passive* [*sic*] sense that Bayer embraces. Promise, as I have claimed elsewhere, offers both presence and *discloses* a future in such a way as to pry creation just a bit more open."[13] The problem with Jacobsen's argument is that it undercuts the "performative nature of promise" by removing the contextual conditions necessary for a performative as such.

Austin's *How to Do Things with Words* has authorized the work of many recent homileticians.[14] For Austin, contextual conditions are *precisely* those conditions that *must* be fulfilled to authorize a speech act as perlocutionary or performative. Austin labels these "felicity conditions," and it is only when one's words conform to these a priori conditions that a promise counts as a promise. How can it be (for Jacobsen) that a

---

11. See J. L. Austin, *How to Do Things with Words*, 2nd ed., ed. J. G. Urmson and Marina Sbisà (Cambridge, MA: Harvard University Press, 1999), 22, where Austin cites an example of an actor on the stage uttering "I do" in a staged marriage. Such an example he deems "parasitic" on "real" performative speech.

12. For example: "That is, a promise not only announces or informs as to a future state of affairs but does so in such a way as to constitute a new state of affairs in the present." Kay, *Preaching and Theology*, 123.

13. David Schnasa Jacobsen, "Promise as an Event of the Gospel in Context: Toward an Unfinished Homiletical Theology of Grace and Justice" (papers presented at the Annual meeting for the Academy of Homiletics, San Antonio, TX, November 2016), 75. The Bayer text that Jacobsen references is *Theology the Lutheran Way*, trans. and ed. Jeffrey G. Silcock and Mark C. Mattes (Grand Rapids, MI: Eerdmans, 2007).

14. For homiletical examples, see Charles L. Bartow, *God's Human Speech: A Practical Theology of Proclamation* (Grand Rapids, MI: Eerdmans, 1997); John M. Rottman, "Performative Language and the Limits of Performance in Preaching," in *Performance in Preaching: Bringing the Sermon to Life*, ed. Jana Childers and Clayton L. Schmit (Grand Rapids, MI: Baker Academic, 2008), 67–86; Jared E. Alcántara, *Crossover Preaching: Intercultural-Improvisational Homiletics in Conversation with Gardner C. Taylor* (Downers Grove, IL: InterVarsity, 2015), 91–138; and James F. Kay, "Preacher as Messenger of Hope," in *Slow of Speech and Unclean Lips: Contemporary Images of Preaching Identity*, ed. Robert Stephen Reid (Eugene, OR: Cascade Books, 2010), 13–34.

promise is "the incalculable from the outside" if calculation is always already necessary on the inside (for Austin)? One could argue that the presence of God that Jacobsen is so intent on asserting (hence four major essays on the same subject) is only ever able to "become present in the moment" by reducing God to a metaphysical a priori: the condition necessary for promising as such.[15]

Homiletical theologies are in trouble because theologies are troubling. Who among us possesses the temerity to speak of God, to objectify God in speech, to totalize God through propositions, to objectify God's "Word" as promise? Luke Powery helpfully moves us away from such trouble by leaning into the trouble of God as gift, prayer, and song.[16] Such acts do not attempt to recuperate language as sameness. If we really want to prove our unwavering confidence in God as a promise-maker, then homiletics should *bears witness* (*martureó*) to this hope to the point of death. This is the direction we should head as modes of *doing theology* in/as preaching.

The Death of Preaching

Prepositions matter. They situate us in relation to nouns and verbs—the being and doing of life. In titling this section of my book "the death *of* preaching" I signify both preaching's death and our participation in death inasmuch as we bear the task of preaching.

I wish to underscore what I've been arguing all along: that in and through preaching, preachers are *caught up in* death. At the same time and according to the same conditions, preachers mount an assault against death's regime. To borrow George Steiner's phrasing, sermons are at once "rehearsals for death" and affronts against the "obstinacies of the impenetrable." He avers, "It is the lucid intensity of its meeting with death that generates in aesthetic forms that statement of vitality, of life-presence, which distinguishes serious thought and feeling from the trivial and the opportunistic."[17] Preaching (and Steiner makes a similar case for aesthetics and poetics) is as much transgressive as

---

15. Jacobsen, "Promise as an Event," 75.
16. See Luke Powery, "In Our Own Native Tongue: Toward a Pentecostalization of Homiletical Theology," in *Homiletical Theology in Action: The Unfinished Theological Task of Preaching*, ed. David Schnasa Jacobsen (Eugene, OR: Cascade Books, 2015), 72–84; Powery, *Dem Dry Bones: Preaching, Death, and Hope* (Minneapolis: Fortress Press, 2012); and Powery, *Spirit Speech: Lament and Celebration in Preaching* (Nashville: Abingdon, 2009).
17. George Steiner, *Real Presences: Is There Anything in What We Say?* (London: Faber & Faber, 1989), 141. "It is the facticity of death, a facticity wholly resistant to reason, to metaphor, to revelatory representation, which makes us 'guest'workers,' *frontaliers*, in the boarding houses of life" (140).

ingressive—indeed, every ingress is a transgress. On a purely structural-physiological level, preachers infringe upon death's domain with each inhalation.

In the face of death, preaching is at once object and subject. On the objective side, preaching abides in death's domain. Here, death is both the *terminus a quo* and *terminus ad quem* of sermon preparation and delivery, and we can do nothing to stay preaching's slippage beyond this "mortal coil." But we try. Through Christendom, and especially through modern Christendom, we've been taught to employ our homiletical technologies to sustain preaching, to protect preaching from death. This is a mistake. What preachers must come to terms with in/at the wake of postmodernism is that we are nothing more than homiletical *frontaliers*, migrant workers laboring on foreign soil.[18]

But the death of preaching is also subjective. We are caught up in the "event" of preaching—if we may speak of preaching as an *event*.[19] In it we are seized in the mysterious workings of the God who has called us (to die). Much as we have been invited into Christ's death and resurrection, in preaching we fight against the powers of death when we—paradoxically—plunge into the waters of death, willingly submitting to the fold of divine mystery that is beyond understanding, beyond articulation, beyond decidability.

The Apostle Paul guides us here. The death of preaching participates in the semantic undecidability in which Paul sometimes revels. Much as the "righteousness of God" (*dikaiosynē Theou*) in Romans 3:21, the "message of faith" (*akoés pisteōs*) in Galatians 3:2, and the "faith of Christ Jesus" (*pisteōs Christou Iēsou*) in Galatians 2:16 point to Paul's (deliberate) linguistic polysemy, the death of preaching aims to speak in one breath to preaching's demise along with our own *in* preaching.[20] I wish to suggest that the death of preaching participates in this same generative semantic ambivalence and theological uncertainty. The death of preaching is simultaneously active and passive, objective and

---

18. On the "wake of postmodernism" and its philosophical implications, see Josh Toth, *The Passing of Postmodernism: A Spectroanalysis of the Contemporary* (Albany: SUNY Press, 2011) and Josh Toth and Neil Brooks, "Introduction: A Wake and Renewed?" in *The Mourning After: Attending the Wake of Postmodernism*, ed. Josh Toth and Neil Brooks (Amsterdam: Editions Rodopi B. V., 2007), 1–14.

19. Lowry hits the mark when he writes, "Preaching is an offering intended to evoke an event that cannot be coerced into being." Eugene Lowry, *The Sermon: Dancing the Edge of Mystery* (Nashville: Abingdon, 1997), 37.

20. The grammatical terms for this are the subjective genitive and objective genitive. The former names the *subject* of the action contained in another noun; the latter names the *direct object* of the action contained in another noun. For this distinction in the letters of Paul, see Richard B. Hays, *The Faith of Jesus Christ: The Narrative Substructure of Galatians 3:1–4:11*, 2nd ed. (Grand Rapids, MI: Eerdmans, 2002), 161.

subjective. It operates in the middle voice, as Caputo might put it.[21] The fatal flaw of modern Christian preaching is that we are trying to keep preaching from meeting its Maker.

Far too much contemporary preaching smacks of kerygmatic atheism. Have you ever stopped to ask yourself during a sermon whether the truth of God's existence or death mattered to the sermon? Not to the preacher, of course; you will find very few preachers who would respond to the death of God with a shrug. I'm talking about the preaching itself, what is going on in and through the sermon. This is not identical to the sermon's content, and this distinction will become apparent as we proceed through this section.

Homiletical atheism points to a failure to trust the God who called us and has promised to sustain us in and through our preaching. Even as we profess confidence in the Spirit's abiding presence, our actions speak louder than our words. (This is ironic considering that the aphorism "practice what you preach" should probably catch a preacher's attention.) We live out our theologies by how we preach; preaching is *doing theology*, and not just by what we choose to preach on. That is why I'm suggesting that any kerygmatic theology worthy of the name ought to be a thanatology—or, better, a *thanato-poetics*.

Preaching *must* die! This is our task—nay, our summons. Of necessity. By necessity. Preaching is obliged to die. To itself. For the other.

I insist: preaching must die. The insistence implied in this *must* situates me as one in-sisting, as one standing (*sistere*) upon (*in*) preaching's grave, as it were. But in insisting I am also invoking an intervention by and according to a certain radical homiletics; I am in-voking an intervention: In one and the same gesture, I am calling (*vocare*) upon (*in*) preaching to die and coming (*venire*) in between (*inter*) preaching and its death—which is where I believe homileticians are called to stand.

My insistence upon the death of preaching im-plies and im-plicates preaching in death, preaching as death. Thus, my approach in this book has been to ply apart preaching from its constitutive elements (language, the preacher, scripture, God) *and* fold in (*plicare* means "to fold" in Latin) a certain thanato-poetics that has been excised from homiletical theologies. This has been accomplished by force—as if the force of

---

21. Thus, the death of preaching is not an event in and of itself, but a naming of the unnamable getting itself said and done, perchance, in the event. See Caputo, *The Insistence of God*, 30, 48, and Caputo, *Hoping Against Hope: Confessions of a Postmodern Pilgrim* (Minneapolis: Fortress Press, 2015), 202n16.

death were not always already the force of preaching. Such is nothing less than the troubling of preaching and death.

My thesis has been simple: *preaching is born to meet its Maker*. Preaching must die (to itself), for in its untimely departure we catch a glimpse (perchance) of something else, something we *can't* preach. It is this something else, this radical alterity trembling at preaching's core and on its periphery, that I hope to retrieve for preaching in/as the wake of postmodernism. My method has followed from this aim. Herein, I sought to trouble the foundations of preaching, to expose it to the trouble always already at work on the inside of preaching and death, preaching as (a form of) death.[22]

Dying to Preach: A Summons

Preaching is not dogma. It is not pop-wisdom. It is not teaching. Nor is it seven-steps-to-a-happy-marriage. It's not a Hallmark card, spouting sappy, prepackaged sentiments! Preaching is kamikaze discourse. Preaching digs along the fault lines of our theological, ethical, cultural, political, economic, and ecclesiological infrastructures until the whole damn thing implodes. Preaching is a screwworm fly that burrows deep into our theological brain matter and lays eggs that drive us mad for justice. Preaching is a wormhole that utterly reorients our relation to time and matter, to eternity and all that matters.

Get the picture? Are you still with me?

Preaching is not itself life. From the preacher's point of view, preaching is more death-dealing than life-giving.[23] In other words, when preaching leans into its innermost possibility, preaching participates in the kenotic self-emptying of the preacher and their words in order for God to resurrect new life out of the dead bones of language, speech, hermeneutics, and theology.[24] At the same time, as preaching

22. See Jacques Derrida, "The Force of Law: The 'Mystical Foundation of Authority'," in *Deconstruction and the Possibility of Justice*, ed. Drucilla Cornell, Michel Rosenfeld, and David Gray Carlson (New York: Routledge, 1992), 8: "The questioning of foundations is neither foundationalist nor anti-foundationalist. Nor does it pass up opportunities to put into question or even to exceed the possibility or the ultimate necessity of questioning, or the questioning form of thought, interrogating without assurance or prejudice the very history of the question of its philosophical authority. For there is an authority—and so a legitimate force in the questioning form of which one might ask oneself whence it derives such great force in our tradition."

23. As Luke Powery puts it, in direct confrontation to the "homiletical quarantining of death" displayed in prosperity gospel preaching, "Existential and liturgical realities demonstrate that death is prominent as a context for preaching. . . . preaching that ignores death is irresponsible, a theological lie and unable to declare real hope. In fact, it is Spiritless preaching." Luke A. Powery, "Haunting Echoes for Homiletics: Why the Spirituals Matter for Preaching," *Homiletic* 37, no. 2 (2012): 9.

meets its Maker it initiates a boldness that subverts theological and ecclesial systems that bar certain kinds of people from the pulpit. Preaching ought to trigger a "bold humility," as I've put it above and elsewhere.[25]

Preaching, in and of itself, is nothing but human words. Otherwise than Being. Much as John the Baptist recognized that he was not himself the light, but a mere *witness* to the light, so too is preaching no more than a signpost, an outstretched finger (I'll let you decide which finger) to the threshold of life, which is, of course, death. Accordingly, a sermon is an artifact of human faithfulness.[26] It is a fallout zone, still leaking radiation. To behold a sermon after it has been preached is not unlike the river valleys glimpsed on Mars's surface, bearing witness to the possibility of life in spite of its own desiccated desolation.

The starting point of preaching is an aporia. We may not pass because the route is impassable. The mode of kamikaze discourse we call preaching opens with death. Where it might lead us and our congregants remains a mystery.

Resurrection, Perhaps

This book has celebrated preaching's death and has summoned preachers to participate therein. More concretely, it has taken seriously Jesus's paradoxical words that the key to participating in God's kin(g)dom is to lean into those elements that seem least powerful, least efficacious, and to trust that the God who is in the business of making all things new (Rev 21:5) will honor our homiletical sacrifices. This has not been a trick. It's not a sly gimmick whereby we wink and smirk at one another as we speak of death and weakness and failure. To borrow a line from Caputo, "The trick will be not to compromise the cross by turning weakness, folly, and non-being into cunning stratagems, making them into long-term investments in an economy of salvation in

24. NB: Kenosis is troubled by much feminist scholarship. Recent contributions by scholars like Anna Mercedes, *Power For: Feminism and Christ's Self-Giving* (London: T & T Clark, 2011), draw our attention to the power arising from such acts as a power "that leans toward others and offers itself to them" (7). Such "power for" the other can actually lead to human flourishing rather than further subjugating and silencing already marginalized bodies/voices.

25. See Jacob D. Myers, *Making Love with Scripture: Why the Bible Doesn't Mean How You Think it Means* (Minneapolis: Fortress Press, 2015), 123–26 and Myers, "Writing Spiritually," in *Writing Theologically,* ed. Eric D. Barreto (Minneapolis: Fortress Press, 2015), 148–51.

26. Karl Barth, *The Church Dogmatics,* I/1, ed. G. W. Bromiley & T. F. Torrance, trans. G. W. Bromiley, 2nd ed. (Edinburgh: T & T Clark, 1975), 47: "Talk about God in the Church seeks to be proclamation to the extent that in the form of preaching and sacrament it is directed to man [*sic*] with the claim and expectation that in accordance with its commission it has to speak to him the Word of God to be heard in faith."

which God and theology turn out to be the winners. . . . Theology is not about winning."[27] Neither is preaching!

The stiff drink of homiletical hemlock I've been brewing in these pages does not go down smoothly. It burns like moonshine, or Drano. Preaching has more in common with Russian roulette than big-game hunting. That's what this book has been about—helping preaching meet its Maker.[28]

Preaching was not made to live because it is neither living nor life itself. At most, preaching is a witness, a sign, a crimson X marking a demolition site. The church has developed sophisticated technologies in modernity to give preaching the semblance of life. But like other technologies, homiletical life support does not foster abundant life. The body that lives without the soul is just a shell, a zombie—and our world could do with fewer zombies.[29] Such technologies belie the truth: preaching was born under a death sentence. It was born to die. Only when preaching embraces its own death is it able to truly live. The whole thing is paradoxical, I know. But what did you expect for we who are summoned to follow Jesus?

This book has questioned the underlying ideological assumptions that prop up contemporary homiletical theories. It is a bold manifesto against preaching in support of preaching. It situates preaching's innate rationality against the so-called rationality of modern Christianity. Hereby, it supports a way of preaching that moves counter to the "wisdom of this world" (1 Cor 2:6).[30] It joins in God's self-revealed counter-logic of superabundance that saturates and thereby breaks open worldly systems of thought and practice.[31] At base, this book has tried to give preaching the good death it deserves. More specifically, it sought to help Christ-followers (particularly those serving in post-

---

27. John D. Caputo, *The Folly of God: A Theology of the Unconditional* (Salem, OR: Polebridge, 2016), 5.

28. See Karl Barth, *Homiletics*, trans. Geoffrey W. Bromiley and Donald E. Daniels (Louisville: Westminster John Knox, 1991), 50: "God himself [*sic*] wills to reveal himself. He himself wills to attest his revelation. He himself—not we—has done this and wills to do it. Preaching, then, takes place in listening to the self-revealing will of God. Preachers are drawn into this event. . . . The event becomes a constituent part of their own existence." See also Dietrich Ritschl, *A Theology of Proclamation* (Richmond, VA: John Knox, 1960).

29. See here Brian K. Blount's superb book *Invasion of the Dead: Preaching Resurrection* (Louisville: Westminster John Knox, 2014).

30. For a more in-depth treatment on this "wisdom" in Paul's Epistle, see my upcoming essay. "Wise Speech: 1 Corinthians 2:1–16," in *In Tongues of Mortals and Angels: A De-Constructive Theology of God Talk in Acts and Paul*, Eric D. Barreto, Jacob D. Myers, and Thelathia Nikki Young (Minneapolis: Fortress Press, forthcoming).

31. See Paul Ricoeur, "The Logic of Jesus, The Logic of God," in *Figuring the Sacred: Religion, Narrative, and Imagination*, ed. Mark I. Wallace, trans. David Pellauer (Minneapolis: Augsburg Fortress, 1995), 279–83.

Christian contexts) participate in a kerygmatic quietus poised toward the hope and possibility of resurrection.

Homiletics is only theological to the degree that it is thanatological; it orients us to God inasmuch as it orients us to death. If my wager that preaching was born to die holds, then joining in preaching's deconstruction offers us the means of helping preaching die well. We need not be afraid of deconstruction; it is merely an orientation toward what is always already taking place within texts and traditions. And what is preaching if not a way of situating our lives and our words—our very breath—among texts and traditions within the context of Christian worship?

Deconstruction, to the degree that it "is" anything, that it "does" anything, unwittingly serves preaching inasmuch as it exposes us to our (often) unexamined presuppositions, prejudices, and elisions that we employ to construct frameworks for meaning-making. If left unchecked, all ideologies—homiletical ideologies included—can become idolatries. And just as idolatries take the place of the God who may come, ideologies are nothing less than acts of inhospitality. As we move forward, leaning into the hope of revelation, perhaps, we must heed Derrida's reminder: "The other may come, or he may not. I don't want to programme him, but rather to leave a place for him to come if he comes. It is the ethic of hospitality."[32] Such is also the ethic of preaching.

---

32. Jacques Derrida and Anne Dufourmantelle, *Of Hospitality*, trans. Rachel Bowlby (Stanford: Stanford University Press, 2000), 83.

Bibliography

Alcántara, Jared E. *Crossover Preaching: Intercultural-Improvisational Homiletics in Conversation with Gardner C. Taylor.* Downers Grove, IL: InterVarsity, 2015.

Allen, Ronald J. *Hearing the Sermon: Relationship, Content, Feeling.* St. Louis: Chalice, 2004.

_____. *Interpreting the Gospel: An Introduction to Preaching.* St. Louis: Chalice, 1998.

_____. *Preaching and the Other: Studies of Postmodern Insights.* St. Louis: Chalice, 2009.

_____. "Preaching as Mutual Critical Correlation through Conversation." In *The Purposes of Preaching*, edited by Jana Childers, 1–22. St. Louis: Chalice, 2004.

_____. *Preaching is Believing: The Sermon as Theological Reflection.* Louisville: Westminster John Knox, 2002.

_____. *Sermon Treks: Trailways to Creative Preaching.* Nashville: Abingdon, 2013.

_____. "Shaping Sermons by the Language of the Text." In *Preaching Biblically: Creating Sermons in the Shape of Scripture*, edited by Don M. Wardlaw, 29–59. Philadelphia: Westminster, 1983.

Ambrose. "De Fide Ad Gratianum." In *Nicene and Post-Nicene Fathers.* Vol. 10, *Ambrose: Selected Works and Letters*, edited by Philip Schaff and translated by H. de Romestin. Series 2. Edinburgh: T & T Clark, 2009.

Anthony, Benjamin Jay. "Christ in Boston: The Death and Afterlife of Phillips Brooks." PhD diss., Vanderbilt University, 2015.

Anderson, Carol. *White Rage: The Unspoken Truth of our Racial Divide.* New York: Bloomsbury, 2016.

Anzaldúa, Gloria. *Borderlands/La Frontera: The New Mestiza.* San Francisco: Aunt Lute Books, 1987.

_____. "*La Conciencia de la Mestiza*: Towards a New Consciousness." In *Feminisms: An Anthology of Literary Theory and Criticism*, edited by Robyn R. Warhol and Diane Price Herndl, 765–75. New Brunswick, NJ: Rutgers University Press, 1997.

The Apostolic Fathers: I Clement, II Clement, Ignatius, Polykarp, Didache. Loeb Classical Library. Volume 24. Edited and translated by Bart D. Ehrman. Cambridge, MA: Harvard University Press, 2003.

Aristotle. *Categories. On Interpretation. Prior Analytics.* Loeb Classical Library. Volume 325. Translated by H. P. Cooke and H. Tredennick. Cambridge, MA: Harvard University Press, 1938.

_____. *Metaphysics: Books I–IX.* Loeb Classical Library. Volume 271. Translated by H. Tredennick. Cambridge, MA: Harvard University Press, 1935.

Augustine. *Confessions.* Translated by Henry Chadwick. Oxford: Oxford University Press, 2009.

_____. "Epistle 137: To Volusian." In *Fathers of the Church.* Vol. 3, *St. Augustine Letters 131-164.* Translated by Sister Wilfrid Parsons SND. Washington, DC: Catholic University of America Press, 1953.

_____. *On Christian Teaching.* Translated by R. P. H. Green. Oxford: Oxford University Press, 2008.

_____. *On the Holy Trinity.* In *Nicene and Post-Nicene Fathers*, vol. 3, edited by Philip Schaff and translated by Stephen McKenna, 1–228. New York: Cosimo, 2007.

_____. *On the Trinity.* Translated by Stephen McKenna. Washington, DC: Catholic University of America Press, 1963.

_____. "Sermon 188." In *Augustine in His Own Words*, Edited by William Harmless, translated by Edmund Hill, 128–30. Washington, DC: Catholic University of America Press, 2010.

Austin, J. L. *How to Do Things with Words.* 2nd ed. Edited by J. G. Urmson and Marina Sbisà Cambridge, MA: Harvard University Press, 1999.

Baldwin, James. *Nobody Knows My Name.* New York: Vintage Books, 1993.

Barreto, Eric D. "Negotiating Difference: Theology and Ethnicity in the Acts of the Apostles." *Word and World* 31, no. 2 (Spring 2011): 129–37.

Barth, Karl. *The Church Dogmatics*, I/1. Edited by G. W. Bromiley and T. F. Torrance. Translated by G. W. Bromiley. Edinburgh: T & T Clark, 1975.

_____. *The Church Dogmatics*, II/1. Edited by G.W. Bromiley and T. F. Torrance. Translated by T. H. L. Parker, W. B. Johnston, Harold Knight, and J. L. M. Haire. Edinburgh: T & T Clark, 1957.

_____. *The Church Dogmatics: Lecture Fragments*, IV/4. Translated by Geoffrey W. Bromiley. Grand Rapids, MI: Eerdmans, 1981.

_____. *Credo*. Eugene, OR: Wipf & Stock, 2005.

_____. *The Epistle to the Romans*. 6th ed. Translated by Edwyn C. Hoskyns. London: Oxford University Press, 1933.

_____. *God in Action: Theological Addresses*. Eugene, OR: Wipf & Stock, 2005.

_____. *Homiletics*. Translated by Geoffrey W. Bromiley and Donald E. Daniels. Louisville: Westminster John Knox, 1991.

_____. "No! Answer to Emil Brunner." In *Karl Barth: Theologian of Freedom*, edited by Clifford Green, 151–67. Minneapolis: Fortress Press, 1991.

_____. *The Word of God and the Word of Man*. Translated by Douglas Horton. Gloucester, MA: Peter Smith, 1978.

Bartlett, David L. *Between the Church and the Bible: New Methods for Biblical Preaching*. Nashville: Abingdon, 1999.

Bartow, Charles L. *God's Human Speech: A Practical Theology of Proclamation*. Grand Rapids, MI: Eerdmans, 1997.

Bauman, Zygmunt. *Liquid Love: On the Frailty of Human Bonds*. Cambridge: Polity, 2003.

_____. *Liquid Modernity*. Cambridge: Polity, 2007.

_____. *Liquid Times: Living in an Age of Uncertainty*. Cambridge: Polity, 2006.

Bayer, Oswald. *Theology the Lutheran Way*. Translated and edited by Jeffrey G. Silcock and Mark C. Mattes. Grand Rapids, MI: Eerdmans, 2007.

Bennington, Geoffrey, and Jacques Derrida. *Jacques Derrida*. Translated by Geoffrey Bennington. Chicago and London: University of Chicago Press, 1993.

Benveniste, Émile. *Problems in General Linguistics*. Translated by Mary Elizabeth Meek. Coral Gables, FL: University of Miami Press, 1971.

Bergson, Henri. "Images and Bodies." In *Key Writings*, edited by John Mullarkey and Keith Ansell Pearson, 103–50. London: Bloomsbury Academic, 2014.

Bhabha, Homi K. *The Location of Culture*. London: Routledge, 1994.

Blanchot, Maurice. *The Work of Fire*. Translated by Charlotte Mandell. Stanford: Stanford University Press, 1995.

_____. *The Step Not Beyond*. Translated by Lynette Nelson. Albany: SUNY Press, 1992.

Bloch, Jean-Richard. *Destin du siècle*. Paris: Presses Universitaires de France, 1996.

Blount, Brian K. *Invasion of the Dead: Preaching Resurrection*. Louisville: Westminster John Knox, 2014.

Boff, Leonardo. *Church, Charism, and Power: Liberation Theology and the Institutional Church*. Translated by John W. Diercksmeier. Eugene, OR: Wipf & Stock, 2012.

Bonhoeffer, Dietrich. *Worldly Preaching: Lectures on Homiletics.* Edited and translated by Clyde E. Fant. New York: Crossroad, 1991.

The Book of Confessions. Louisville: Office of the General Assembly Presbyterian Church (USA), 1999.

Bordo, Susan. *The Male Body: A New Look at Men in Public and in Private.* New York: Farrar, Straus & Giroux, 1999.

_____. *Unbearable Weight: Feminism, Western Culture and the Body.* Berkeley: University of California Press, 1993.

Boroditsky, Lera. "Lost in Translation." *The Wall Street Journal,* July 23, 2010.

Boroditsky, Lera, and Alice Gaby. "Remembrances of Times East: Absolute Spatial Representations of Time in an Australian Aboriginal Community." *Psychological Science* 21, no. 11 (November 2010): 185–89.

Boroditsky, Lera, Orly Fuhrman, and Kelly McCormick. "Do English and Mandarin Speakers Think About Time Differently?" *Cognition* 118, no. 1 (Oct 2011): 123–29.

Braxton, Brad R. *No Longer Slaves: Galatians and African American Experience.* Collegeville, MN: Liturgical Press, 2002.

Brooks, Gennifer Benjamin. *Black United Methodists Preach!* Nashville: Abingdon, 2012.

Brooks, Phillips. *Lectures on Preaching Delivered Before the Divinity School of Yale College in January and February 1877.* New York: E. P. Dutton, 1894.

Brothers, Michael. *Distance in Preaching: Room to Speak, Space to Listen.* Grand Rapids, MI: Eerdmans, 2014.

Brown, Sally A., and Luke A. Powery. *Ways of the Word: Learning to Preach for Your Time and Place.* Minneapolis: Fortress Press, 2016.

Brown, Teresa L. Fry. "An African American Woman's Perspective: Renovating Sorrow's Kitchen." In *Preaching Justice: Ethnic and Cultural Perspectives,* edited by Christine M. Smith, 43–61. Eugene, OR: Wipf & Stock, 2008.

_____. *Can A Sistah Get A Little Help?: Encouragement for Black Women in Ministry.* Cleveland: Pilgrim, 2008.

_____. *Delivering the Sermon: Voice, Body, and Animation in Proclamation.* Minneapolis: Fortress Press, 2008.

_____. *Weary Throats and New Songs.* Nashville: Abingdon, 2003.

Browne, R. E. C. *The Ministry of the Word.* London: SCM, 1958.

Brueggemann, Walter. *Finally Comes the Poet: Daring Speech for Proclamation.* Minneapolis: Augsburg Fortress Press, 1989.

_____. *Ice Axes for Frozen Seas: A Biblical Theology of Provocation.* Edited by Davis Hankins. Waco, TX: Baylor University Press, 2014.

_____. *Texts Under Negotiation: The Bible and Postmodern Imagination.* Minneapolis: Fortress Press, 1993.

_____. *Theology of the Old Testament: Testimony, Dispute, Advocacy.* Minneapolis: Fortress Press, 2005.

_____. *The Word Militant: Preaching a Decentering Word.* Minneapolis: Fortress Press, 2007.

Brunner, Emil. *The Christian Doctrine of God.* Vol. 1, *Dogmatics.* Translated by Olive Wyon. Eugene, OR: Wipf & Stock, 2014.

Burghardt, Walter, SJ. "Preaching, Role of." In *The New Dictionary of Catholic Social Thought,* edited by Judith A. Dwyer, 777–80. Collegeville, MN: Liturgical Press, 1994.

Butler, Judith. *Bodies That Matter: On the Discursive Limits of "Sex."* London: Routledge, 2011.

_____. *Gender Trouble.* London: Routledge, 1990.

_____. *Subjects of Desire: Hegelian Reflections in Twentieth-Century France.* New York: Columbia University Press, 2012.

Buttrick, David. *A Captive Voice: The Liberation of Preaching.* Louisville: Westminster John Knox, 1994.

_____. *Homiletic: Moves and Structures.* Philadelphia: Fortress Press, 1987.

Campbell, Charles L. *Preaching Jesus: New Directions for Homiletics in Hans Frei's Postliberal Theology.* Grand Rapids, MI: Eerdmans, 1997.

_____. *The Word Before the Powers: An Ethic of Preaching.* Louisville: Westminster John Knox, 2002.

Caputo, John D. *Against Ethics: Contributions to a Poetics of Obligation with Constant Reference to Deconstruction.* Bloomington: Indiana University Press, 1993.

_____. *Deconstruction in a Nutshell: A Conversation with Jacques Derrida.* New York: Fordham University Press, 1997.

_____. *The Folly of God: A Theology of the Unconditional.* Salem, OR: Polebridge, 2016.

_____. *Hoping Against Hope: Confessions of a Postmodern Pilgrim.* Minneapolis: Fortress Press, 2015.

_____. *The Insistence of God: A Theology of Perhaps.* Bloomington: Indiana University Press, 2013.

_____. *More Radical Hermeneutics: On Not Knowing Who We Are.* Bloomington: Indiana University Press, 2000.

_____. "Teaching the Event: Deconstruction, Hauntology, and the Scene of Pedagogy." *Philosophy of Education* (2012): 25.

_____. *The Weakness of God: A Theology of the Event.* Bloomington: Indiana University Press, 2006.

_____. *What Would Jesus Deconstruct? The Good News of Postmodernism for the Church.* Grand Rapids, MI: Baker Academic, 2007.

Carvalhaes, Claudio. "*Communitas*: Liturgy and Identity," *International Review of Mission* 100, no. 392 (April 2011): 37–47.

_____. *Eucharist and Globalization: Redrawing the Borders of Eucharistic Hospitality.* Eugene, OR: Pickwick, 2013.

Chapell, Bryan. *Christ-Centered Preaching: Redeeming the Expository Sermon.* 2nd ed. Grand Rapids, MI: Baker Academic, 2005.

Childers, Jana. *Performing the Word: Preaching as Theater.* Nashville: Abingdon, 1998.

_____. "The Preacher's Creative Process: Reaching the Well." In *Performance in Preaching: Bringing the Sermon to Life*, edited by Clayton J. Schmit and Jana Childers, 153–68. Grand Rapids: Baker Academic, 2008.

_____. "Seeing Jesus: Preaching as Incarnational Act." In *The Purposes of Preaching*, edited by Jana Childers, 23–47. St. Louis: Chalice, 2004.

Chrétien, Jean-Louis. *Under the Gaze of the Bible.* Translated by John Marson Dunaway. New York: Fordham University Press, 2015.

Chopp, Rebecca S. *The Power to Speak: Feminism, Language, God.* New York: Crossroad, 1989.

Cixous, Hélène. *"Coming to Writing" and Other Essays.* Edited by Deborah Jenson. Translated by Sarah Cornell. Cambridge: Cambridge University Press, 1992.

_____. "The Laugh of the Medusa." Translated by Keith Cohen and Paula Cohen. *Signs: Journal of Woman in Culture and Society* 1, no. 4 (1976): 875–93.

_____. *The Newly Born Woman.* Translated by Betsy Wing. Minneapolis: University of Minnesota Press, 2001.

_____. *Three Steps on the Ladder of Writing.* Translated by Sarah Cornell and Susan Sellers. New York: Columbia University Press, 1993.

Claypool, John R. *The Preaching Event.* Waco, TX: Word Books, 1980.

Coates, Ta-Nehisi. *Between the World and Me.* New York: Spiegel & Grau, 2015.

Cochrane, Kira. *All the Rebel Women: The Rise of the Fourth Wave of Feminism.* London: Guardian Books, 2003.

Collins, Patricia Hill. *On Intellectual Activism.* Philadelphia: Temple University Press, 2013.

Cone, James H. "Theology's Great Sin: Silence in the Face of White Supremacy." *Union Seminary Quarterly Review* 55 (2001): 1–14

Conley, Verena Andermatt. *Hélène Cixous: Writing the Feminine.* Expanded ed. Lincoln: University of Nebraska Press, 1991.

Copeland, Jennifer E. *Feminine Registers: The Importance of Women's Voices for Christian Preaching.* Eugene, OR: Cascade Books, 2014.

Craddock, Fred B. *As One Without Authority.* Rev. ed. St. Louis: Chalice, 2001.

_____. "Inductive Preaching Renewed." In *The Renewed Homiletic*, edited by O. Wesley Allen Jr., 41–55. Minneapolis: Fortress Press, 2010.

_____. *Overhearing the Gospel.* Rev. ed. St. Louis: Chalice, 2002.

_____. *Preaching.* 25th anniversary ed. Nashville: Abingdon, 2010.

_____. "The Sermon and the Uses of Scripture." *Theology Today* 42, no. 1 (April 1985): 7–14.

Crawley, Ashon. "Breathing Flesh and the Sound of Black Pentecostalism." *Theology and Sexuality* 19, no. 1 (2013): 49–60.

Crockett, Clayton. "The Death of God, Death, and Resurrection." In *Resurrecting the Death of God: The Origins, Influence, and Return of Radical Theology*, edited by Daniel J. Peterson, G. Michael Zbaraschuk, 141–54. Albany: SUNY Press, 2014.

Culler, Jonathan D. *Ferdinand De Saussure.* Rev. ed. Ithaca, NY: Cornell University Press, 1986.

DeLeers, Stephen Vincent. *Written Word Biomes Living Word: The Vision and Practice of Sunday Preaching.* Collegeville, MN: Liturgical Press, 2004.

Derrida, Jacques. *Adieu to Emmanuel Lévinas.* Translated by Pascale-Anne Brault and Michael Naas. Stanford: Stanford University Press, 1999.

_____. "Afterword: Toward an Ethic of Discussion." In *Limited Inc.*, translated by Samuel Weber, 111–60. Evanston, IL: Northwestern University Press, 1998.

_____. *Dissemination.* Translated by Barbara Johnson. Chicago: University of Chicago Press, 1981.

_____. "The Ends of Man." In *Margins of Philosophy*, translated by Alan Bass, 109–36. Chicago: University of Chicago Press, 1982.

_____. "The Force of Law: The 'Mystical Foundation of Authority'." In *Deconstruction and the Possibility of Justice*, edited by Drucilla Cornell, Michel Rosenfeld, and David Gray Carlson, 3–67. New York: Routledge, 1992.

_____. *The Gift of Death.* Translated by David Wills. Chicago: University of Chicago Press, 1995.

_____. *The Gift of Death and Literature in Secret.* Translated by David Willis. 2nd ed. Chicago: University of Chicago Press, 2008.

_____. *Given Time: I. Counterfeit Money.* Translated by Peggy Kamuf. Chicago: University of Chicago Press, 1994.

_____. "How to Avoid Speaking: Denials." In *Languages of the Unsayable: The Play of Negativity in Literature and Literary Theory*, edited by Sanford Budick and Wolfgang Iser, translated by Ken Frieden, 3–70. Stanford: Stanford University Press, 1987.

_____. "Letter to a Japanese Friend." In *A Derrida Reader: Between the Blinds*, edited by Peggy Kamuf, translated by David Wood and Andrew Benjamin, 269–76. New York: Columbia University Press, 1991.

_____. *Memoires for Paul de Man*. Translated by Cecile Lindsay, Jonathan Culler, and Eduardo Cadava. New York: Columbia University Press, 1986.

_____. *Of Grammatology*. Corr. ed. Translated by Gayatri Chakravorty Spivak. Baltimore: Johns Hopkins University Press, 1997.

_____. *Rogues: Two Essays on Reason*. Translated by Pascale-Anne Brault and Michael Naas. Stanford: Stanford University Press, 2005.

_____. *"Sauf le nom (Post-Scriptum)."* In *On the Name*, edited by Thomas Dutoit, translated by David Wood, John P. Leavey Jr., and Ian McLeod, 35–88. Stanford: Stanford University Press, 1995.

_____. *Specters of Marx: The State of the Debt, the Work of Mourning and the New International*. Translated by Peggy Kamuf. New York: Routledge, 1994.

_____. *Speech and Phenomena; And Other Essays on Husserl's Theory of Signs*. Translated by David B. Allison. Evanston, IL: Northwestern University Press, 1973.

_____. *Without Alibi*. Edited and translated by Peggy Kamuf. Stanford: Stanford University Press, 2002.

Derrida, Jacques, and Anne Dufourmantelle. *Of Hospitality*. Translated by Rachel Bowlby. Stanford: Stanford University Press, 2000.

Derrida, Jacques, and Maurizio Ferraris. *A Taste for the Secret*. New York: Polity, 2001.

Didier, Eribon. *Insult and the Making of the Gay Self*. Translated by Michael Lucey. Durham, NC: Duke University Press, 2004.

Diprose, Rosalyn. *Corporeal Generosity: On Giving with Nietzsche, Merleau Ponty, and Levinas*. Albany: SUNY Press, 2002.

Du Bois, W. E. B. *The Souls of Black Folk*. New Haven, CT: Yale University Press, 2015.

Dyson, Michael Eric. *Tears We Cannot Stop: A Sermon to White America*. New York: St. Martin's, 2017.

Elliot, T. S. *The Four Quartets*. New York: Houghton Mifflin, 1943.

Ebeling, Gerhard. *Word and Faith*. Philadelphia: Fortress Press, 1963.

Eckhart, Meister. *Meister Eckhart: Teacher and Preacher*. Edited and translated by Bernard McGuinn. New York: Paulist, 1986.

_____. *Meister Eckhart: The Essential Sermons, Commentaries, Treatises, and Defense*. Translated by Edmund Colledge and Bernard McGinn. New York: Paulist, 1981.

English, Donald. *An Evangelical Theology of Preaching*. Nashville: Abingdon, 1996.

Eslinger, Richard L. *A New Hearing: Living Options in Homiletic Method*. Nashville: Abingdon, 1987.

_____. *The Web of Preaching: New Options in Homiletic Method*. Nashville: Abingdon, 2002.

Fanon, Frantz. *Black Skin, White Masks.* Translated by Richard Philcox. New York: Grove, 2008.

Farley, Edward. *Practicing Gospel: Unconventional Thoughts on the Church's Ministry.* Louisville: Westminster John Knox, 2003.

Farris, Stephen. *Preaching That Matters: The Bible and Our Lives.* Louisville: Westminster John Knox, 1997.

Fausey, Caitlin M., and Lera Boroditsky. "Who Dunnit? Cross-Linguistic Differences in Eye Witness Memory." *Psychon Bull Rev* 18 (2011): 150–57.

Fink, Eugen. *Sixth Cartesian Meditation: The Idea of a Transcendental Theory of Method.* Translated by Ronald Bruzina. Bloomington: Indiana University Press, 1995.

Florence, Anna Carter. *Preaching as Testimony.* Louisville: Westminster John Knox, 2007.

_____. "Put Away Your Sword! Taking the Torture Out of the Sermon." In *What's the Matter With Preaching Today?*, edited by Mike Graves, 93–108. Louisville: Westminster John Knox, 2004.

Fosdick, Harry Emerson. "What's The Matter With Preaching?" *Harper's* (July 1928): 133–41.

Foss, Chris. "'There is No God Who Can Keep Us From Tasting': Good Cannibalism in Hélène Cixous's *The Book of Promethea*." In *Scenes of the Apple: Food and the Female Body in Nineteenth- and Twentieth-Century Women's Writing*, edited by Tamar Heller and Patricia Moran, 149–66. Albany: SUNY Press, 2003.

Foucault, Michel. *Ethics, Subjectivity and Truth: Essential Works of Foucault, 1954–1984.* Edited by Paul Rabinow. New York: New Press, 1997.

_____. *The Order of Things: An Archeology of the Human Sciences.* Translated by Alan Sheridan. London: Routledge, 1989.

_____. *Power/Knowledge: Selected Interviews & Other Writings, 1972–1977.* Edited by Colin Gordon. New York: Pantheon Books, 1980.

_____. "The Subject and Power." In *Power: Essential Works of Foucault*, edited by James Faubion, translated by Robert Hurley, 326–48. New York: New Press, 2000.

_____. "Truth and Power." In *The Foucault Reader*, edited by Paul Rabinow, translated by Christian Hubert, 51–75. New York: Pantheon Books, 1984.

Francis. *The Joy of the Bishops: Evangelii Gaudium.* Dublin: Veritas, 2013.

Frank, Thomas. "Closing Salvo: Dark Age." In *Commodify Your Dissent: Salvos From the Baffler*, edited by Thomas Frank and Matt Weiland, 255–74. New York: Norton, 1997.

Furtick, Steven. *Greater: Dream Bigger. Start Smaller. Ignite God's Vision for Your Life.* Colorado Springs: Multnomah Books, 2012.

Gilbert, Kenyatta R. *The Journey and Promise of African American Preaching*. Minneapolis: Fortress Press, 2011.

Glissant, Édouard. *Caribbean Discourse: Selected Essays*. Translated by J. Michael Dash. Charlottesville: University of Virginia Press, 1999.

———. *Introduction à une poétique du divers*. Paris: Gallimard, 1996.

———. *Poetics of Relation*. Translated by Betsy Wing. Ann Arbor: University of Michigan Press, 1997.

Gadamer, Han-Georg. *Philosophical Hermeneutics*. Edited and translated by David E. Linge. Berkeley: University of California Press, 1976.

Goffman, Erving. *The Presentation of the Self in Everyday Life*. Garden City, NY: Doubleday, 1959.

González, Justo L. *Santa Biblia: The Bible through Hispanic Eyes*. Nashville: Abingdon, 1995.

González, Justo L., and Catherine Gunsalus González. *Liberation Preaching: The Pulpit and the Oppressed*. Nashville: Abingdon Press, 1980.

González, Justo L., and Pablo A. Jiménez, eds. *Púlpito: An Introduction to Hispanic Preaching*. Nashville: Abingdon, 2005.

Gorgias. *Philosophic Classics*. Vol. 1, *Thales to Ockham*. Edited by Walter Kaufmann. Translated by Kathleen Freeman. New Jersey: Prentice Hall, 1968.

Grau, Marion. "Erasing Economy: Derrida and the Construction of Divine Economies." *CrossCurrents* 52, no. 3 (Fall 2002): 360–70.

Gross, Nancy Lammers. *If You Cannot Preach Like Paul . . .* Grand Rapids, MI: Eerdmans, 2002.

Hancock, Angela Dienhart. *Karl Barth's Emergency Homiletic, 1932-1933: A Summons to Prophetic Witness at the Dawn of the Third Reich*. Grand Rapids, MI: Eerdmans, 2013.

Hankins, Davis. Introduction to *Ice Axes for Frozen Seas: A Biblical Theology of Provocation*, by Walter Brueggemann, 1–19. Edited by Davis Hankins. Waco, TX: Baylor University Press, 2014.

Harris, James H. *Preaching Liberation*. Minneapolis: Fortress Press, 1995.

———. *The Word Made Plain: The Power and Promise of Preaching*. Minneapolis: Augsburg Fortress, 2004.

Hart, John W. *Karl Barth vs. Emil Brunner: The Formation and Dissolution of a Theological Alliance, 1916-1936*. New York: Peter Lang, 2001.

Hays, Richard B. *The Faith of Jesus Christ: The Narrative Substructure of Galatians 3:1—4:11*. 2nd ed. Grand Rapids, MI: Eerdmans, 2002.

Hegel, G. W. F. *Hegel's Science of Logic*. Translated by A. V. Miller. New York: Humanity Books, 1991.

Heidegger, Martin. *On the Way to Language*. Translated by Peter D. Hertz. New York: Harper & Row, 1982.

Helsel, Carolyn Browning. "The Hermeneutics of Recognition: A Ricoeurian Interpretive Framework for Whites Preaching on Racism." PhD diss., Emory University, 2014.

_____. "A Word to the 'Whites': Whites Preaching about Racism in White Congregations." *Word and World* 31, no. 2 (Spring 2011): 196–203.

Henderson-Espinoza, Robyn. "Difference, Becoming, and Interrelatedness: A Material Resistance Becoming," *CrossCurrents* 66, no. 2 (June 2016): 281–89.

Herzog, Frederick. *Liberation Theology.* New York: Seabury, 1972.

Hidalgo, Jacqueline M. "Reading from No Place: Toward a Hybrid and Ambivalent Study of Scriptures." In *Latino/a Biblical Hermeneutics: Problematics, Objectives, Strategies*, edited by Francisco Lozada Jr. and Fernando F. Segovia, 165–86. Atlanta: SBL, 2014.

Hilkert, Mary Catherine. *Naming Grace: Preaching and the Sacramental Imagination.* New York: Continuum, 1997.

Hooke, Ruthanna B. "The Personal and Its Others in the Performance of Preaching." In *Preaching and the Personal*, edited by J. Dwayne Howell, 19–43. Eugene, OR: Pickwick, 2013.

_____. "The Spirit-Breathed Body: Divine Presence and Eschatological Promise in Preaching." Paper presented at the Annual Meeting for the Academy of Homiletics, San Antonio, TX, November 2016.

_____. *Transforming Preaching.* New York: Church Publishing, 2010.

hooks, bell. *Feminism is for Everybody: Passionate Politics.* London: Pluto, 2000.

_____. *Outlaw Culture: Resisting Representations.* New York: Routledge, 1994.

_____. *Teaching to Transgress: Education as the Practice of Freedom.* New York: Routledge, 1994.

_____. *The Will to Change: Men, Masculinity, and Love.* New York: Atria Books 2004.

Hudson, Mary Lin. "To Die and Rise Again: Preaching the Gospel for Liberation." In *Preaching as a Theological Task: World, Gospel, Scripture: In Honor of David Buttrick*, edited by Thomas G. Long and Edward Farley, 112–21. Louisville: Westminster John Knox, 1996.

Huyssen, Andreas. *After the Great Divide: Modernism, Mass Culture, Postmodernism.* Bloomington: Indiana University Press, 1986.

Irenaeus. *On the Apostolic Preaching.* Translated by John Behr. Crestwood, NY: St. Vladimir's Theological Seminary Press, 1997.

Irigaray, Luce. *Between East and West: From Singularity to Community.* Translated by Stephen Pluháek. New York: Columbia University Press, 2002.

_____. *Democracy Begins Between Two.* Translated by Kirsteen Anderson. New York: Routledge, 2001.

_____. *The Forgetting of Air in Martin Heidegger*. Translated by Mary Beth Mader. Austin: University of Texas Press, 1999.

_____. *In the Beginning She Was*. London: Bloomsbury Academic, 2013.

_____. *Sexes and Genealogies*. Translated by Gillian C. Gill. New York: Columbia University Press, 1993.

_____. *Thinking the Difference: For a Peaceful Revolution*. Translated by Karin Montin. New York: Routledge, 1994.

_____. *This Sex Which is Not One*. Translated by Catherine Porter. Ithaca, NY: Cornell University Press, 1985.

_____. *To Be Two*. Translated by Monique M. Rhodes and Marco F. Cocito-Monoc. New York: Routledge, 2001.

_____. *To Speak is Never Neutral*. Translated by Gail Schwab. New York: Routledge, 2002.

Isenberg, Nancy. *White Trash: The 400-Year Untold History of Class in America*. New York: Viking, 2016.

Jackson-Jordan, Elizabeth Ann. "Clergy Burnout and Resilience: A Review of the Literature." *Journal of Pastoral Care and Counseling* 67, no. 1 (March 2013): 1–6.

Jacobsen, David Schnasa. "The Promise and Cross: Homiletical Theology, the Vocative Word *Extra Nos*, and the Task of a Revisionist Eschatology." In *Homiletical Theology in Action: The Unfinished Theological Task of Preaching*, edited by David Schnasa Jacobsen, 108–30. Eugene, OR: Cascade Books, 2015.

_____. "Promise as an Event of the Gospel in Context: Toward an Unfinished Homiletical Theology of Grace and Justice." Paper presented at the Annual Meeting for the Academy of Homiletics, San Antonio, TX, November 2016.

_____. "The Promise of Promise: Retrospect and Prospect of a Homiletical Theology." *Homiletic* 38, no. 2 (2013): 3–16.

_____. Review of *Hoping Against Hope: Confessions of a Postmodern Pilgrim*, by John D. Caputo. *Homiletic* 41, no. 1 (2016): 91–92.

_____. Review of *The Insistence of God: A Theology of Perhaps*, by John D. Caputo. *Homiletic* 39, no. 2 (2014): 57.

_____. "The Unfinished Task of Homiletical Theology." In *Homiletical Theology: Preaching as Doing Theology*, edited by David Schnasa Jacobsen, 39–55. Eugene, OR: Cascade Books, 2015.

Jacobsen, David Schnasa, and Robert Allen Kelly. *Kairos Preaching: Speaking Gospel to the Situation*. Minneapolis: Fortress Press, 2009.

Jantzen, Grace M. *Becoming Divine: Towards a Feminist Philosophy of Religion*. Bloomington and Indianapolis: Indiana University Press, 1999.

Jameson, Fredric. *Postmodernism, or, The Cultural Logic of Late Capitalism*. Durham, NC: Duke University Press, 1991.

Johnson, Christopher. *System and Writing in the Philosophy of Jacques Derrida.* Cambridge: Cambridge University Press, 1993.

Jones, Robert P. *The End of White Christian America.* New York: Simon & Schuster, 2016.

Kafka, Franz. "Letter to Oskar Pollak, January 27, 1904." In *Letters to Friends, Family, and Editors,* edited by Max Brod, translated by Richard Winston and Clara Winston, 15–16. New York: Schocken Books, 1977.

Kant, Immanuel. *Critique of Pure Reason.* Edited and translated by Paul Guyer and Allen W. Wood. Cambridge: Cambridge University Press, 1998.

Kay, James F. "Preacher as Messenger of Hope." In *Slow of Speech and Unclean Lips: Contemporary Images of Preaching Identity,* edited by Robert Stephen Reid, 13–34. Eugene, OR: Cascade Books, 2010.

_____. *Preaching and Theology.* St. Louis: Chalice, 2007.

Kearney, Richard. *Anatheism: Returning to God after God.* New York: Columbia University Press, 2011.

_____. "Deconstruction, God, and the Possible." In *Derrida and Religion: Other Testaments,* edited by Yvonne Sherwood and Kevin Hart, 297–308. New York: Routledge, 2005.

_____. *The God Who May Be: A Hermeneutics of Religion.* Bloomington: Indiana University Press, 2001.

Kearns, Laurel, and Catherine Keller. *Ecospirit: Religions and Philosophies for the Earth.* New York: Fordham University Press, 2007.

Keller, Catherine. *The Face of the Deep: A Theology of Becoming.* London: Routledge, 2003.

Keller, Timothy. *Preaching: Communicating Faith in an Age of Skepticism.* New York: Viking, 2015.

Kierkegaard, Søren. *Fear and Trembling.* Vol. 6, *Repetition.* Kierkegaard's Writings. Translated by Edna H. Hong and Howard V. Hong. Princeton, NJ: Princeton University Press, 1983.

_____. *Papers and Journals: A Selection.* Translated by Alastair Hannay. London: Penguin Books, 1996.

_____. *The Sickness Unto Death: A Christian Psychological Exposition for Upbuilding and Awakening.* Vol. 19 of Kierkegaard's Writings. Edited and translated by Howard V. Hong and Edna H. Hong. Princeton, NJ: Princeton University Press, 1983.

Kim, Eunjoo Mary. *Preaching in an Age of Globalization.* Louisville: Westminster John Knox, 2010.

_____. *Preaching the Presence of God: A Homiletic from an Asian American Perspective.* Valley Forge, PA: Judson, 1999.

Lacan, Jacques. *Écrits: A Selection*. Translated by Bruce Fink. New York: Norton, 1977.

LaRue, Cleophus J. *I Believe I'll Testify: The Art of African American Preaching*. Louisville: Westminster John Knox, 2011.

_____. *The Heart of Black Preaching*. Louisville: Westminster John Knox, 1999.

_____. *Rethinking Celebration: From Rhetoric to Praise in African American Preaching*. Louisville: Westminster John Knox, 2016.

Levinas, Emmanuel. *Otherwise Than Being: Or, Beyond Essence*. Translated by Alphonso Lingis. Pittsburgh: Duquesne University Press, 1998.

_____. "The Paradox of Morality: An Interview with Emmanuel Levinas." In *The Provocation of Levinas: Rethinking the Other*, edited by Robert Bernasconi and David Wood, translated by Andrew Benjamin and Tamra Wright, 168–80. London: Routledge, 1988.

_____. *Proper Names*. Translated by Michael B. Smith. Stanford: Stanford University Press, 1996.

Lewis, Karoline M. *John*. Fortress Biblical Preaching Commentaries. Minneapolis: Fortress Press, 2014.

Lindbeck, George A. *The Nature of Doctrine: Religion and Theology in a Postliberal Age*. Louisville: Westminster John Knox, 1984.

Lischer, Richard. "Preaching as the Church's Language." In *Listening to the Word: Essays in Honor of Fred Craddock*, edited by Thomas G. Long and Gail R. O'Day, 113–30. Nashville: Abingdon, 1993.

_____. *A Theology of Preaching: The Dynamics of the Gospel*. Revised ed. Eugene, OR: Wipf and Stock, 2001.

Locke, John. *An Essay Concerning Human Understanding*. Edited by Peter Nidditch. Oxford: Oxford University Press, 1979.

Long, Thomas G. "Can I Get a Witness?" *Vision* 10, no. 1 (Spring 2009): 20–27.

_____. "No News is Bad News." In *What's the Matter with Preaching Today?*, edited by Mike Graves, 145–57. Louisville: Westminster John Knox, 2004.

_____. *Preaching and the Literary Forms of the Bible*. Philadelphia: Fortress Press, 1988.

_____. *Preaching From Memory to Hope*. Louisville: Westminster John Knox, 2009.

_____. "Shaping Sermons by Plotting the Text's Claim Upon Us." In *Preaching Biblically: Creating Sermons in the Shape of Scripture*, edited by Don M. Wardlaw, 84–100. Philadelphia: Westminster, 1983.

_____. "The Use of Scripture in Contemporary Preaching." *Interpretation* 44, no. 4 (October 1990): 341–52.

_____. *The Witness of Preaching*. 3rd ed. Louisville: Westminster John Knox, 2016.

Lorde, Audre. *Sister Outsider: Essays and Speeches.* Berkeley, CA: Crossing Press, 2007.

Lose, David J. *Preaching at the Crossroads: How the World—and Our Preaching—Is Changing.* Minneapolis: Fortress Press, 2013.

Lowe, Walter. *Theology and Difference: The Wound of Reason.* Bloomington: Indiana University Press, 1993.

Lowry, Eugene. *The Homiletical Plot: The Sermon as Narrated Art Form.* Expanded ed. Louisville: Westminster John Knox, 2001.

_____. *The Sermon: Dancing the Edge of Mystery.* Nashville: Abingdon, 1997.

MacKendrick, Karmen. "Sharing God's Wounds: Laceration, Communication, and Stigmata." In *The Obsessions of Georges Bataille: Community and Communication,* edited by Andrew J. Mitchell and Jason Kemp Vinfree, 133–46. Albany: SUNY Press, 2009.

Malcolmson, William L. *The Preaching Event.* Philadelphia: Westminster, 1968.

Marion, Jean-Luc. *Being Given: Toward a Phenomenology of Givenness.* Translated by Jeffrey L. Kosky. Stanford: Stanford University Press, 2002.

Mauss, Marcel. *The Gift: The Form and Reason for Exchange in Archaic Societies.* Translated by W. D. Halls. London: Routledge, 1990.

McCabe OP, Herbert. "The Eucharist as Language." *Modern Theology* 15, no. 2 (April 1999): 131–41.

_____. "The Logic of Mysticism." In *God Still Matters.* London: Continuum, 2005.

McClintock Fulkerson, Mary. *Changing the Subject: Women's Discourses and Feminist Theology.* Eugene, OR: Wipf & Stock, 2001.

McClure, John S. "Collaborative Preaching and the Bible: Toward a Practical Theology of Memory." In *Preaching and the Personal,* edited by J. Dwayne Howell, 56–70. Eugene, OR: Pickwick, 2013.

_____. *Other-wise Preaching: A Postmodern Ethic for Homiletics.* St. Louis: Chalice, 2001.

_____. "Preacher as Host and Guest." In *Slow of Speech and Unclean Lips: Contemporary Images of Preaching Identity,* edited by Robert Stephen Reid, 119–42. Eugene, OR: Cascade Books, 2010.

_____. *The Roundtable Pulpit: Where Leadership and Preaching Meet.* Nashville: Abingdon, 1995.

McClure, John S., Ronald J. Allen, Dale P. Andrews, L. Susan Bon, Dan P. Moseley, and G. Lee Ramsey Jr. *Listening to Listeners: Homiletical Case Studies.* St. Louis: Chalice, 2004.

McCullough, Amy P. "Her Preaching Body: A Qualitative Study of Agency, Meaning and Proclamation in Contemporary Female Preachers." PhD diss., Vanderbilt University, 2012.

McKenzie, Alyce M. "Out of Character! Preaching Biblical Wisdom in a Secular Age." *Journal for Preachers* 22, no. 4 (1999): 44–50.

_____. *Preaching Proverbs: Wisdom for the Pulpit.* Louisville: Westminster John Knox, 1996.

_____. "Wisdom as a Resource for Preaching in a Time of War." *Journal for Preachers* 28, no. 1 (2004): 21–27.

McMickle, Marvin A. *Shaping the Claim: Moving from Text to Sermon.* Minneapolis: Fortress Press, 2008.

Mead, G.H. *G.H. Mead: A Reader.* Edited by Filipe Carreira da Silva. London: Routledge, 2012.

Medina, José. *Language: Key Concepts.* London: Continuum, 2005.

_____. *The Epistemology of Resistance: Gender and Racial Oppression, Epistemic Injustice, and Resistant Imaginations.* Oxford: Oxford University Press, 2012.

_____. *Speaking from Elsewhere: A New Contextualist Perspective on Meaning, Identity, and Discursive Agency.* Albany: SUNY Press, 2006.

Mercedes, Anna. *Power For: Feminism and Christ's Self-Giving.* London: T & T Clark, 2011.

Miller, Joshua. *Hanging by a Promise: The Hidden God in the Theology of Oswald Bayer.* Eugene, OR: Pickwick, 2015.

Mitchell, Henry H. *Black Preaching: The Recovery of a Powerful Art.* Nashville: Abingdon, 1990.

Moltmann, Jürgen. *Theology of Hope: On the Ground and Implications of a Christian Eschatology.* Translated by James W. Leitch. Minneapolis: Fortress Press, 1993.

Moore, Stephen D. "Que(e)rying Paul: Preliminary Questions." In *Auguries: The Jubilee Volume of the Sheffield Department of Biblical Studies,* edited by David J. A. Clines and Stephen D. Moore, 250–74. Sheffield, UK: Sheffield Academic Press, 1998.

Moore, Stephen D., and Yvonne Sherwood. *The Invention of the Biblical Scholar: A Critical Manifesto.* Minneapolis: Fortress Press, 2011.

Moss, Otis, III. *Blue Note Preaching in a Post-Soul World: Finding Hope in an Age of Despair.* Louisville: Westminster John Knox, 2015.

Mulligan, Mary Alice, and Ronald J. Allen. *Make the Word Come Alive: Lessons from Laity.* St. Louis: Chalice, 2005.

Muñoz, José Esteban. *Cruising Utopia: The Then and There of Queer Futurity.* New York: NYU Press, 2009.

Myers, Jacob D. "Before the Gaze Ineffable: Intersubjective *Poesis* and the Song of Songs." *Theology and Sexuality* 17, no. 2 (May 2011): 139–60.

_____. "Dying to be Creative: Playing in/with the Homiletical Hiatus." *Homiletic* 38, no. 2 (2013): 17–29.

_____. "The Erotic Approach: Homiletical Insights from the Work of Georges Bataille." *Theology and Sexuality* 19, no. 1 (2013): 26–37.

_____. *Making Love with Scripture: Why the Bible Doesn't Mean How You Think It Means.* Minneapolis: Fortress Press, 2015.

_____. "Preaching Philosophy: The Kerygmatic Thrust of Paul Ricoeur's Philosophy and its Contribution to Homiletics." *Literature and Theology* 27, no. 2 (May 2013): 208–26.

_____. "Toward an Erotic Liturgical Theology: Schmemann in Conversation with Contemporary Philosophy." *Worship* 87, no. 5 (September 2013): 387–413.

_____. "Wise Speech: 1 Corinthians 2:1-16." In *In Tongues of Mortals and Angels: A De-Constructive Theology of God Talk in Acts and Paul*, by Eric D. Barreto, Jacob D. Myers, and Thelathia Nikki Young. Minneapolis: Fortress Press, forthcoming.

_____. "Writing Spiritually." In *Writing Theologically,* edited by Eric D. Barreto, 135–51. Minneapolis: Fortress Press, 2015.

Nagel, Thomas. *The View From Nowhere.* Oxford: Oxford University Press, 1986.

Nieman, James R., and Thomas G. Rogers. *Preaching to Every Pew.* Minneapolis: Fortress Press, 2001.

Oakes, Kenneth. *Karl Barth on Theology and Philosophy.* Oxford: Oxford University Press, 2012.

Ong, Walter J. *Orality and Literacy.* London: Routledge, 1982.

_____. *The Presence of the Word.* New Haven, CT: Yale University Press, 1967.

Pape, Lance B. *The Scandal of Having Something to Say: Ricoeur and the Possibility of Postliberal Preaching.* Waco, TX: Baylor University Press, 2013.

Passmore, John. *Recent Philosophers.* London: Duckworth, 1985.

Pasquarello, Michael III. *Christian Preaching: A Trinitarian Theology of Proclamation.* Grand Rapids, MI: Baker Academic, 2006.

_____. *Sacred Rhetoric: Preaching as a Theological and Pastoral Practice of the Church.* Grand Rapids, MI: Eerdmans, 2005.

Paulhan, Jean. *The Flowers of Tarbes.* Translated by Michael Syrotinski. Urbana: University of Illinois Press, 2006.

Plato. *The Republic.* Rev. ed. Loeb Classical Library. Volume 237. Translated by Paul Shorey. Cambridge, MA: Harvard University Press, 1930.

Pontifical Bible Commission. *The Interpretation of the Bible in the Church.* Rome: Liberia Editrice Vaticana, 1993.

Powery, Luke. *Dem Dry Bones: Preaching, Death, and Hope.* Minneapolis: Fortress Press, 2012.

_____. "Haunting Echoes for Homiletics: Why the Spirituals Matter for Preaching." *Homiletic* 37, no. 2 (2012): 4–15.

_____. "In Our Own Native Tongue: Toward a Pentecostalization of Homiletical Theology." In *Homiletical Theology in Action: The Unfinished Theological Task of Preaching*, edited by David Schnasa Jacobsen, 72–84. Eugene, OR: Cascade Books, 2015.

_____. *Spirit Speech: Lament and Celebration in Preaching.* Nashville: Abingdon, 2009.

Pseudo-Dionysius. *The Mystical Theology.* In *Pseudo-Dionysius: The Complete Works*, edited by Paul Rorem, translated by Colm Luibheid, 133–42. New York: Paulist, 1987.

Randolph, David James. *The Renewal of Preaching in the Twenty-First Century.* 2nd ed. With commentary by Robert Stephen Reid. Eugene, OR: Wipf & Stock, 2008.

Reid, Robert Stephen. "Commentary." In *The Renewal of Preaching in the Twenty-First Century*, 2nd ed., 113–38. Eugene, OR: Wipf & Stock, 2008.

_____. *Slow of Speech and Unclean Lips: Contemporary Images of Preaching Identity.* Eugene, OR: Cascade Books, 2010.

Ricoeur, Paul. *The Conflict of Interpretations: Essays in Hermeneutics.* Edited by Don Ihde. Translated by Peter McCormick. Evanston, IL: Northwestern University Press, 1974.

_____. *Figuring the Sacred: Religion, Narrative, and Imagination.* Edited by Mark I. Wallace. Translated by David Pellauer. Minneapolis: Augsburg Fortress, 1995.

_____. "From Metaphysics to Moral Philosophy." Translated by David Pellauer. *Philosophy Today* 40 (1996): 443–59.

_____. "The Hermeneutical Function of Distanciation." In *Hermeneutics and the Human Sciences: Essays on Language, Action, and Interpretation*, edited and translated by John B. Thompson, 131–44. Cambridge: Cambridge University Press, 1981.

_____. "The Metaphorical Process as Cognition, Imagination, and Feeling." *Critical Inquiry* 5, no. 1 (Autumn 1978): 143–59.

_____. *Oneself as Another.* Translated by Kathleen Blamey. Chicago: University of Chicago Press, 1992.

_____. *Time and Narrative.* Vol. 3. Chicago: University of Chicago Press, 1988.

Rimbaud, Arthur. "À Georges Izambard (Charleville, 13 mai 1871)." In *Rimbaud: Complete Works, Selected Letters, A Bilingual Edition*, rev. ed., edited by Seth Whidden, translated by Wallace Fowlie, 370. Chicago: University of Chicago Press, 2005.

Ritschl, Dietrich. *A Theology of Proclamation.* Richmond, VA: John Knox, 1960.

Rivera, Mayra. *Poetics of the Flesh.* Durham, NC: Duke University Press, 2015.

Robinson, Haddon W. *Biblical Preaching: The Development and Delivery of Expository Messages.* 3rd ed. Grand Rapids, MI: Baker Academic, 2014.

Rose, Lucy Atkinson. "Conversational Preaching: A Proposal." *Journal for Preachers* 19, no. 1 (Advent 1995): 26–30.

_____. *Sharing the Word: Preaching in the Roundtable Church.* Louisville: Westminster John Knox, 1997.

Rottman, John M. "Performative Language and the Limits of Performance in Preaching." In *Performance in Preaching: Bringing the Sermon to Life*, edited by Jana Childers and Clayton L. Schmit, 67–86. Grand Rapids, MI: Baker Academic, 2008.

Sampson, Melva L. "Fetching Spiritual Power: Black Women's Preaching Bodies as African Centered Womanist Oratory." PhD diss., Emory University, 2016.

Saussure, Ferdinand de. *Course in General Linguistics.* Edited by Charles Bally, Albert Sechehaye, and Albert Riedlinger. Translated by Roy Harris. Chicago: Open Court, 1983.

Schoonmaker, Geoffrey Noel. "Preaching About Race: A Homiletic for Racial Reconciliation." PhD diss., Vanderbilt University, 2012.

Smith, Adam. *Wealth of Nations.* Edited by Charles J. Bullock. New York: Cosimo, 2007.

Smith, Christine M. "Preaching as an Act of Resistance." In *The Arts of Ministry: Feminist Womanist Approaches*, edited by Christie Cozad Neuger, 39–59. Louisville: Westminster John Knox, 1996.

_____. *Preaching as Weeping, Confession, and Resistance: Radical Responses to Radical Evil.* Louisville: Westminster John Knox, 1992.

_____. *Weaving the Sermon: Preaching in a Feminist Perspective.* Louisville: Westminster John Knox, 1989.

Smith, Steven G. *The Argument to the Other: Reason Beyond Reason in the Thought of Karl Barth and Emmanuel Levinas.* Chico, CA: Scholars Press, 1983.

Snider, Phil. *Preaching After God: Derrida, Caputo, and the Language of Postmodern Homiletics.* Eugene, OR: Cascade Books, 2012.

_____. "Speech In Support of Council Bill 2012-226." August 20, 2012. https://tinyurl.com/aybckj4.

Spivak, Gayatri. *The Post-colonial Critic.* New York: Routledge, 1990.

Stanley, Andy. *Enemies of the Heart: Breaking Free from the Four Emotions That Control You.* Colorado Springs: Multnomah Books, 2011.

Steiner, George. *Real Presences: Is There Anything in What We Say?* London: Faber & Faber, 1989.

Still, Judith. *Feminine Economies: Thinking Against the Market in the Enlightenment and the Late Twentieth Century.* Manchester: Manchester University Press, 1997.

_____. "A Feminine Economy: Some Preliminary Thoughts." In *The Body and the Text: Hélène Cixous, Reading and Teaching*, edited by Helen Wilcox et al., 49–60. New York: St. Martin's, 1990.

Stott, John. *Between Two Worlds: The Challenge of Preaching Today.* Grand Rapids, MI: Eerdmans, 1982.

Strauss, Claude Lévi. *The View From Afar.* Translated by Joachim Neugroschel and Phoebe Hoss. Chicago: University of Chicago Press, 1992.

Taylor, Charles. *Human Agency and Language: Philosophical Papers I.* Cambridge: Cambridge University Press, 1989.

_____. "The Politics of Recognition." In *Multiculturalism: Examining the Politics of Recognition*, edited by Amy Gutmann, 25–74. Princeton: Princeton University Press, 1994.

_____. *A Secular Age.* Cambridge, MA: Harvard University Press, 2007.

_____. *Sources of the Self: The Making of Modern Identity.* Cambridge: Cambridge University Press, 1989.

Thomas, Frank A. *They Like to Never Quit Praisin' God.* Rev. ed. Cleveland: Pilgrim, 2013.

_____. *Introduction to the Practice of African American Preaching.* Nashville: Abingdon, 2016.

Thompson, Lisa L. "'Now that's Preaching!' Disruptive and Generative Preaching Practices." *Practical Matters* 8 (April 2015): 73–84.

Timmerman, Daniël. *Heinrich Bullinger on Prophecy and the Prophetic Office (1523-1538).* Göttingen: Vandenhoeck & Ruprecht, 2015.

Toth, Josh. *The Passing of Postmodernism: A Spectroanalysis of the Contemporary.* Albany: SUNY Press, 2011.

Toth, Josh, and Neil Brooks. "Introduction: A Wake and Renewed?" In *The Mourning After: Attending the Wake of Postmodernism*, edited by Josh Toth and Neil Brooks, 1–14. Amsterdam: Editions Rodopi B. V., 2007.

Travis, Sarah. *Decolonizing Preaching: The Pulpit as Postcolonial Space.* Eugene, OR: Cascade Books, 2014.

_____. "Troubled Gospel: Postcolonial Preaching for the Colonized, Colonizer, and Everyone in Between." *Homiletic* 40, no. 1 (2015): 46–54.

Troeger, Thomas H. *Imagining a Sermon.* Nashville: Abingdon, 1990.

Troeger, Thomas H., and Leonora Tubbs Tisdale. *A Sermon Workbook: Exercises in the Art and Craft of Preaching.* Nashville: Abingdon, 2013.

Turner, Mary Donovan. "Disrupting a Ruptured World." In *Purposes of Preaching*, edited by Jana Childers, 131–40. St. Louis: Chalice, 2004.

Turner, Mary Donovan, and Mary Lin Hudson. *Saved from Silence: Finding Women's Voice in Preaching*. St. Louis: Chalice, 1999.

Turner, Michael A. *A Peculiar Prophet: William H. Willimon and the Art of Preaching*. Nashville: Abingdon, 2010.

Turner, William Clair, Jr. *Preaching That Makes the Word Plain: Doing Theology in the Crucible of Life*. Eugene, OR: Wipf & Stock, 2008.

Voelz, Richard W. "Silence and Deficiency: Contemporary Pictures of Youth and Preaching." *Encounter* 76, no. 1 (2016): 21–49.

_____. *Youthful Preaching: Strengthening the Relationship between Youth, Adults, and Preaching*. Eugene, OR: Cascade Books, 2016.

Ward, Richard F. *Speaking of the Holy: The Art of Communication in Preaching*. St. Louis: Chalice, 2001.

Waznak SS, Robert P. *An Introduction to the Homily*. Collegeville, MN: Liturgical Press, 1998.

Webb, Joseph M. *Preaching Without Notes*. Nashville: Abingdon, 2001.

Webb, Stephen H. *The Gifting God: A Trinitarian Ethics of Excess*. New York: Oxford University Press, 1996.

Willimon, William H. *The Intrusive Word: Preaching to the Unbaptized*. Grand Rapids, MI: Eerdmans, 1994.

_____. *Pastor: The Theology and Practice of Ordained Ministry*. Nashville: Abingdon, 2002.

_____. *Peculiar Speech: Preaching to the Baptized*. Grand Rapids, MI: Eerdmans, 1992.

_____. *Proclamation and Theology*. Nashville: Abingdon, 2005.

Wilson, Paul Scott. *God Sense: Reading the Bible for Preaching*. Nashville: Abingdon, 2001.

_____. *The Practice of Preaching*. 2nd ed. Nashville: Abingdon, 2007.

_____. *Preaching and Homiletical Theory*. St. Louis: Chalice, 2004.

_____. "Preaching as God's Event." *Vision* 10, no. 1 (Spring 2009): 12–19.

_____. *Preaching as Poetry: Goodness, Beauty, and Truth in Every Sermon*. Nashville: Abingdon, 2014.

Winch, Peter. *The Idea of a Social Science and its Relation to Philosophy*. 2nd ed. London: Routledge, 1990.

Wise, Tim. *White Like Me: Reflections on Race from a Privileged Son*. 3rd ed. Berkeley, CA: Soft Skull Press, 2011.

Wittgenstein, Ludwig. *Philosophical Investigations*. 4th ed. Translated by G. E. M. Anscombe, P. M. S. Hacker, and Joachim Schulte. Malden, MA: Wiley-Blackwell, 2009.

_____. *Tractatus Logico-Philosophicus*. Translated by D. F. Pears and B. F. McGuiness. London: Routledge, 1961.

Yarber, Angela. *The Gendered Pulpit: Sex, Body, and Desire in Preaching and Worship.* Cleveland, TN: Parson's Porch Books, 2013.

York, Hershael W., and Bert Decker. *Preaching with Bold Assurance: A Solid and Enduring Approach to Engaging Exposition.* Nashville: B & H, 2003.

Young, Thelathia Nikki. *Black Queer Ethics, Family, and Philosophical Imagination.* New York: Palgrave Macmillan, 2016.

Index of Scripture

Index of Names and Subjects

Grau, Marion, 70, 138, 139n156, 184, 188

Habermas, Jürgen, 119
Harry Potter, 7, 12
Heideggerian infrastructure, 2
Heimdall, 48, 49
Hidalgo, Jacqueline, 69, 69n46, 189
homiletics, xii, 1–5, 3n8, 4n12, 7, 9, 11n27, 12, 13n37, 14–16, 20, 20n7, 21n11, 23, 29, 32, 35–38, 43, 48, 50, 52–53, 56, 57n4, 58, 58n9, 71–73, 76, 85n90, 86, 90, 92, 96n10, 98, 101, 102n27, 104, 104n39, 108, 112, 118–20, 122n106, 123n108, 125n114, 128, 128n122, 132, 134–39, 143–44, 147–49, 151, 153n28, 156, 158–62, 162n54, 163, 163n58, 165–67, 167n68, 168–69, 169n74, 170–72, 172n82, 173–75, 179, 181, 183, 189–90, 193, 195, 197; echognomic, 135; of presence, 147, 172–74; postliberal, 112; African American, 150; Roman Catholic, 116–17, 151; radical, 6n16, 160–61, 163, 165–66, 170–72
Hooke, Ruthanna, 59, 60n15, 95n7, 153n28, 189
hooks, bell, 79, 80n73, 80n77, 174, 174n91, 189
horcrux, 7–12
Hudson, Mary Lin, 40, 40n65, 74, 74n60, 80n74, 82, 83n83, 189, 198

identity, 4n11, 5n13, 9n22, 27n27, 32n42, 35n51, 37, 39, 44, 49, 49n88, 55–56, 56n2, 57n3, 58n6, 58n8, 58n10, 59nn13–14, 60n16,

61n18, 61n20, 68n38, 68nn40–41, 69, 69n44, 71nn51–52, 73n59, 74n61, 75n64, 76n65, 76n66, 78–83, 85–92, 92n111, 96n8, 110, 112–13, 112n71, 122, 127, 133, 135, 156n38, 166, 168; double-consciousness, 70, 70n48; new consciousness, 69, 70n47, 179; no place, 39n64, 69, 69n46, 167, 189; performing, 64, 81, 184; *terra incognita*, 69, 73–74
Ikon (Belfast, Ireland), 171
imago Dei, 64
Irigaray, Luce, 1, 1n2, 17, 17n1, 18, 18n2, 19n5, 22, 22n14, 27n27, 30–32, 30n35, 31nn36–38, 32n40, 32nn42–43, 33n44, 34n48, 37nn57–58, 38, 38nn59–60, 39n63, 40, 40nn67–68, 41n71, 50–53, 50nn91–92, 51nn94–96, 52n97, 53n99, 78n71, 91, 91n110, 92n112, 127, 154n30, 157n40, 167n67, 189
iterable, 35, 37, 156n37

Jacobsen, David Schnasa, 1n3, 163n58, 171n74, 190, 196
Jennings, Willie James, 47, 47n86
Jiménez, Pablo, 110–11, 110n65, 188
Jones, Robert, 70, 71n49, 191

Kant, Immanuel, 20n7, 61, 65n30, 95, 191
Kay, James, 19n5, 191
Kearney, Richard, 8, 8n20, 140, 140n160, 148n16, 169, 169n74, 191
Keller, Timothy, 10, 10n26, 191
kerygmatic economy, 95, 116, 123, 129, 139